Write in Style

Write in Style is aimed at everyone for whom clarity and accuracy of expression are important skills. Accessible and often entertaining, this book offers sound, practical advice on all types of writing from essays and articles to minutes and reportage. The main areas covered are:

- Sentences, punctuation and paragraphs
- Finding and using the right style
- How to write essays, reports, minutes and summaries
- A comprehensive guide to English grammar

This new edition includes a revised and expanded section on report writing, and a new chapter on writing and computers. Each section includes illustrations, examples and exercises to help you put the techniques and skills into practice.

Write in Style is the ideal guide for A-level and undergraduate students, and for professionals who want to improve their English.

Dr. Richard Palmer is Head of English at Bedford School, an ISI Schools Inspector and an examiner for the International Baccalaureate. He has also been an examiner for GSCE and A-Level and the Open University. His other books include *Brain Train: Studying for Success*, also published by Routledge.

Other titles from Routledge

Brain Train
Studying for success
2nd Edition
Richard Palmer

Effective Speaking
Communicating in speech
Christopher Turk

Effective Writing
Improving scientific, technical and
business communications
2nd Edition
Christopher Turk and John Kirkman

Good Style
Writing for science and technology
John Kirkman

How to Get an MBA
Morgen Witzel

Scientists Must Write
A guide to better writing for
scientists, engineers and students
2nd Edition
Robert Barrass

Students Must Write
A guide to better writing in
coursework and examinations
2nd Edition
Robert Barrass

Study!
A guide to effective study, revision
and examination techniques
2nd Edition
Robert Barrass

Writing at Work
A guide to better writing in
administration, business and
management
Robert Barrass

For more information about these and other titles published by Routledge please
contact:

Routledge, 11 New Fetter Lane, London EC4P 4EE.
Tel: 020 7583 9855; Fax: 020 7842 2303; or visit our web site at
www.Routledge.com

Write in Style

A guide to good English

Second edition

Richard Palmer

London and New York

First published 1993 by E & FN Spon
Reprinted 1994, 1995, 1999

Second edition first published 2002
by Routledge
11 New Fetter Lane, London EC4P 4EE

Simultaneously published in the USA and Canada
by RoutledgeFalmer
29 West 35th Street, New York, NY 10001

RoutledgeFalmer is an imprint of the Taylor & Francis Group

© 1993, 2002 Richard Palmer

Typeset in Goudy by
Keystroke, Jacaranda Lodge, Wolverhampton
Printed and bound in Great Britain by
Biddles Ltd, Guildford and King's Lynn

British Library Cataloguing in Publication Data
A catalogue record for this book is available from the British Library

Library of Congress Cataloging in Publication Data
A catalog record for this book has been requested

ISBN 0–415–25263–6

Reviews of the 1st edition

'an accessible and lively guide to English style and usage.'

Secondary and Higher Education Journal

'Richard Palmer . . . has a formidable grasp of the language and illustrates his points with some fascinating quotations.'

Bradford Telegraph & Argus

'. . . brisk, attractive and undogmatic, and a distinguishing feature of the whole book is his obvious enjoyment of his task. This book would undoubtedly help any trainee scientist to improve his skill in transferring information in English – and to enjoy doing so.'

Journal of Fluid Mechanics

'Anyone looking for a ready source of ideas to stretch KS4 English pupils and to extend the range in their writing needs search no further!'

'His book provides the necessary underpinning for any writer: confidence in handling language to its best effect in a register appropriate to the given task and audience.'

'. . . individual lovers of the language will also find much in it to delight and test them.'

Journal of the Headmasters' Conference Schools

Contents

List of exercises

For Annie, as always; for my mother and father,
Tony and Ethel Palmer; and to the memory of
Raymond Wilson (1925–75)

Acknowledgements

Countless people have helped me with this book – those who taught me, those I have taught with, and those whom I have taught.

It was my great good fortune as a sixth former at Dulwich College to be taught by Raymond Wilson, then Head of English, later Professor of Education at Reading University. It was he who kindled – indeed ignited – my life-long love of English, and of teaching too. I mourn his passing, as I do that of my first Head of Department, Reggie Watters, for whose wise expertise and generosity I remain deeply grateful. Peter Clayton and Christopher Rowe were enormously helpful in my time as a student teacher at King Edward VI School, Norwich, as were subsequent colleagues Edward Baines, Tim Kirkup and the late Tom Keeley; I would additionally like to salute and thank all members, past and present, of my Department at Bedford School. And I am no less indebted to my many thousands of students over the years: they have constantly stimulated and increased my interest in all things literary and linguistic, and I hope they all enjoyed my classes as much as I did.

I would also like to thank Roger Allen, Michael and Louise Tucker, John Fleming, John White, Brendan Law, Colin Brizicki, Wendy Pollard, Jane Richardson, Robert Kapadia, and, especially, Louise Berridge, whose detailed criticisms and suggestions have been invaluable; Tim Raynor and Jacky Max at NatWest ICT Learning & Development; the late Philip Read for commissioning the original edition; John Penny for his wonderful illustrations; and finally my wife and daughters for their love and patience while the book was being written.

Thanks are due to the following for permission to reproduce material:

The Random House Group and The Hemingway Foreign Rights Trust for permission to reproduce material from *Big Two-Hearted River* by Ernest Hemingway.

The Guardian for permission to reproduce material from:

John Naughton's column of 14 April, 1996

Statistic, 1963

Clive James's TV Column of 2 March, 1980

Private Eye for permission to reproduce material from *Private Eye* magazine, 1986.

A.M. Heath & Co. Ltd. for permission to reproduce material from *Catch-22*, by Joseph Heller.

American Zoetrope for permission to transcribe and reproduce material from the film, *Apocalypse Now*.

The Birmingham Evening Mail for permission to reproduce a report from 6 December, 1986.

The Publishers have made every effort to contact the copyright holders of material reproduced in this book, but this has not been possible in every case. We would welcome correspondence from individuals or companies that we have been unable to trace.

Preface

The pleasure principle and the work ethic

We put our love where we have put our labour.

Ralph Waldo Emerson

When work is a pleasure, life is a joy. When work is a duty, life is slavery.

Maxim Gorky

Men seldom give pleasure when they are not pleased themselves.

Samuel Johnson

1988 saw the publication of the Kingman Report into the learning and teaching of English. Reviewing it in a leading article,[1] *The Guardian* assumed as a proven fact that there are two extreme factions in the English teaching profession. One is characterized by a 'yearning for more learning by rote' and a 'return to traditional grammar lessons'; the other is distinguished by its 'belief that rules should not be taught but absorbed'.

The editorial went on mildly to berate Kingman for steering a timid course between those extremes. Yet it was itself remarkably indecisive. It scoffed at the notion of 'learning by osmosis', but was also certain that 'a return to traditional grammar lessons would not raise standards'. Not only did it fail to supply the answers it found absent in the Report: it seemed to accept that one must be 'for creativity' or 'for accuracy' – that the controlling emphasis must fall either on enjoyment and pleasurable absorption or on discipline and earned knowledge.

I found that puzzling then, and I continue to do so now. Surely it is not a question of either/or but of both/and?

[*]

Those words formed the opening of my 1993 Preface; the intervening years have only increased the bewilderment expressed in that short third paragraph.

---

1 *The Guardian*, 30 April, 1988, p. 18.

Moreover, the last decade has witnessed a deepening of the crisis Kingman identified despite, or more likely because of, the many changes there have been in education, introduced on an almost yearly basis and at all levels. In most instances it is doubtful whether they have been successful; in one or two it is quite clear that they have not been. As I write, the A/S and A2 system introduced in 2000 to replace the old A Level is a complete shambles – its much-vaunted claim to increase breadth while retaining depth a manifest fiction, its organization chaotic and the very meaning of the first batch of A/S scores indecipherable. But an even bigger, though perhaps less comically obvious, failure has been the National Curriculum (NC). About to come 'on stream' when Kingman reported, it has proved arguably the most expensive disaster in British educational history.

The NC 'guaranteed' to make every UK pupil technologically literate by making Technology a compulsory core subject. This did not happen. The latter initiative proved quite impossible to effect and the desired goal is as far off now as it was fifteen years ago. It also 'guaranteed' to raise dramatically standards of ordinary literacy and numeracy in our young people. That did not happen either. Indeed, just a few years ago came the launch of new literacy and numeracy strategies, including the creation of the Literacy Hour and the Numeracy Hour; while they have proved one of the few truly successful educational initiatives of our time, the fact that such programmes were deemed urgently necessary amounts to 'official' confirmation of the NC's failure.

No less eloquent in its different way is that dismal phenomenon, SPAG. Standing for 'Spelling, Punctuation And Grammar' and supposedly a decisive NC innovation, SPAG turned out to involve merely the award of bonus marks in any paper involving the use of continuous English. The maximum such award was and remains 5 marks, tagged on to papers already marked out of 100; since a candidate had to be flawless to get 5 and terminally illiterate to score 0, the initiative was rendered even less meaningful. What had been advertised as ensuring a notable rise in young writers' technical accuracy soon boiled down to a manoeuvre as tacky and ridiculous as the acronym itself.

So far I have offered essentially general observations, though they are based on my secondary and tertiary teaching experience (including talking to many other teachers and their students) and on my private experience as a reader of letters, circulars, reports, newspapers, Ceefax and all the rest of it. But the deepening crisis in 'English' mentioned above was brought home to me a few years ago in a peculiarly direct way. In 1996 1 was engaged by NatWest Bank's IT Learning & Development section in London to run a series of courses entitled *English for Professionals*. The experience was a most rewarding one for me, and I hope it proves analogously so for readers, since it has prompted a number of additions and expansions in this new edition. However, my chief point here is to draw attention to how sad it was – even appalling – that a major commercial organization *needed* to employ someone like me. Its dedicated and intelligent personnel had not received such training at school or college and felt its absence deeply – to an extent where they were happy to attend a sequence of two-hour classes at the end of a hard day's work.

That citing of 'happy' and the implicit accompanying tribute to their discipline returns me to my initial plea for a both/and approach. It is doubly wrong to reject learning by osmosis on the one hand and direct grammatical training on the other. Both are essential; both can be made pleasurable and productive; each complements the other without being enough on its own.

It is incorrect to assume that no effective learning can be achieved by osmosis – that is, through a process of absorption. Children become fluent in their native tongue by the age of 4 or 5, without any formal training or conceptual understanding of the structures they employ. Later on they become competent in reading, an activity that self-evidently depends upon absorption. And this 'absorption' operates in two ways, signalled by the two separate applications of that word. 'To absorb' means to soak up, to take in fully; but we also regularly speak of being absorbed in an activity – captivated by it, lost in concentrated attention and wonder. In sum: 'absorption' involves profound pleasure as well as assimilation of knowledge. It is a truism that reading is one of life's great pleasures: my point here is that pleasure brings not only its own reward but a lot of other ones too. It is both fun and instructive.

Nevertheless, it is perfectly absurd to claim that you can master all English skills and requirements solely by osmosis. No one can master anything in such a way. You cannot become a competent pianist just by listening to Vladimir Ashkenazy or Oscar Peterson: you've got to do a lot of active work as well, starting with learning the notes and how to get your fingers to manipulate them accurately and pleasingly. Nor can you become a good cook just by watching someone else prepare a succulent meal. The once-modish phrase 'hands-on experience' describes the position very well: everyone needs direct practical involvement to become accomplished at anything. That includes the use of language.

Grammar teaching got a bad name some forty years ago, through being carried out in a dry and unpleasurable way. Those who dislike the prospect of reviving it do so, I suspect, because they confuse content with the methods they remember from their own schooldays.[2] But there is no reason why learning grammar cannot be fun, even exciting. Most people enjoy learning about how things work; why should language be any different? Moreover, since language is common to us all, something we use virtually all the time, finding out how it works should be especially rewarding.

Bernard Levin has suggested that the English language is the greatest work of art that the human species has yet produced. One of the chief purposes of a work of art is to stimulate pleasure – so there is no reason why mastering a language should be dull or merely hard work. Indeed, I would argue that mastery – of anything – is impossible under such arid conditions. The range of skills involved in becoming an accomplished writer and speaker means that care, discipline

---

2 Or those of their parents; you are now quite old if you remember the regular formal teaching of grammar!

and concentration are always necessary; but these qualities can and must be accompanied by a sense of pleasure. There are many kinds of good writing, and many different ways in which one can write well; all are nevertheless characterized by the delight in words they both take and communicate.

The last few paragraphs have discussed a process of learning which no matter how rewarding has never been easy. But it could be that it's even more difficult now than it was ten years ago. As befits a culture that has become blame-centred and obsessed with litigation, everyone is so much more *accountable*. Professionals of all kinds are being asked to do far more in the way of reporting, record-keeping and the like, and the pressures on them (including those of longer hours and ever-more tasks to attend to) mount by the year.[3] Students are tested more often and more stringently than ever before, and in an increasing variety of ways; there have also been signal alterations to the way syllabuses at 16+ and tertiary levels are designed, administered and assessed. Small wonder that the word 'stress' seems to be on so many people's lips.

For students (and their teachers) those pressures are nastily reflected in such now-standard terminology such as

aims and objectives
attainment targets
assignments
bullet points
delivery
tasks

– vocabulary which smacks as much of a bombing mission as an educational programme. The same mixture of the joyless and the sinister characterises the latest developments in GCSE English, which is now a tedious and philistine enterprise in thrall to political correctness. That is less surprising (though no less regrettable) if one considers these two extracts from educational documents published by the government, both of which combine a maximum of ugliness with a minimum of clarity or indeed meaning:

> **. . . What we want to achieve through the establishment of the Learning Academy is to make learning a dynamic, strategically focused activity that is integrally aligned to the organic growth of the Department.[4]**

> ### *Evaluation*

> **This measures what was, is, and could be, and to which some worth is then ascribed and from which develops actions (to do more of, to do less of,**

3 That is one reason why Chapter 13 on Reports is now four times longer than its 1993 counterpart.
4 Job advertisement placed by the Department for Education & Skills, 2001.

to develop, to strengthen), resulting in different and better behaviour, attitudes and perceptions of reality.[5]

I hope this book represents a step in a better direction, and indeed the right one. The accent is firmly on pleasure, as indicated by the sub-title above; I have much enjoyed writing what follows, and if that enjoyment is not communicated to or shared by the reader, then I've failed. But if fun is an essential requirement, so is skill – the ability to apply knowledge in a precise and effective way. For those who, like that *Guardian* leader-writer commenting on Kingman, remain unconvinced that a spirited interest in how language works is fundamental to truly accomplished writing, I would offer two crisp quotations. The first is a remark made by Eddie 'Lockjaw' Davis, a superb tenor saxophonist who chose to spend a period of his career away from the bandstand, working as a booking agent and band-manager. When he later resumed playing, he maintained that his time away made him a better player and a more fully-rounded man, saying:

The better he knows the product, the better the salesman.

The analogy is telling: the better you know how language operates, the better you'll be able to 'sell' it – and yourself – when writing.

The advice given by Artemus Ward is much more peremptory:

A writer who can't write in a grammerly manner better shut up shop.

Anyone who thinks that the conventions and rules of English don't matter is not going to get very far as a writer, no matter how modest his or her goals. Without a working knowledge of how the signals and structures of language operate and an understanding of why they have been agreed, you are most unlikely to communicate what you might imagine you're saying.

It takes time to acquire the kind of confidence whereby one looks forward to writing as a source of delight rather than as a forbidding task or chore. But it can be done – and one of the better ways is to go back to that time when the magic of words first strikes us: childhood. Charles Baudelaire defined 'genius' as

childhood recaptured at will

and while genius is beyond the scope of most of us, we will still benefit enormously if we can invest adult activity with the fresh excitement that distinguishes childhood pursuits. Of course, very young writers have many limitations: I am not advocating a return to 'the cat sat on the mat' practice. But young children embody in their use of language two qualities that older writers forget at their peril: they

5 From *NVQ Teacher Training Guidance Notes*, 1996.

have a clear idea of what they want to say and a pleasure-based verve in the way they say it.

My aim is therefore twofold. Naturally, I want to be helpfully instructive, enabling you to write with confidence and clarity. The tasks, techniques and skills this book explores are many and wide-ranging, and I believe its advice contains something of value to all writers of 15 years and above, whatever their particular needs. But I also want you to enjoy yourself while reading the material and, perhaps, attempting some of the exercises I include. I am convinced that students – of any age or ability – learn faster and better if they have a good time while they work, which is why the host of examples are designed to give pleasure as well as instruction. The combination of absorbed amusement and challenging work has rarely had other than a successful outcome. And what better way to start than to have some undemanding but illuminating fun at someone else's expense?

Part I

Engage brain and ear before writing

Chapter 1

Disasters

Troubles hurt the most when they prove self-inflicted.
Sophocles, *Oedipus Rex*

Destructive criticism is one of life's great pleasures, and a seriously undervalued one. As we grow up, we are often brainwashed into thinking that the only reputable type of criticism is 'constructive' – that is, essentially admiring but containing some suggestions as to how what has been done could be made even better. But when something is awful, why not say so? Children do; maybe that's why they have so much fun, and embarrass po-faced adults so often! So let's take an enjoyable look at four passages that turned out rather less well than their authors intended.

1 In this set of instructions the writer gets into a hilarious mess through not thinking clearly or 'hearing' the words.

> When feeding the baby with a bottle, it must be held at a steep angle with the bottom tilted up and the neck held firmly down, otherwise an air-bubble will form in the neck. Do not allow the baby to drink all the feed at once, but give it a rest sometimes so that it can get the wind up. Finally, when the baby has finished the bottle, place it under the tap straight away, or allow it to soak in a mild solution of Milton, to prevent infection. If the baby does not thrive on fresh milk it should be powdered or boiled.

A formal analysis of why this goes wrong would show that the loose use of pronouns sets up a farcical ambiguity. But a simpler explanation is that the writer is **lazy**. There has been no attempt to imagine how the words will 'sound', how they will affect the reader. Given that the passage is instructional, presumably intended to assist an inexperienced parent, that is a severe fault.

***

Exercise 1
Rewrite the above passage so that it makes clear and uncomical sense. You'll find my suggested version in Appendix I.

2 The next extract, taken from an A Level English examination script, suffers from inadequate thought too, though in a different way.

> Fielding, having once been a playwrite [sic][1], moved into novels. In this novel he was not merely trying to parody *Pamela*, by Richardson, but his was make [sic] some clear social comments. To do this he had to use caricatures and situations, and this obviously could lead to a certain amount of disconnection of events.

Even if we ignore the spelling mistake and the brief dive into illiteracy in the second line, this is an unholy mess. The candidate is not stupid, and underneath the drivel there is a sense of some useful points trying to emerge. But they are all jumbled together, linked by a 'logic' presumed to be adequate but which in fact is non-existent. The writer needed to be aware of a very valuable principle:

Never begin a sentence until you are sure of what you want to say in it *and* of how it will end.

If obeying that principle means that you write shorter sentences for a while, never mind. Better that than to land yourself in the kind of quagmire we've just waded through.

3 Finally, we now encounter a writer who does not patronize his readers so much as ignore them completely. The suffering narrator here is Bertie Wooster, struggling with a work of philosophy his fiancée has thrust upon him to improve his mind: the passage comes from P. G. Wodehouse's story *Jeeves Takes Charge*.

> I opened *Types Of Ethical Theory*, and I give you my honest word this was what hit me:
> 'Of the two antithetic terms in the Greek philosophy one only was real and self-subsisting; and that one was Ideal Thought as opposed to that which it has to penetrate and mould. The other, corresponding to our Nature, was in itself phenomenal, unreal, without any permanent footing, having no predicates that held true for two moments together; in short, redeemed from negation only by including indwelling realities appearing through.'
> Well, I mean to say, what?

Bertie may be a 'silly ass' [Jeeves, his manservant, describes him elsewhere as 'mentally negligible'] but his reaction is a model for all put-upon readers. Equally

---

1 'Sic' means 'thus': it is used when quoting a passage containing grammatical errors, so that the reader will realize that the original writer committed the error, not the quoter. 'Sic' is therefore a splendidly economical way of saying, 'Yes, he/she really did write it this way!'

'Never begin a sentence until you are sure how it will end'.

unanswerable is Ernest Hemingway's observation that a writer's greatest gift – and, by association, a reader's too – is 'a built-in, shock-proof shit detector'. In Bertie's position we might urge the author to call in Dyno-Rod as soon as possible.

Readers must be prepared to do some work from time to time, naturally, but they also have the right to expect that things are not made needlessly difficult for them. No subject is so elusive or challenging that it cannot be rendered reasonably clear and enjoyable for an audience. The failure to do so means only one thing, ultimately: the writer doesn't care about his audience, being enclosed in a mere ego-trip.

I've entitled this section 'Disasters'. Two other terms defining such embarrassing incompetence are 'Howlers' and 'Colemanballs'. Virtually anyone who has sat an exam, filled in a form or composed a report has at some time committed a 'howler' – that is, a *written* error where there is a crucial gap between intention and result. You and I may not have sunk to the depths of these exam bloomers

Vacuum: a large empty space where the Pope lives.

Trees break wind for up to 200 yards.

It was dark when I was aroused by my alarm-clock.

Music sung by two people at the same time is called a duel.

or these (insurance) form-filling ones

I had been driving for forty years when I fell asleep at the wheel.

Coming home I drove into the wrong house and collided with a tree I haven't got.

The pedestrian had no idea in which direction to run, so I ran over him.

or such idiocy as attends these newspaper headlines

Something Went Wrong In Jet Crash, Expert Says

Squad Helps Dog Bite Victim[2]

Man Found Dead In Graveyard

But we should bear in mind that lapses of this kind can embarrass any writer just as much and as often as any speaker – which is where 'Colemanballs' comes in. That now-famous *Private Eye* term, originally inspired by the daft remarks of television commentator David Coleman but subsequently extended to include any and all such blunders, chiefly signifies *oral* gaffes. Three of my abiding favourites are:

We are not prepared to stand idly by and be murdered in our beds.

The Reverend Ian Paisley

If Tchaikovsky were alive today he'd be turning in his grave

Radio 1

We're waiting for the pole-vault over the satellite.

David Coleman

Of course, broadcasting is a pressured, heat-of-the-moment business, and such slips are bound to occur sooner or later, however articulate and skilful the speaker may normally be. That makes them as forgivable as funny, and the exercise overleaf that features ten further dangers is best attempted in that spirit. But there's a serious point at issue as well as amusement:

All successful communication requires unwavering alertness.

Never let your tongue or your hand get ahead of your brain.

Or as Kingsley Amis unimprovably puts it:

The price of a good style is eternal vigilance.

---

2 All this needs to make it entirely satisfactory is a hyphen between 'Dog' and 'Bite'. The structure 'Dog-Bite' transforms what were respectively a separate noun and verb into a compound adjective qualifying 'Victim'. An interesting example of the power – and importance – of precise punctuation!

Exercise 2

Ten comically inadequate remarks follow. In each case:

(a) Work out **why** it fails/is ridiculous
(b) Rewrite it so that it is clear and not able to be laughed at. Keep as close as you can to the original idea and wording.

1   **With the very last kick of the game, McDonald scored with a header.**

Alan Parry

2   **We thought this story incredible – very convincing.**

Lord Asa Briggs

3   **The Channel Tunnel project seems to be getting off the ground again.**

Sir Alistair Burnett

4   **Here we are in the Holy Land of Israel – a Mecca for tourists.**

David Vine

5   **She really set the pool alight tonight.**

Anita Lonsborough, talking about a swimmer

6   **To win a Gold Medal, you've got to come first.**

David Coleman

7   **I thought 2–0 was an accurate reflection of the scoreline.**

John Toshack

8   **Tell me, what's your gut feeling in your heart of hearts?**

Radio 4's *Today* programme

9   **Obviously you do other things as well as dedicating your life 24 hours a day to ballet.**

Mike Read

10   **The atmosphere is amazing: you could cut the tension with a cricket stump.**

Murray Walker

My suggested answers are on page 225.

The original's 'gut feeling in your heart of hearts' is an example of a **mixed metaphor**, which is a construction where two separate images collide, with confusing and/or ludicrous results. For example:

We're skating on thin ice and will soon be out of the frying pan and into the fire.

Both the images are clichés, of course, which doesn't help; but the biggest problem is the marriage of ice/water and heat. If one visualizes the overall scenario, absurdity ensues – a picture of a skater in danger suddenly repositioned in boiling fat and additionally threatened by a large blaze. The latter would surely cause the **thin ice** to melt at once anyway, wouldn't you say?

Another example comes from a Radio 4 news bulletin: I nearly included it in my very first section, 'Disasters':

The policy of non-intervention is a hot potato which has left the Government with egg on its face.

A hot potato means an urgent problem; to be left with **egg on one's face** means to be embarrassed or to look foolish. The trouble is, of course, that potatoes aren't famous for being made out of eggs; a potentially vigorous statement is again ruined by the visual absurdity the images evoke.

Mixed metaphors are invariably a symptom of the failure to 'engage brain before writing' or to both 'hear' and 'see' the words chosen. As noted, they are often an additionally unfortunate consequence of relying on hackneyed phrases.

Chapter 2

Triumphs

Style is a magic wand, and turns to gold everything it touches.
Logan Pearsall Smith

We've just looked at various examples of how not to write. Now let's redress the balance by considering some admirable passages. My illustrations have been chosen to match the types of writing included in the previous section: a passage of instructional prose; the beginning of a student essay; a newspaper article; an advanced philosophical discourse.

1 Taken from Sir Izaak Walton's masterpiece, *The Compleat Angler*.

How To Dress A Chub For Table
First scale him, and then wash him clean, and then take out his guts; and to that end make the hole as little and as near to his gills as you may conveniently, and especially make clean his throat from the grass and weeds that are usually in it, for if that be not very clean, it will make him to taste very sour; having so done, put some sweet herbs into his belly, and then tie him with two or three splinters to a spit, and roast him, basted often with vinegar, or rather verjuice[1] and butter, and with a good store of salt mixed with it.

If he is thus dressed, you will find him a much better dish of meat than you, or most folk, even the Anglers themselves do imagine; for this dries up the fluid watery humour with which all Chubs do abound.

This has considerable charm and it flows easily. Its chief quality, however, is its *clarity*: the careful organization and precise detail create a foolproof guide.

2 The start of an A Level essay on *As I Lay Dying*, a novel by William Faulkner.

---

1 'Verjuice' is the juice of an unripe fruit.

As the title so bluntly suggests, the novel is concerned wholly with death. It is void of any romanticism, and death itself is treated with little religious significance; it is the finality of death in a world ruled by nature and the unforgiving gods of ancient times that we are shown. This, indeed, is a radical and epic treatment of life's most important event, but the epic nature of the book is constantly undermined: the single most important sentence in the novel confirms my opening statement in its grotesque simplicity – 'My father used to say that the reason for living was to get ready to stay dead a long time.' The triviality of life: the finality of death without salvation or damnation.

Those that do not know Faulkner's novel will have to take my word for it that the content here is first class. But I hope any reader will appreciate the quality of its **style**. The concepts are large and the argument ambitious; yet notice how straightforward and logical the thinking and writing are. The first sentence sets up everything with fierce clarity, and then all the major implications are pursued with vigorous, stark persuasiveness. Finally, it is an excellent introduction as well as very fine in its own right: one would want to read on, avidly.

3 An extract from one of Alistair Cooke's *Letters From America*, part of an appreciation of US Chief Justice Earl Warren, who died in July 1974.

I'd always taken for granted that the ultimate truth about old people had been spoken by Aristotle twenty-three hundred years ago. Which is: 'Unlike the young, the old have lived long' – nobody like Aristotle for getting down to fundamentals – 'they have often been deceived, they have made many mistakes of their own, they have seen the pain caused by positive men, and so they are positive about nothing. And when they err, they err in all things by extreme moderation.'

As time went on, and I was able to watch young politicians age and mellow and grow positive about nothing, I noticed that very rarely there was a man who mellowed, like over-ripe fruit, into acidity. They were usually men who'd seemed to be committed all their lives to a bland, comfortable conservatism. And then something happened, something unexplained by the geriatric experts. It wasn't that they grew into a familiar type of the peppery conservative but that they grew at once more mellow and more radical.

Both comfortable to read and fascinating, the writing is masterly in its apparent effortlessness. In fact, it is very shrewdly crafted for all its air of spontaneity. Its sentences are intelligently varied in length; there are agreeable changes in tone, including one nicely understated joke; it is flawlessly punctuated (which always assists understanding). Above all, there is a central awareness of how the words will sound. That may hardly seem surprising, since the piece was conceived as a radio talk; the crucial point is that it reads as well as it sounds, **and vice**

versa. During this book I shall be stressing a great deal the importance of 'voice' in one's writing, and now seems a good time to record another fundamental principle:

All good writing *sounds* equally good when read aloud; and all good talking will *read* well if transcribed.

Sadly, the same relationship characterizes **bad** writing and talking. If you want proof, refer back to any of the pieces in the previous section.

4 A paragraph from 'The Vision Of A Child', one of five philosophical lectures collected in David Newsome's *Two Classes Of Men: Platonism and English Romantic Thought*.

We may grant that distinctions of measure and discernment of categories are important to the imaginative poet as well as to the scientist. Just because he has them, the poet is a philosopher in a sense that a child can never be. Coleridge recognized this in his careful analysis of the loosing and binding power of the imagination, as we have seen, and his approval of the statement of H. S. Reimarus that 'we have no conception, not even of single objects, except by means of the similarity we perceive between them and other objects'. F. D. Maurice, likewise, pointed to the inability of a child to make refined distinctions, arising from the infant state when all men are called 'father' and all women 'mother'. But the particular genius of the child – and to Coleridge a child possesses genius rather than talent – was the combination of simplicity, innocence and sensibility which enabled it to penetrate to the essence of what it observed, without being able to explain the process in intellectual or rational terms.

Here Newsome addresses some fundamental principles and phenomena of perception, as part of a searching reappraisal of the work of a major English poet. Nobody would call the writing 'easy': such major concerns demand fierce concentration on the reader's part. But that concentration is rapidly rewarded, because the prose is both logical and vibrant, with a couple of homely examples the better to fix things in one's mind.

If you refer back to the passage Bertie Wooster had to endure (page 4), you should at once be aware of a crucial difference. The more one studies the prose there, the muddier it becomes; equivalent attention to Newsome's work quickly brings enlightenment. And Newsome's scale of reference is no smaller or less profound than that of the 'companion piece'. His ideas are large and his focus ambitious, but one senses that he is anxious to share them with us; in contrast, Bertie's tormentor seems to be indulging some private game that shuts out his audience. Huge or complex ideas need not remain inaccessible to the 'ordinary reader'. Indeed, I would argue that if those ideas cannot be expressed to the satisfaction and understanding of such a reader, they are probably not that important or worthwhile after all.

Summary

Successful writing depends on a lot of things, but we have already identified three of the most important.

1   All good writing is *clear*; to achieve clarity you must work out in advance what you want to say in each sentence and each paragraph. You cannot afford to 'just write': tough-minded preliminary planning is essential if your work is to please and illuminate.
2   All good writing has a proper sense of its audience. You should assume your reader is intelligent, or not actually a moron; on the other hand, do not *over*estimate his or her abilities. At every turn you should keep your readers awake, interested, stimulated; but you should also ensure that they are comfortable, aware of what you're doing and where you're going. In short, make your reader your respected but gratified *companion*.
3   All good writing has a strong sense of 'voice'. Effective prose, no less than successful poetry, is attractive to ear and eye alike. Writing that is pleasing has a natural rhythm and melodiousness, qualities that characterize a pleasant speaking voice; in addition, the presence of good 'voice' automatically renders one's writing more personal, warmer and clearer.

With these central things firmly in mind, let us now take a close look at how language works.

Part II

Foundations

Chapter 3

Introduction

Style, like the human body, is especially beautiful when the veins are not prominent and the bones cannot be counted.

Tacitus

It is flesh which makes a body both beautiful and individual. Few people other than rampant ghouls find skeletons aesthetically delightful, and I've yet to find anyone who found them sensually attractive. And whereas each human body seems unique, each skeleton looks identical to all but an expert eye.

Consider what happens to the body, however, if any of its bones is deformed or deficient in some other way. Not only does the frame appear forlorn and full of pain; the flesh on it often looks comparably unhealthy. Just as good bone structure and skin tone can enhance healthy flesh and transform it into beauty, so any flaws in the body's basic structure seem eventually to infect it throughout.

It is the same with language. The ultimate aim of this book is to help you achieve an elegant, precise and individual style in all that you write – to give your writing the functional beauty that characterizes a healthy body. But that cannot be done until the skeleton is in good shape. The foundations or 'bones' of your language must be sound if its flesh – what you want to say and how you wish to say it – is to prosper.

Of course, flesh and bone go together. A fleshless skeleton may not be much to look at, but then neither is flesh on its own: it is so much dead meat. Writers who ignore the basic structures and concentrate on disembodied style don't just fail to write well: they end up butchering the language they claim to nurture and enjoy. The sections which follow look at the bones and ligaments of language (the sentence and the clause) and its essential joints (punctuation and paragraphing).

Chapter 4

Bone structure

4.1   WHAT IS A SENTENCE?

The sentence is the single most important linguistic structure: it is, if you like, the backbone of all writing. And it is disturbing how much **invertebrate** writing one encounters. Many otherwise quite capable writers either do not understand what a sentence is or are incapable of applying that understanding at all times.

One reason for this is that the sentence is a very difficult concept to explain and therefore to master. There are only three 'rules' which pertain, and each is of limited value.

1   **All sentences must begin with a capital letter and end with a full stop.**
2   **All sentences must express a complete thought.**
3   **All sentences must contain a subject and a finite verb.**

Comfortably straightforward, aren't they? No? You're absolutely right!

The first rule is one of the first things most of us learn at primary school. It seems elementary: using a capital letter is simple, and we all know what a full stop is. But the rule is not much use on its own:

Manchester United.   **Write In Style.**

Those start with capital letters, and I've [legitimately] placed a full stop after each one. They are not sentences, however; to establish why not, we need to consider rules 2 and 3.

I've often felt that rule 2 ought to be more helpful than it actually is. 'A complete thought' **seems** to be a clear and precise term: in this pair of examples it is obvious that the first is incomplete, making no sense whatsoever.

The man in a yellow.   **The girl in rags.**

But in what way is the second 'a complete thought'? It makes a certain amount of sense, yes, but only in terms of naming, of identification. Like 'Manchester United' and 'Write In Style', 'The girl in rags' prompts us to ask something like 'Well, so what?' or 'What about her?' As they stand, all three are in a kind of limbo, requiring further information to satisfy us fully.

That's where rule 3 comes in. Each of these four examples obeys rules 1 and 2; only one of them matches the requirement laid down by rule 3. Which is it?

(a) The mechanic in the oil-stained overall.
(b) The Hound of the Baskervilles.
(c) The dog bites the milkman.
(d) British Aerospace.

The answer is (c), which is an authentic **sentence**; the others are **phrases**.

In (c) an event takes place: something happens, firmly located in time. In this case that time is the present, but the sentence could equally be set in the past –

The dog bit the milkman.

or the future –

the dog will bite the milkman.

Bites, bit and **will bite** denote an action or a process – which is what all 'verbs' do. In addition, that action or process is identified in terms of time – hence 'finite', located within a definite tense/area of time. Finally, to be fully 'finite', a verb must be accompanied by a **subject** – and this tricky concept needs a little exploration.

In 'English studies' we use the term **subject** in two quite separate ways, and this can forgivably cause students a lot of confusion. In its broader, more general sense, **subject** means **topic**. In these remarks

(a) **Can you remember the subject of this chapter?**
(b) **He is bored: we should change the subject.**

subject refers to what the chapter or the conversation is about: strictly speaking, the term should be expanded to **subject matter**.

But **subject** has a narrower, technical meaning too. In grammatical terms, **subject** means that which governs the verb – the person or thing 'in charge' of the action or process described. In that earlier sentence

The dog bites the milkman

'the dog' is the 'doer' of the action (**bites**). It is the **grammatical subject**.

As a summary for the time being, let's see how the two separate meanings of **subject** apply to my three most recent examples.

(a) Can you remember the subject of this chapter?

> Topic/subject matter: the question of what the chapter is about.
> Grammatical subject: 'you'[+ finite verb 'can remember'].

(b) He is bored: we should change the subject.

> Topic/subject matter: the speaker's desire to talk about something else.
> Grammatical subjects: i) 'He' [+ finite verb 'is'].
>   ii) 'we' [+ finite verb 'should change']

(c) The dog bites the milkman.

> Topic/subject matter: An incident involving a dog, a milkman and an act of biting*
> Grammatical subject: 'The dog' [+ finite verb 'bites'].

* You might find this explanation clumsy, vague or pompous. I rather hope you do: I phrased it in that way to highlight further the complete separateness of the two meanings of **subject**. For I could re-arrange the words in that sentence so that the **subject matter** definition still applied but the **grammatical subject** was radically different:

(d) The milkman bites the dog.

That still concerns 'a dog, a milkman and an act of biting'; but now it is the 'milkman' who is 'in charge' of the action: he is 'the doer', not the dog!

To qualify as a sentence, therefore, a verbal structure must possess three principal properties. It must describe an action or process that is located in a specific time-zone; the 'doer' [grammatical subject] must be identified; and the thought expressed must be complete, fully satisfying. If you are not yet comfortable with the first two, then please read through the material again. If you're happy about those two but continue to find the concept of 'a complete thought' problematic, it is time to introduce another term: the clause.

4.2 SENTENCE AND CLAUSE: WHAT'S THE DIFFERENCE?

When uncertain about a meaning, most sensible people refer to a good dictionary. *The Shorter Oxford* defines 'sentence' as:

A series of words in connected speech or writing, forming the grammatically complete expression of a single thought.

And 'clause' as:

A short sentence; a distinct member of a sentence, one containing a subject and a predicate.[1]

The trouble is that unless you already know the difference, I suspect that this pair of definitions is not only of little help but probably increases your confusion! The most we can deduce from them is that

All sentences are clauses, or contain several clauses; but a single clause does not necessarily form a sentence.

And a fat lot of help **that** seems to be, no doubt prompting the reaction, 'Thanks a whole bunch!' I hope I can clear things up by studying some examples, in the form of a little exercise.

Exercise 3
Which of these is a sentence, which a clause?

1   Although you broke the window.
2   I forgive you.
3   I have a hunch that.
4   You dislike cheese.

All four start with capitals and end with full stops; all four have a subject and a finite verb – as follows:

	Subject	Finite verb
1	you	broke
2	I	forgive
3	I	have
4	You	dislike

But do all four express a **complete** thought?

---

1 Don't worry about the term 'predicate'. It is defined as 'the statement made about a subject'; in effect this simply means everything in the sentence or clause apart from the subject. By definition, the predicate includes a finite verb.

I hope you can see that 1 and 3 do not – we need more information for them to satisfy fully. Both are left hanging in the air. In 1 the use of 'although' sets up an expectation that is not fulfilled, while 3 is even more frustrating, leaving us entirely ignorant of what this 'hunch' is about. Both 2 and 4 are complete. They may be somewhat bald, even uninteresting; nevertheless, they require nothing else to make complete grammatical and intellectual sense.

However, it is relatively easy to make 1 and 3 part of an authentic sentence: we can merge them with 2 and 4.

5   **Although you broke the window, I forgive you.**
6   **I have a hunch that you dislike cheese.**

These make complete sense, and are now, perhaps, more interesting! 5 and 6 now consist of two clauses – each has two subjects and two finite verbs. And both consist of a **main clause** and a **subordinate clause**. The latter term describes a clause that cannot stand on its own –

Although you broke the window . . .
I have a hunch that . . .

Subordinate clauses are 'grammatical juniors', dependent on the main clause for complete sense. They are not 'subordinate' in any other way; they need not be stylistically inferior, and indeed may be more informative than the main clause they depend on, as in this example:

7   **If you go on with a diet that consists exclusively of cottage cheese, dry toast and Brazil nuts, I shall worry.**

The main clause is **I shall worry**: it is, I think, rather feeble in view of what precedes it, a sad anticlimax to what was promising to be a fairly arresting sentence. But although that previous clause is much more interesting in every other way, it remains grammatically subordinate: it could not stand on its own.

If we return to my metaphor of grammar as a skeleton, we could say that sentences/main clauses are **bones**, and that subordinate clauses are **ligaments**. Bones may well be the basis of everything, but without ligaments they remain stiff and limited; it is often the ligaments, or the 'junior' members of a sentence that give it charm and impact. Once those bones and ligaments are in good shape, the chances are high that the flesh that covers them – the actual material and individual words chosen – will be sound and pleasing.

The next section looks at how a number of professional writers create widely different shapes and effects out of the basic properties we've so far covered.

4.3 BIG BONES OR LITTLE BONES: HOW LONG SHOULD A SENTENCE BE?

'How long is a piece of string' is often cited as the classic useless question, and to ask 'How long should my sentences be?' might seem equally idiotic. In fact it is both intelligent and important. For once you've understood how and why your sentences work, you can **fashion** them to your taste – and that partly involves a decision about how long and complex, or short and snappy, they need to be for your purposes. Effective writing comes in all shapes and sizes: the key is in judging which shape and size is most appropriate to a given task.

Please read this passage from Ernest Hemingway's *Big Two-Hearted River*.

> He took out his knife, opened it, and stuck it in the log. Then he pulled up the sack, reached into it, and brought out one of the trout. Holding him near the tail, hard to hold, alive, in his hand, he whacked him against the log. The trout quivered, rigid. Nick laid him on the log in the shade and broke the neck of the other fish in the same way. He laid them side by side on the log. They were fine trout.
>
> Nick cleaned them, slitting them from the vent to the tip of the jaw. All the insides and the gills and the tongue came out in one piece. They were both males, long grey-white strips of milt, smooth and clean. All the insides clean and compact, coming out all together. Nick tossed the offal ashore for the minks to find.
>
> He washed the trout in the stream. When he held them back in the water they looked like live fish. Their colour was not gone yet . . .

And so on. I admire this a good deal, but I've chosen it for this section because it is precariously close to being monotonous. There is some variety – but only in that some sentences are even shorter than others!

Hemingway is famous for this kind of style. In the example chosen, the profusion of full stops is designed to make the reader focus on each simple action and perception, and in its stark way it is a very physical piece.[2] I think it works well, but it is a most unwise model. In your own writing it is best to aim for a greater variety of sentence-length.

The next passage goes to the opposite extreme.

> When the director in the field sends the executive in there's got to be a professional set-up. We didn't have one.

---

2 The hero, Nick, is in fact still suffering from trauma, so the simple style is movingly appropriate, his stiff halting sentences analogous to the tentative steps someone might take when first walking after breaking a leg. Another example of such surface simplicity hiding deeper truth and trauma can be found in Aston's speech at the end of Act II of Harold Pinter's *The Caretaker*.

I suppose Loman had thought of a dozen angles of attack and obviously the one he'd chosen was the one he thought was right and he was wrong.

'I think you're showing an unreasonable bias towards – '

'Is that so?' I was really very fed up. 'We've been called in by a panic directive to clear up the wreck of an operation that went off half-cocked and killed one man and exposed another and by a bit of luck I missed a bomb and last night they picked Fyson out of Tunis harbour and it'd be nice to think that when they grilled him he didn't break but the last time I saw him his nerve had gone so they wouldn't have had any trouble. How safe's our base now, Loman? . . .'

from *The Tango Briefing* by Adam Hall

If a homework-marker would criticize Hemingway for too many short sentences, then Hall would be equally castigated for writing an eight-line sentence devoid of punctuation. Yet I consider this excellent writing. The narrator, Quiller, is very annoyed, and his outburst is the result of cumulative frustration. It explodes in a single 'breathless' rush, which makes the absence of punctuation entirely appropriate.

Once again, however, that is not a model I'd advise you to copy. Creative writers can break 'rules' in this way provided they succeed as a result. That is also true for you and me, but in most of your discursive, non-fiction writing it is better to stick to a middle course than emulate either of those extremes.

That middle course will be easier to negotiate if you stay constantly alert to your readers' pleasure and comfort. The following passage does this very well; it makes the subject come alive by **varying** the rhythms and shape of the prose.

This extract occurs at the end of a portrait of 'Arnold' by John Wain, in his book *Dear Shadows*.

Long before the mile was covered, Arnold was wilting. There was simply no strength left in that old body which had weathered malnutrition and disease seventy years earlier and had gone on at a cracking pace ever since. We walked more and more slowly. I was about to suggest that he sit down while I fetched the car when we heard behind us the drumming engine of a tractor. It came up, towing behind a flat wagon which had been emptied of its load. We flagged it down. The driver, a good-natured young fellow, let us scramble up on to the wagon, and sitting on its smooth boards, dusty with fragments of straw and chaff, we finished our excursion. Arnold looked round with satisfaction at the landscape, and remarked that this would be a good way of taking a holiday: touring the British Isles by tractor and trailer.

That was the last of my excursions with Arnold. His bed, and then the grave, claimed him in the first height of summer, the time of year he loved so much, and his life ended among springing green leaves and clamorous birds. But I remember him jolting along behind the tractor, enjoying the fun of it, finding zest in that last outing as he found zest in all the others.

I was very proud of Arnold. He was my father.

The last sentence reveals Arnold's identity for the first time – a wonderfully touching ending.[3] Elsewhere there is again a variety in sentence-length pleasing in its richness and also appropriate. The shorter sentences tend to be about Arnold's weakness – his own 'shortness' of breath and stamina – while the longer ones meander gracefully, reflecting the gentle panorama of the landscape. Wain is always alert to why a specific length or rhythm is apposite, and how it will benefit the reader.

SENTENCE LENGTH: SOME CONCLUDING GUIDELINES

It is impossible to give watertight advice on how long and how varied your sentences should be. As we've just seen, different kinds of writing require different things and express different priorities. However, there are guidelines which can be of assistance in shaping your sentences; they all hinge on the need to 'hear' what you're writing and to calculate its effect on others.
[Note: ** denotes an illustration or exercise to follow.]

1   It is usually a good idea to make your first sentence reasonably short. This is not an absolute rule, naturally, but your readers will be grateful if you ease them into your material with crisp straightforwardness.
2   Too many short sentences will quickly tire and irritate your readers.**
3   Equally, avoid too many long sentences. These tire readers in a different way, and you risk bewildering and eventually losing them.
4   Avoid constructing sentences that are too complex or needlessly intricate.**
5   It is often wise to follow a sentence containing a lot of information with a short one that, while not duplicating your material, summarizes or clarifies it.**
6   Make sure each new sentence actually says something. Mere repetition of already-established material is of no use, however elegant your style. Deliberate repetition for effect is another matter, but it is a difficult skill and should in any case be used sparingly.

Finally, two 'golden principles':

1   Trust the *feel* of your prose. By all means be self-critical and alert to danger, but if, all precautions admitted, you're convinced that the three successive long [or short] sentences you've written are effective and pleasing, *keep them in.* Slavishly to write one long, two short, or one long, one short, one long

---

3 Incidentally, it is also a perfect example of the power of a short paragraph, a technique to be examined later.

and so on, is just silly. To approach your prose as if it is some kind of elaborate Morse code is no way to achieve competence, let alone true 'style'.

2   Assume your readers are intelligent. Don't patronize; don't be indifferent either. You can expect them to be prepared to do some work, but try to make their working environment as comfortable and stimulating as you can.

Illustrations and exercises

Passage A: Exercise 4

This is potentially a vigorous piece, but it is marred by too many short sentences. Keeping as close as you can to the original, try recasting it so that it acquires proper fluency. My suggested version is on page 226.

Prohibition was known as 'The Great Experiment'. The experiment was a remarkable one. It occurred in the United States of America. It took place in the years 1920–33. The sale and consumption of alcohol was prohibited throughout those years. But the people's liking for alcohol did not disappear. Therefore alcohol was distilled illegally. It was sold in 'Speakeasies'. 'Speakeasies' were clubs owned by gangsters. Some of those gangsters became enormously powerful. Al Capone of Chicago was for a time considered to be the most powerful man in the country. He was eventually imprisoned for tax evasion. The gangsters' control nevertheless continued. The experiment came to an end in 1933. By this time the damage had been done. America has had to live with organized crime ever since.

Passage B: Exercise 5

This next sentence is much too 'fiddly' and intricate. The writer has not done enough prior planning, and tries to cram too much in, with increasingly confusing results for the reader. Try re-writing it so that it is clear; use two sentences if you wish. Again, my suggested version is on page 226.

Counsel maintained that the accused, if he had, as was alleged by some, though not the most reliable of the witnesses for the prosecution, taken the articles in question, had been subject to temporary lapses of memory as a result of shell-shock sustained during the war.

Passage C

No exercise this time – just an example of how to 'clinch' and clarify information listed in a long sentence with a snappily short one. It comes from Joseph Heller's *Catch-22*.

> One day Clevinger had stumbled while marching to class; the next day he was formally charged with 'breaking ranks while in formation, felonious assault, indiscriminate behaviour, mopery, high treason, provoking, being a smart guy, listening to classical music' and so on. In short, they threw the book at him.

I have described sentences and clauses as the bones and ligaments of writing; if you construct them well, you will invariably produce a sound and durable 'skeleton'. But before we can go on to consider the 'muscle and flesh' that make the body of your writing come fully alive, a detailed study of punctuation and paragraphing is needed. For these are 'joints', essential if your prose is to be flexible and attractive.

Chapter 5

Joints

5.1   PUNCTUATION: WEIGHT-TRAINING

Towards the end of Kingsley Amis's 1966 novel, *The Anti-Death League*, Jagger, a senior Government investigator, explains how he came to determine the authorship of a seditious poem that had been circulated within a top-secret Defence establishment.

> 'Whereas there are a number of illiteracies in spelling, the punctuation is correct all through. Now that's odd, you see. For every twenty people who can spell there's hardly one who can punctuate. Pretty well everyone who can punctuate can spell as a matter of course. So our man isn't really semi-literate: he's just pretending to be.'

The argument may be overstated, but I think it is substantially true.

As a teacher I have come across hundreds of students – children and adults – who only rarely make errors in spelling or grammar but whose punctuation is either incompetent or dangerously limited. And I fear that nowadays this is also true of many professional communicators. In the newspapers and periodicals you read, you won't find much misspelling or many grammatical errors, but you will find a lot of wretched punctuation. Even the book-publishing trade is no longer reliable: on many occasions over the years I have been sent books to review awash with errors that ought to embarrass a decent GCSE student.

Something even more significant is suggested in the extract above. Jagger implies, in effect, that the skills of punctuation are harder to master than those of spelling, that they are subtler and more elusive. I think that is true too. Poor spelling is highly **visible**; so is bad grammar. Poor punctuation obtrudes less perceptibly; perhaps for that reason it matters less?

On the contrary: punctuation is the most important of all 'bread and butter' skills. Good grammar and correct spelling are not exactly incidental, naturally, and any proficient writer needs to be flawless in both. But bad punctuation is insidious, just as good punctuation is at times hardly noticeable. A spelling mistake may leap out of the page at you and interrupt the flow of your reading. That is

'Poor spelling is highly visible'.

regrettable, but unless the mistake is comically bad, it is improbable that you will fail to grasp what the intended word is. Similarly, a sudden dive into bad grammar will deflect and irritate, but it's unlikely to destroy meaning completely.

But inadequate punctuation can rapidly cause disaster. A writer who ignores essential full stops or uses the comma as the sole, carry-all signal [two common flaws in the work I encounter] will soon create a mess that is either permanently incomprehensible or requiring much arduous 're-coding' before understanding dawns. To use a building simile, punctuation is like mortar: unless you put it in correctly every time, your bricks will eventually collapse, leaving only a wrecked heap.

Before going any further, I want to list all the punctuation devices available, and to grade them according to 'weight'.[1] For once you understand the relative strength of each one, you'll be in a good position to decide which you should use when a punctuation point is needed.

There are twelve grades of pause used when punctuating. I list them in ascending order of status; to the right is my idea of their weight as pauses, on a scale of to 1 to 20.[2]

1 I am not at the moment concerned with the punctuation of speech and quotation. These techniques are important [they are fully covered in Chapter 17] but they have nothing to do with pause and **weight** of pause, my focus here.
2 You will see that it does not include the **hyphen** or the **forward-** or **backward-slash**. Needless to say, those devices are very useful and should be part of any writer's armoury; however, they do not signify any kind of *pause*, which is my present concern.

I would imagine that numbers 10–20 are larger units/pause signals than most of you will currently be concerned with; number 7 has a section to itself later. What I most wish to make clear about the remainder is threefold:

- That the comma – the commonest and also the most wildly overused punctuation point – is very much the weakest.
- That the full stop, although it is [rightfully] used a great deal, is a very 'senior' pause, several times stronger than the comma. Indeed, for most writers there is only one larger device – the paragraph.
- That there are a number of invaluable devices in between the comma and the full stop which should be a regular part of every writer's equipment.

We shall return to those six devices shortly; first, it is likely that numbers 3 and 9 need explanation.

Ellipsis

The definition of this term in the *Shorter Oxford English Dictionary* runs

> **The omission of one or more words in a sentence, which would be needed to express the sense completely**

and that, certainly, is the function you will come across or use most often, especially when quoting. If I were to apply ellipsis to the sentence you have just read, it might appear as

> **The definition of this term in the *Shorter Oxford English Dictionary* . . . is the function you will . . . use most often.**

The practice allows you to retain the governing sense of a remark while editing it for your own purposes. It is a small (albeit very neat) device, which is why I have called number 3 **the weak ellipsis**.

But ellipsis has two other applications that the *SOED* does not list – one weak, one strong. The former can be used to signify not just an edited remark but one that is never *finished*; perhaps the commonest example occurs in dialogue, when one speaker interrupts another:

> 'What I want . . .'
> 'I don't *care* what you want.'

In such a case you could use the dash instead – which is why the list above allots the two devices the same score – but the latter is so valuable as the equivalent of a strong comma[3] that its integrity in that respect should be preserved. Using the weak ellipsis enables you to do so, and it is an elegant method in its own right.

In striking contrast, **the strong ellipsis** is a very weighty pause – a kind of 'big brother' to the paragraph. It is most often used in novels to denote a significant lapse in time; in non-fiction writing it can be a deftly economical way of signalling the need for further thought and action or that the way forward is shrouded in uncertainty:

> **It would be good to see him heeding this advice . . .**
> **As to what we do next . . .**

To be used sparingly anyway, **the strong ellipsis** is unlikely to strike writers engaged on academic or professional tasks as an appropriate device very often, if at all. But it is always worthwhile to know what a punctuation signal denotes, and I would hope that you'll now be comfortable with ellipsis in all its three applications even if your need is to decode it as a reader rather than use it yourself.

Next, let us see how bad punctuation can destroy potentially competent writing.

A Mind the stop[4]

These four instances of inadequate or incorrect punctuation are in order of increasing length. The first appeared in a popular Sunday newspaper. Can you put it right?

> *Passage A: Exercise 6*
> Lady X refuses all blandishments to go on the stage or into films. Though her sister, Lady Y, is an actress. Appearing in *People Of Our Class*.

---

3 See page 32.
4 I have borrowed this neat phrase from G.V. Carey, who made it the title of his classic monograph on punctuation skills. See Further Reading.

It should be written as one sentence. As it stands, it is jerky, damaging flow and meaning by separating components that belong naturally together. You may by now see that the second and third 'sentences' do not meet the three criteria laid down in the previous chapter: strictly speaking, they are not sentences at all.

You could restore flow and grammatical accuracy in several ways: the simplest is to substitute the first two full stops with commas:

> Lady X refuses all blandishments to go on the stage or into films, though her sister Lady Y is an actress, appearing in *People Of Our Class*.

That first example suffered from absurdly overweighted pauses. What's wrong with this second one?

Passage B: Exercise 7
It should be noted that plastics can vary considerably in ruggedness they can be heavy or thin, plastic dials and knobs can have a metal sleeve to take the screw or they can be just plastic, the latter are the more likely to pull off in your hand.

Please attempt these two tasks.

1   Read Passage B aloud. Obey as if your life depended on it the pauses and the punctuation signals; if **no** pause is signalled, obey that too. I'd be very surprised if it sounded 'right' as you spoke the words. The passage induces breathlessness, doesn't it? And didn't you find you were rapidly approaching a point where the meaning was so misty as to seem lost?
2   With a piece of paper to hand, read it aloud again, as slowly as you like, and write down
     (a) every word that you think requires a signalled pause after it;
     (b) the 'weight' of the pause you think is best – comma, full stop or something in between.

Then write out the piece in its complete 'improved' form. My suggested version follows in a moment.

Passage B was a piece of instructional prose. I would not say that clarity is more important in such writing than elsewhere – clarity is **always** of prime importance, whatever the task. But I'm sure you know how maddening, imprecise or confusing instructions can be, especially if you've just spent a lot of money on some new hardware [hi-fi equipment, super-de-luxe lawn mower] and find yourself at the mercy of instructions originally written in Japanese and translated by someone not fully at home with English! Instructional writing needs to be absolutely precise; it is therefore essential that the shape and rhythm of the prose match that ordered process.

So, to come to my own version of the breathless flurry above, the information must be clearly and calmly presented one step at a time. In this case, full stops are ideal, although there also needs to be a colon where the original included no punctuation whatever. My corrections are underlined.

> It should be noted that plastics vary considerably in ruggedness: they can be heavy or thin. Plastic dials and knobs can have a metal sleeve to take the screw or they can just be plastic. The latter are the more likely to pull off in your hand.

Now we have three clear, telling sentences instead of one hopelessly entangled one. All it took to effect such a decisive change was a little reflection and a moment or two of putting oneself in the reader's place.

Those first two examples are straightforward illustrations of poorly-judged pauses, at either end of the scale. The final one is marred by a sense of headlong rush compounded by technical inadequacy. Though the flaws are analogous to those noted in A and B they are even more damaging because the passage is so much longer.

Passage C: Exercise 8

Cholesterol, a steroid alcohol found in certain fluids and substances, stored by the body, is a potentially deadly phenomenon, it promotes arteriosclerosis, this precipitates high blood pressure, which increases the chances of having a heart
5   attack, or angina, or a host of similarly dangerous conditions, its main carriers are foods we eat regularly, like butter, cheese, milk and salt, let alone things like cream and rich puddings.
   If you have too many of these, and I haven't yet mentioned eggs or anything fried, oil and dripping are simply loaded
10 with cholesterol, your arteries harden prematurely, this makes it more difficult for the blood to flow, obviously enough, they also get coated and, in general, unhealthy, contaminated and weak, you run a high risk, at the very least, of premature illness, or incapacity, or even death.

I have come across many hundreds of paragraphs like those over the years, and all of them suffered from what happens here. Not only does the passage become increasingly tiresome to read: the writer's control over his material and over his very thinking gets progressively weaker.

In this case, there's a wealth of detailed information: the writer evidently knows what he's talking about. But he hasn't worked out how best to deploy his material:

by halfway his sense of destination is cloudy and his ability to register separate points has almost vanished. In lines 8–10, for instance, he desperately inserts something he should have included earlier, and then adds a larger point about oil and dripping. However, such poor planning would matter less if the punctuation were better.

The root of the problem is simple but very serious – most of the commas are **wrong**.

The comma is the weakest possible pause; most of the time the writer should have chosen a stronger alternative. As it is, the prose is a series of incontinent spasms in which the commas buzz across our eyes like the spots one sees after a racking cough. And this is not just a matter of taste or reader-comfort: those guidelines are underscored by the fundamental fact that

It is grammatically incorrect to separate two clauses with <u>only</u> a comma.

With that essential principle in mind, re-write the piece. Read the passage aloud as it stands: you should find that your delivery will help you to decide how long each pause needs to be. Plenty of devices are at your disposal; you need not overdo the full stop, but I'll be surprised if you don't use more than the solitary instance the original provides! You may find that certain minor changes in word order are advisable, that the paragraphing would benefit from slight modification, and that a few words need to be added or substituted. But in essence you should be able to transform the piece into clarity and elegance simply by choosing correct and varied punctuation. My suggested version is on page 226.

Passage C was infested with a chronic condition sadly prevalent in much writing today: I call it 'the yob's comma'. The next section is dedicated to a full diagnosis of that condition and, I hope, its cure; this section closes with a detailed study of each punctuation device.

Weights and measures: an annotated 'hierarchy' of punctuation

1 The comma
Denotes a brief, hardly perceptible pause. If used with a conjunction [**and, but, for** etc.] it acquires the same weight as a semi-colon; otherwise it should be chosen only to separate individual words or phrases. **Never** use it on its own to divide two full clauses.

2 The dash
Equivalent to a 'strong' comma. The dash is very useful towards the end of a clause or sentence when the writer wishes to stress an additional and important point.

3 Brackets/a pair of dashes
Used to isolate a thought or piece of information that is worth including but is

secondary to the main thrust of the material. The pair of dashes is slightly the weightier, but essentially they do the same work.[5]

4 The semi-colon

As might be deduced from its form [; – a full stop above a comma] its weight is almost exactly halfway between the comma and the full stop. It should be used to separate two clauses whose subject matter is closely related. Intelligent use along these lines prevents overuse of the comma and also preserves the full stop for when a significantly large pause is required.

5 The colon

Identical to 4 in both weight and sad underuse nowadays. Whereas the semi-colon denotes a pause between two related clauses, the colon separates two that directly interlock – i.e. each is to an extent dependent on the other for full sense or impact.

6 The full stop

A major pause: it should therefore be used as sparingly as possible. If you do want your reader to pause significantly, then of course use it, but be ready to take advantage of 4 and 5 as more lightweight alternatives. A profusion of full stops prohibits flow and can irritate.

7 The question and exclamation marks

As the full stop at their base might suggest, these have the same weight as a full stop but are also specific signals. Any time a question is asked or implied, a question mark is obligatory. Exclamation marks are used to highlight remarks that should surprise or amuse. Beware, however, of using them too often for 'jokes'. The practice is not a bad one, but the reader might soon tire of seeing every third sentence or so advertised as a 'laugh'.

In speech punctuation, exclamation marks should be used if the tone and especially the volume of the speaker are strong (see Chapter 21).

All these devices are examined further during the remainder of this chapter, including plenty of illustrations of their correct use. It's also worth pointing out that I've been using every kind of punctuation device throughout this book. If you're unsure of how they work or are not yet clear about what I mean by 'weight of pause', you might find it helpful to re-read a couple of my paragraphs and work out how my punctuation works. It's quite possible that you'll find some mistakes or less than perfect choices; if so, write and let me know. I'll be interested and grateful (albeit somewhat ashamed) and you'll feel terrific!

---

5 The dash has a dubious status in some circles. I imagine this stems from primary-school days, when the dash is discouraged lest it become the only punctuation used. That is fair enough at such an early stage; adults will find the dash a most valuable 'heavy' alternative to the comma. It does roughly the same work but visually highlights the subsequent material in a very neat fashion.

5.2 'PUNK-TUATION' (I): THE YOB'S COMMA

> The notes I handle no better than many pianists. But the pauses between the notes – ah, that is where the art resides.
>
> Artur Schnabel

The single biggest and most common punctuational disease is the abuse of the comma. Like many diseases, however, its symptoms are not always obvious to the patient, who indeed may not even recognize them until it is too late. I've already referred several times to 'weight of pause' and the need to 'hear' how your writing will strike the reader; I'm also uncomfortably aware that unless you half-instinctively know what I mean by all that, you may as yet be not too much the wiser. A couple of analogies may help to clarify matters.

Nearly everyone listens to music at some time or another, and music depends on **rhythm**, from the simplest nursery rhyme to the most grandly-scored symphonic masterpiece. Rhythm involves the use of space, pauses and changes of emphasis; even a tone-deaf person will register such things, and can certainly respond to the use of **dynamics** [changes in volume].

It doesn't take much imagination to realize how dull any kind of music would quickly become if there were no variety in volume or rhythm. Admittedly, there are a few works in all musical genres [rock, jazz and classical] which turn monotony in to an hypnotic virtue; that indeed seems to be the *sole* aim and function of an idiom currently so popular, rap music. By and large, however, lack of variety leads to grinding tedium. So to be of enjoyable, music must intrigue and engage the listener, and it achieves that partly by the use of 'rests', changes from *piano* to *forte*, and the use of a sudden increase in volume [*sforzando*]. In short, every piece of

'Music must intrigue and engage the listener'.

music has, in addition to the notes on the page, a host of 'secondary' but essential instructions denoting required volume, weight of touch and sound, design of phrasing and so forth.

Punctuation does the same kind of work. It **orchestrates** your words in the way that a composer orchestrates his notes; you assist and grip your reader by varying your pauses, and making that variety part of a pleasing overall structure that makes satisfying sense.

The 'yob's comma' destroys that possibility. If you provide merely a deluge of single-weight pauses, your writing will become monotonous and rapidly lose both meaning and impact. If there is no differentiation between one phrase and another, one point and another, one sentence and another, the result can only be visual anarchy and visible meaninglessness.

To use a second and briefer analogy: imagine how boring would be a football match where the only kind of pass attempted was a soft five-yard effort. [Yes, I know some of you find football boring anyway: bear with me for a moment!] The rhythm and excitement of football lie in the rich variety of its movement, the potential range of length and 'weight' of passes. A good side will employ any number of different devices: the long through pass, the deft headed pass, the 'wall' pass, the back pass, the 'one-two', the swerve pass with the outside of the foot, and so on. It is through such variation that players hope to achieve – literally – their goal.

Your aim as a punctuator is much the same. You should aim to use the most appropriate device for the task of the moment, just as do the footballer and composer. A footballer won't last long if all he uses is the delicate five-yard pass; you'll be in similar trouble if the only 'weight' of pause you use is the weakest.

Now to some illustrations and exercises.

Yob's comma: recognition, rules and remedies

Take a good look at this sentence.

   1 **It was a fine day, the sun was shining.**

It seems O.K., doesn't it? The two clauses appear so closely linked that the comma appears to be adequate as a separating device. Well, as I hope you may have realized from earlier examples, the comma is not enough. To repeat a fundamental principle:

> **It is always wrong to divide two clauses with <u>only</u> a comma, no matter how closely related in subject matter they may be.**

You may remember that this rule can be also expressed in a different way:

> **If the subject and the verb are changed, more than a comma is needed between the relevant clauses.**

In Example 1 there are two subjects [it and **sun**] and two finite verbs [**was** and **was shining**]. Therefore we need something stronger than a comma. Virtually any substitution would be correct, but some alternatives are stylistically better than others. Let's consider them in ascending order of aptness.

> **1a It was a fine day. The sun was shining.**

This is grammatically correct, but it isn't very good: the sentences are too closely related for such a major pause to be appropriate. Furthermore, to continue writing in such a way for even a short time would render one's prose infuriatingly jagged.

> **1b It was a fine day, and the sun was shining.**
> **or It was a fine day, for the sun was shining.**

This is much better: the connection is made fluently and comfortably. In fact, several other conjunctions would fit – **since**, **because**, even **while**. So there's no flaw or problem about this method; it's just that there are still better ways.

> **1c It was a fine day – the sun was shining.**

Here we find an almost perfect example of the correct use and value of the dash. The root sentence consists of two such closely related clauses that the weakest correct device above the [banned] comma might be considered ideal. Not everyone approves of the dash, however, so perhaps the best version of all is . . .

> **1d It was a fine day; the sun was shining.**

This is flawless and mud-proof. It signals the clauses' close connection while recognizing their separate grammatical integrity. It elegantly avoids both the excessive abruptness of a full stop and the inadequate comma. It is, in short, a classic model of how and why the semi-colon should be used.

Perfect though 1d is, there remains one other way to punctuate the sentence. If you think that the two clauses are not just related but mutually dependent, you should use the colon:

> **1e It was a fine day: the sun was shining.**

There is no real difference between (1d) and (1e): it is a matter of taste, based on your judgment of 'voice'. If you think the 'speaker' was concerned to stress the interlocking nature of the clauses, use the colon; otherwise, the semi-colon shades it. Such a subtle matter deserves a brief further section to itself.

Colon or semi-colon?

What is your opinion of the way this passage is punctuated?

> In one respect they were better off in this camp. There was a doctor in attendance. Some of the children were treated for malnutrition. The commonest complaints among the adults were exhaustion and heat-stroke.

There are four sentences. They are quite dramatic in themselves, and together they quickly paint a powerful picture. However, such clipped brevity could easily become irksome if continued for any length of time.

If we study the sentences as a sequence, we can see that they divide into two pairs: the first and second go together, as do the third and fourth. But these 'pairs' are subtly different.

The first two sentences interlock. The former is of course complete in itself as a grammatical structure, but in addition it fulfils a hint or expectation raised by **In one respect** in the latter. To put it another way, the information about the doctor answers the question raised in our minds as to why these people were **better off**. In such cases of 'fulfilment' or 'answering', the colon is the perfect separating device[6]:

> In one respect they were better off in this camp: there was a doctor in attendance.

The second pair does not function in quite the same way. Once again, the separating full stop is excessive in weight; but these sentences do not interlock so much as balance each other. There is no dependent or fulfilling logic operating: it is more a case of 'On the one hand . . . and on the other'. In such instances the semi-colon is the ideal device:

> Some of the children were treated for malnutrition; the commonest complaints among the adults were exhaustion and heat stroke.

If you have not as yet used either colon or semi-colon with any regularity or comfort, my advice would be to ignore for the time being the distinction between them: just get into the habit of using one of them on occasions when that degree of 'weight' is required. As you become more adept at this, you should soon feel

---

6 The colon is also used to introduce 'lists'. This is much more straightforward than the 'interlocking' signal discussed above, and can I hope be explained via a single example:

> You will need the following things for your trip to Wales: a tent, a sleeping bag, eating utensils, a signed photograph of Tom Jones, the sheet music of 'Bread of Heaven', and a large brown paper bag.

confident enough to use both; when that time arrives, this summarizing formula may further assist you.

> Colon: links sentences on the basis 'Given A, then B'. Often it can replace 'because' or longer *causal* phrases.
> Semi-colon: links sentences that balance each other without being directly complementary. It is most often used as an alternative to comma + conjunction.

The exercise at the end of this section includes plenty of practice on these two subtle devices; now it is time to look at a longer and more complicated 'yob's comma' model.

What is wrong with the punctuation here?

> **2 There are two things which really annoy me about you, firstly, you never look me in the eye, secondly, you're the untidiest slob I've ever met.**

There are four commas: only two are legitimate [those after **firstly** and **secondly**]. The other two fail to recognize that a new clause has begun, introducing a change in subject and verb. How do we put things right?

The sentence consists of a preliminary announcement

> **There are two things which really annoy me about you . . .**

followed by two clauses which identify what those things are. In other words, that announcement interlocks with the remainder – the ideal situation for a colon.

> **2a There are two things which really annoy me about you: firstly, you never . . .**

Moving on, the comma after **eye** is similarly wrong. Although the subject is the same (**you**), the verb changes from **look** to **are**; there are two good alternatives.

> **2b . . . you never look me in the eye, and secondly . . .**
> Or **2c . . . you never look me in the eye; secondly . . .**

Remember the equation: **comma + conjunction = semi-colon**. Either way is fine; if I suggest that 2c is preferable, it is because

A   Using the semi-colon whenever you can will soon make it an automatic and valuable part of your technical armoury.

B   It prevents the over-use of that very common word 'and', too many instances of which can get on a reader's nerves.

The full amended sentence now reads:

2d There are two things which really annoy me about you: firstly, you never look me in the eye; secondly, you're the untidiest slob I've ever met.

Summary

The 'yob's comma' is a very common and also chronic ailment that disfigures the work of many otherwise proficient writers. The good news is that it can be quite easily cured; all it takes is a certain amount of careful thought, allied to the fundamental grammatical principles I've outlined several times. The bad news is that if such care is not taken, other aspects of your writing will soon begin to disintegrate. Just as a composer who has no sense of rhythm will produce music that makes little sense and has no real impact, so a writer who cannot punctuate competently will eventually be unable to transmit his thoughts properly. 'Punk-tuation' reduces both style and content to ugly inadequacy.

Please try the summarizing exercise; then there is a brief examination of how punctuation can make a decisive difference to meaning, after which we look at another aspect of 'Punk-tuation' – the abuse and non-use of the apostrophe.

Exercise 9
Correct the faulty punctuation in these sentences. You will find my versions on pages 226–7.

1   He was fed up, the bus had left without him.
2   His promotion was not due to any particular skill or merit, he had bought his way up.
3   Stuck out here in the heart of the Yorkshire moors, in the vicinity of a bog, there is no problem parking the car, a little difficulty extricating it may be experienced, though.
4   The fridge worked, the food stayed fresh, the milk remained cold, the little light came on when you opened the door.
5   He was caught in a vicious circle, nobody would hire him as a portrait-painter until he was well known, he couldn't become well known until people hired him.
6   The recent BAFTA awards prove one thing if nothing else, when it comes to excruciating self-indulgence the TV industry has no equals.

5.3 PUNCTUATION & MEANING

By now I hope you are comfortable about the precise weight of pause various punctuation devices signify and how to use the latter to make your written thoughts crisp and easy to follow. If that is the case, you can consider yourself well-schooled in this area, and accurate punctuation should soon become plain sailing for you; in time it may even become instinctive, requiring no conscious thought at all. So far, so very good – except that like most things that can have the vices of its own virtues.

To be able to punctuate automatically, saving time and worry, is a virtue; to imagine that it means you can stop thinking about it is a vice. More than once in this book I shall be alluding to the disparity that can occur between intention and execution – the gap between what one *thinks* one's said and what one has *actually written* – and even the most experienced, technically flawless writers are prone to it. To relax one's vigilance is always risky, and nowhere more so than when punctuating. As a sample proof of that, run your eye over this piece of raw prose:

there was no letter that day he was pleased his wife was worried

How would you punctuate it?

There are at least three ways of doing so accurately, but your answer will (or should!) depend on what you want the resultant sentence(s) to *say*. If you wish to draw a distinction between the man's response to the absence of mail and his wife's, then write

1 There was no letter that day. He was pleased; his wife was worried.

If you want to stress the difference between those reactions *on this particular occasion*, then it should be

1a There was no letter. That day he was pleased; his wife was worried.

Rather clumsy, and maybe not a very likely meaning either, but it's perfectly correct. And if what you wish to denote is the thoroughly unpleasant but intriguing possibility that the man was pleased *because* his wife was worried, then go for

1b There was no letter that day: he was pleased his wife was worried.

Now for a more demanding example – though I'm confident you will also find it entertaining. This next piece of raw prose can be correctly punctuated in two quite separate ways, resulting in two utterly different meanings. I shall label the first version 'Come-on', the second 'Kiss-Off'. Can you work them out? Your decisions begin almost immediately after 'Dear John', which is the only structure common to both. The answers follow.

Dear John

I want a man who knows what love is all about you are generous kind thoughtful people who are not like you admit to being useless and inferior you have ruined me for other men I yearn for you I have no feeling whatever when we're apart I can be forever happy will you let me be yours Gloria

Answers

1   'Come-On'

Dear John,
I want a man who knows
what love is all about. You are
generous, kind, thoughtful. People
who are not like you admit to being
useless and inferior. You have
ruined me for other men. I yearn
for you. I have no feelings whatever
when we're apart. I can be forever
happy – will you let me be yours?

Gloria

2   'Kiss-Off

Dear John,
I want a man who knows what
love is. All about you are generous,
kind, thoughtful people, who are
not like you. Admit to being useless
and inferior. You have ruined me.
For other men, I yearn. For you, I
have no feelings whatever. When
we're apart, I can be forever happy.
Will you let me be?

Yours,

Gloria

Before we move on to the apostrophe, you might try your hand at this confirmatory exercise.

Exercise 10

Each of these sentences is virtually in raw prose form and can acquire two distinctly different meanings, depending on where – and *whether* – stops of some kind are placed. Repunctuate each one twice so that two different meanings clearly emerge. As an 'optional extra', you might like to attempt a brief summary in your own words of what each of the rewrites now means. Answers in Appendix I on page 227.

1   The policeman swore the driver turned across oncoming traffic
2   I have hunted and shot myself and know the dangers of guns
3   Simon thought his mother ought to go to the hospital
4   David decided Susan was no longer up to the job

5.4 'PUNK-TUATION' (II): THE APOSTROPHE – AN ENDANGERED SPECIES

It would be overstating the case to suggest that the correct use of the apostrophe matters as fundamentally as the things we've just been studying. It is nevertheless important. Misuse of it looks amateurish; more significantly, there are times when missed or inaccurate apostrophes damage sense and muddle the reader. Above all, incompetent use of the apostrophe is a telling symptom of a writer's failure to listen to the words, and it can easily lead to further lapses into slovenly and unhelpful writing.

It is commonly believed that the apostrophe has two main functions: to denote the omission of a letter or letters and to denote possession. This is not so: **all apostrophes denote omission**, and the latter function is both inaccurate and redundant.

Most students are aware how the former function works in straight-forward instances. On motorways one finds such abbreviations as **B'ham** for **Birmingham** or **M'chester** for **Manchester**, where the apostrophe saves sign-painters the bother of providing the full name while ensuring that they neatly offer clear directional advice. I also find that practically everyone understands how and why the apostrophe is used to denote sloppy speech:

> **huntin', shootin', fishin'. It was 'orrible.**

However, the apostrophe seems to cause severe difficulty when it comes to denoting possessives and subtle contractions. Such problems can be greatly reduced once it is understood that the apostrophe always signals something which has been left out. To understand why this is so, and how the apostrophe really works, we need briefly 'to boldly go' where few students dare or want to go – back a thousand years and more to Anglo-Saxon.

Anglo-Saxon is the basis of Middle English, Shakespeare's English and modern English. By the time Shakespeare was writing, however, English was far less inflected than it had been in earlier forms. To put it simply for the present: in inflected languages many words change their form according to how they are used grammatically. This invariably involves the use of cases, as is prevalent in Latin and German, and to a lesser extent in French. Modern English remains inflected to a certain degree; one of the cases that remains is the **genitive** – which is where the use of the apostrophe comes in.

In Anglo-Saxon the genitive case was indicated by the ending **-es**, as in

> **Johnes book**   **the Churches land**

The addition originally called for two spoken syllables. The **e** gradually eroded in speech, and in writing this omission was indicated by an apostrophe:

> **John's book**   **the Church's land**

Believe it or not, that simple piece of linguistic history explains everything you need to know about using the apostrophe nowadays. **All** apostrophes denote the omission of a letter, whether the word is a genitive or otherwise: that really is all there is to it.

That said and established, let us at once look at two functions the apostrophe does **not** have, both of which are nonetheless disturbingly prevalent.

1 It must *not* be used as an alternative spelling of ordinary plurals.

Thus, despite the thousands of instances you will see in shops, on menus, in newspaper headlines and on television, it is completely wrong to write such alleged plurals as:

> **potato's** 25p a pound
> Do you like **egg's**?
> Please close all **door's** after you.
> West Indian **cricketer's** get pay rise.

2 It is *not* automatically used in words that include the successive letters '. . . nt . . .'

It is therefore comically illiterate to write:

> I **mean't** to write but forgot.
> The man **lean't** over the balcony.
> Are you going to the **pagean't**?
> No, **Sergean't**, I have not been drinking.

One can understand why these absurdities occur: it's because of such contractions as

> **can't   don't   won't   hadn't**

– all of which use the apostrophe correctly. Writers who insert apostrophes in **both** sets of cases are either not thinking properly or do not know that the apostrophe only signals omission: they respond in a Pavlovian way to the mere sight of the . . . nt . . . formation.

Does it really matter whether we write these out correctly? Well, yes. Misuse of the apostrophe looks amateurish and often ridiculous, and nothing undermines a writer so much as looking a sudden idiot! It can also confuse. It so happens, for example, that there are two nouns, **cant** and **wont**, that don't take the apostrophe:

> 1 **can't**   short for **cannot**. The apostrophe signals the omission of one **n** and the **o**.

1a cant	hypocritical or spurious language; words used out of empty fashion/trendiness.
2 won't	short for **will not**. An admittedly odd contraction: the apostrophe signals the omission of the **o**.[7]
2a wont	habit, custom.

Similarly, to prevent serious confusion one must distinguish between

3 your	belonging to you
3a you're	a contraction of you are
4 their	belonging to them
4a they're	a contraction of they are
4b there're	a contraction of there are[8]

So the apostrophe is not merely an optional decoration. It is an aid to meaning and precision: remove it, and something valuable is lost, as this exercise should demonstrate.

Exercise 11

There follow three pairs of sentences. Each pair is identical save for the presence/absence or position of the apostrophe. Explain the consequent difference in meaning in each case. My suggested explanations can be found below.

1a   The huge cliffs threatened.
1b   The huge cliff's threatened.

2a   He cares less about his children's welfare than his friends'.
2b   He cares less about his children's welfare than his friends.

3a   The village's well has been poisoned.
3b   The villages' well has been poisoned.

Commentary

1a   means that the cliffs threatened something unspecified – presumably a village, a group of people, or suchlike. Here **The cliffs** are the grammatical subject; the finite verb **threatened** is active in mood and in the past tense.

---

7 The change of the original . . . **ill** . . . to a single **o** was evidently considered too complicated to punctuate fully without tiring the reader and sacrificing clarity. Good thinking – as is **fo'csle** for **forecastle**. Strictly speaking, that contraction should be written **fo'c's'le**, but life is too short for such eye-straining fiddliness!

8 Perfectly correct but very rarely used – it looks [and indeed is] too cranky to be helpful. Stick to the full **there are**.

1b   means that something is threatening the huge cliff – erosion and/or the sea, perhaps. **The cliffs** remain the grammatical subject, but the finite verb has changed radically. The apostrophe signifies the omission of the **i**, making the verb **is threatened**: it is passive, not active, and in the present tense, not the past.

These are major changes in grammatical function and consequent meaning – all done by the briefest flick of the pen!

2a   means that he cares less about the welfare of his children than about the welfare of his friends. Put more simply, his friends matter to him more than his children do.

2b   means that his friends care more about the welfare of his children than he does.

The difference here is perhaps less dramatic than in the first pair, but it remains a sizable one.

3a   means that the well which serves the village has been poisoned.

3b   means that the well which serves **several** villages has been poisoned.

The difference in **scale** here is important. A poisoned well is obviously serious anyway, but sentence 3b could indicate a major disaster affecting villages and villagers for miles around.

The last of those three pairs illustrates the use of the apostrophe in plural possessives – the first 'specific problem area' I want to consider.

The apostrophe in plural possessives

What's the difference in meaning here?

1   **The boy's football shirt was filthy.**
2   **The boys' football shirt was filthy.**

The first sentence means that a football shirt belonging to a particular boy was filthy.

The second sentence means that a football shirt belonging to **several** boys was filthy. Presumably they have to take turns in wearing it, while everyone else in the team wears a T-shirt or whatever!

After such a comically unlikely example, let's return for a moment to the serious business of Anglo-Saxon. Remember that the genitive ending was originally **-es**; this applied in plurals as well. Thus:

the dog<u>es</u> bones   the Church<u>es</u>es Bibles

In such cases the 'gradual erosion' referred to earlier led to the dropping of both the **e** and the **s**, creating the modern

the dogs' bones   **the Churches' Bibles**

So plural possessives are, in the main, relaxingly easy: all that is required is an apostrophe after the **s** that signifies the plural number. However, beware of **irregular** plurals. Fortunately, there aren't many of them; less fortunate is the fact that they tend to be in very frequent use.

Men's clothing   **women's rights**   **children's games**

These may be plural **in concept** but they are singular **in grammar**; they must therefore obey the singular possessive form.

Names ending in 's'

Let's introduce this tricky and nowadays quite controversial matter with a little exercise.

Exercise 12
Which of these uses of the apostrophe is wrong?

1   I admire Charles Dicken's novels very much.
2   Really? I find Dickens' work turgid and unfunny.
3   I despise Jone's taste in flashy cars.
4   What you mean is that you wish you had Jones' money.

They **all** are!

Sentences 1 and 3 are, I hope, obviously wrong – although a surprising number of otherwise literate students make this kind of idiotic mistake. I say 'idiotic' because a moment's ordinary thought can prevent it. The names at issue are **Dickens and Jones**; I suppose that somewhere there may be an author called Charles **Dicken** and a car-fancier named **Jone**, but I doubt if the above examples had such obscure figures in mind. 1 and 3 are even more absurd when one recalls that the apostrophe always denotes omission: if asked to work out what letters could possibly be missing in those names, the mind surely boggles.

   Contrary to common usage – which I admit seems increasingly to be receiving 'official' sanction – sentences 2 and 4 are also wrong. They are lazy and unhelpful substitutes for the real thing:

5 Dickens's work   **6 Jones's money**

This is not mere pedantry; if it were, I wouldn't waste your time on it. Forms 5 and 6 are superior because they reflect how the words are **pronounced**: in conversation we would make an extra syllable out of the possessive signal –

    Dickenses work   **Joneses money**

You may notice that these pronunciation models exactly match those original Anglo-Saxon genitive forms; in keeping with modern practice, we omit the **e** when writing, replacing it with an apostrophe.

However, in very long words ending in **s**, it is accepted practice to add only the apostrophe, on the basis that the extra syllable seems to create a real mouthful:

    7 Coriolanus'   **8 Pythagoras'**

Still, it is not wrong to write **Coriolanus's** or **Pythagoras's**: even with such multi-syllabled words we tend to add the extra one in pronunciation, 'real mouthful' or not!

As I mention above, the form taken by 7 and 8 now seems to be accepted usage for all words ending in **s**, and people like me should perhaps concede defeat graciously. But I would encourage you to use the form exemplified by 5 and 6: it is a genuine aid to clarity and precision, and anything that effects such qualities is to be valued and preserved.

Possessive adjectives and pronouns

The apostrophe is **never** used in possessive adjectives or pronouns. The correct forms are:

    Adjectives: my; your; his/her/its; our; their; whose
    Pronouns: mine; yours; his/hers/its[9]; ours; theirs; whose

Only one of these causes trouble – **its** – but it does so in large measure! The problem arises because there is a form **it's**, and virtually everyone confuses the two at some time or another. Here are three separate 'recipes' designed to dispel that confusion once for all.

A By now I'd like to think that you have nailed to your memory the fact that **all apostrophes denote omission**. If you keep that thought uppermost, the distinction ought to be clear:

    its = belonging to it; no omission has been performed.
    it's = it is; the second **i** has been omitted.

---

9 Hardly ever used in this pronoun form, as it happens.

If that isn't clear, try the next.

B If in doubt as to whether to use **its** or **it's**, try mentally substituting **it is** in each case. If it sounds O.K., then **it's** is correct; if you end up with gibberish, you must write **its**.

Examples:

   1 The dog licked **it is** paw. Obvious drivel: you need **its**:
       The dog licked **its** paw.
   2 I must say **it is** nice to see you. No problem: write **it's**:
       I must say **it's** nice to see you.

If that doesn't work, on to the final one.

C A four-stage 'theorem' – convoluted, maybe, but thorough!

   1 **its** is the neuter equivalent of **his** and **her**.
   2 I imagine you would never be tempted to write **hi's** or **he'r**.
   3 So if you remember that the possessive adjective or pronoun **its** follows
       the same formation as **his/her**, you should now get that one right, and
       then . . .
   4 . . . remember to use **it's** in **non**-possessive contexts.

If **none** of those three recipes solves the problem, then I'm afraid there is nothing for it but to learn slowly by getting it wrong again and again until, somehow, it all sinks in!

The apostrophe with abbreviated verbs

In recent years a number of abbreviated verbs have become part of our language, and the apostrophe is a vital ingredient in their correct spelling.

   1 **She OK'd the merger.**
   2 **He was KO'd in the fifth round.**
   3 **They OD'd on barbiturates.**

Unlike those illiterate plurals [**potato's**, **door's** e.g.] discussed earlier, the apostrophe is entirely legitimate here. Indeed, it is **essential**: not to signal the dropping of the **e** invites the reader to 'mispronounce' the verb, with potentially confusing results. For if the **e** is signalled, explicitly or implicitly, one ends up with verbs which sound like

   1a **She 'oaked' the merger.**

2a   **He was 'code' in the fifth round.**
3a   **They 'oded' on barbiturates.**

I can't pretend that such instances would cause anyone a real problem for very long. But it's worth taking the trouble to present these abbreviated verbs in a clear and accurate way – partly because doing so confirms your mastery of the apostrophe and the reasons for its use.

I hope this section has demonstrated that the apostrophe is a handy and badly neglected tool. Although it is true that your writing will be pretty proficient if the only errors you commit concern the apostrophe, using it properly will sharpen your work and add to your readers' precise understanding of it.

5.5 PARAGRAPHING: ART OR SCIENCE?

Proper words in proper places make the definition of a style.

Jonathan Swift

While Swift's remark naturally applies to every aspect of writing, it is particularly germane to the business of paragraphing. The idea of 'proper words in proper places' seems simple enough, but all writers rapidly get to know otherwise. It is very difficult to be sure that one has chosen every word unimprovably **and** placed them all in the best possible position. And the more one writes, the harder it gets. Thousands of writers coin beautiful phrases and fashion exquisite sentences; to achieve the perfect paragraph is something else again. That goal is made all the more elusive by the fact that, unlike the rules of punctuation or even of sentence structure, the skills of paragraphing are not entirely a matter of 'scientific' logic.

For paragraphing is ultimately an art. Its good practice depends on 'feel', voice and instinct rather than on any formula or techniques that can dutifully be learnt. Conversely, its bad practice is as often due to poor instinct or inadequate 'feel' as to anything straightforwardly mechanical. Happily – and somewhat paradoxically – instinct and feel can be substantially improved by training and experience; this chapter offers a number of guidelines that should at least ensure that you never paragraph badly, even if I cannot promise that they will guarantee perfect paragraphs every time.

Perhaps more than any matter analysed so far, paragraphing skills are best understood via illustrations and exercises. As usual, I look first at how **not** to do it.

Avoiding eye-strain

Take a good look – in all senses of that noun – at the three paragraphs which follow. None of them is in my view badly written in any obvious mechanical way; yet all could have been rendered punchier, easier to read, or more aesthetically pleasing. Make a mental note of your reactions as you read, and compare them to mine.

The first example appeared in a local newspaper.

Passage A

Like many other able-bodied people, I had never thought very much about the problems of those confined to wheelchairs.

But after spending just one morning in a chair, I now realize how difficult even a simple shopping trip is for the disabled.

We borrowed a wheelchair from the Red Cross and set out along Station Road. It might be thought that I had an easy job just sitting in a chair being pushed around, but I found the ride both frightening and uncomfortable.

The pavement was very uneven – many slabs were cracked and few were actually aligned with each other. Shock absorbers should be fitted as standard on all wheelchairs.

Added to the problem of bumpy pavements was the fact that Linda, my pusher, took some time to get used to steering the wheelchair up and down the dips in the pavement. She was, of course, further hampered by my weight in the chair.

Kerbstones were another major difficulty. She almost tipped me out several times before she learnt how to negotiate them properly.

Because she had to go down the kerb backwards, I experienced a couple of moments of minor panic, when she had difficulty turning the chair round again in the middle of the road . . .

There is a certain amount to admire here. The 'voice' is clearly audible – concerned and intelligent; the sentences are nicely varied; the vocabulary is appropriately direct and physical.

On the other hand, in the space of just twenty lines there are seven paragraphs, which is excessive. The end of a paragraph signals a pause of some magnitude: after all, the next highest is the end of a chapter. To insist on a major pause every few lines ruins snap and flow; should the writer continue in this vein – and there's obviously a lot more to come, since pusher and passenger haven't even arrived at the shops yet – the reader will surely become fed up with the prose's stop-start jaggedness. It might be argued that such a feature brilliantly reflects the difficulties of locomotion described in the article, but I think that would be over-generous!

You will notice that none of the paragraphs contains more than two sentences, leading to an irritating sense of being pulled away from an idea just as one was becoming gripped by it.

Passage A: **Exercise 13**

Re-design the extract to give it proper flow and a more sensible shape. It might help you to work out first how many 'topics' or specific considerations the writer tackles: that should determine the number of paragraphs you go for. This time my version follows immediately – so try not to look at it until you've decided on your own.

Commentary

I would run together paragraphs 1 and 2, 4 and 5, and 6 and 7; with 3 left as it is, that makes four paragraphs in all. Even now they're on the short side; the subject warrants reasonably terse units, however, and each of the four addresses a distinct topic:

1 An introductory statement about the difficulties of wheelchair-confinement and attitudes to it.
2 A sharp, disturbing summary of what being in a wheelchair actually feels like, even on mundane trips.
3 The problem of pavements.
4 The problem of kerbstones.

Passage B: **Exercise 14**

No prizes for guessing what's wrong with this – it is much too long. How would you 'sub-divide' it? And can you detect any inconsistency in the argument?

Twelfth Night is justly considered as one of the most delightful of Shakespeare's comedies. It is full of sweetness and pleasantry. It is perhaps too good-natured for comedy. It has little satire and no spleen. It aims at the ridiculous
5 rather than the ludicrous. It makes us laugh at the follies of mankind, not despise them, and still less bear any ill will towards them. Shakespeare's comic genius resembles the bee rather in its power of extracting sweets from weeds or poisons than in leaving a sting behind it. He gives the
10 most amusing exaggeration of the prevailing foibles of his characters, but in a way that they themselves, instead of being offended at, would almost join in the humour; he rather contrives opportunities for them to show themselves off

15 in the happiest lights, than renders them contemptible in
the perverse construction of the wit or malice of others. There
is a certain stage of society in which people become conscious
of their peculiarities and absurdities, affect to disguise what
they are, and set up pretensions to what they are not. This
gives rise to a corresponding style of comedy, the object of
20 which is to detect the disguises of self love, and to make
reprisals on these preposterous assumptions of vanity, by
marking the contrast between the real and the affected
character as severely as possible, and denying to those,
who would impose on us for what they are not, even the
25 merit which they have. This is the comedy of artificial life.

Commentary

That was very hard work! As I hint above, length is not the only – or even the main – problem: the paragraph lacks **unity**. It begins by proposing *Twelfth Night*'s essential 'sweetness', yet ends by suggesting that the play is distinguished for its vinegary exposure of artificiality and pretension. All the remarks stimulate, but they do not sit easily together within a single unit. One can sympathize with the reader who wonders irritably if the author could not have made up his mind before starting to write.

Engineering appropriate breaks would have prevented such annoyance. New paragraphs at line 7 [after **towards them**] and at line 15 [after **malice of others**] would signal the distinct shift in focus and allow readers a moment or two to mull over the material in each completed paragraph.

Incidentally, the author is William Hazlitt – one of our finest essayists ever. It's comforting to think that even great writers can get things wrong sometimes!

Both passages subject the reader to needless eye-strain. One jumps around too much; the other offers no respite for too long. Despite containing, in varying degrees, much that is praiseworthy, each would have benefited from more astute paragraphing.

So even if paragraphing is an art and cannot be reduced to a set of prescriptions, it **is** possible to offer some pointers. I must stress that none of what follows is a 'rule': there can always be legitimate exceptions to every guideline I shall suggest. That said, those anxious to acquire an elementary grasp of how to divide their prose into efficient and agreeable units should find them useful.

'It is much too long'.

Designing paragraphs

Your overall piece is your reader's overall environment, which he or she will enjoy and benefit from in direct proportion to how pleasingly you shape it. When designing your paragraphs, all of these suggestions are worth bearing in mind.

1 Each side of the paper [assuming A4 size] should usually contain 2 or 3 paragraphs.
2 Except for occasions when you wish to stress or highlight something, each paragraph should contain **at least three** sentences.
3 A good paragraph normally resembles a miniature chapter or essay: it should be clearly set up, properly developed, and then satisfyingly rounded off.
4 The first and last paragraphs of a piece should usually be fairly short.
5 A paragraph should have unity. You will probably ensure this by staying alert to 3; in addition, you should always be wary of moving in mid-paragraph from

one topic to another. It can happen that the idea you're exploring sparks off another related but different one: this is a pleasing experience, but you mustn't *rush*. Your further idea must wait until you [and the reader] can give it full attention.

6 Try not to start a sentence until you're clear about how it's going to end. This is always important anyway, and I've mentioned it before; if you adopt it as a regular discipline, you will soon acquire a much better 'feel' for when one paragraph should end and another begin.

7 Within reason, try to vary your sentence-length within each paragraph.

8 Good paragraphs tend to have a **nucleus** – a sentence to which all other material can be seen to gravitate.

In the same way, there is no reason why an unusually long or an unusually short paragraph cannot be both pleasing and highly effective. This next example is fully thirty lines long, but it is masterly.

It's hard to make travel arrangements to visit a dream. The voyage I was planning was on a river which existed only in my head. The real Mississippi was an abstraction. I studied it with impatience, feeling that the facts were just so many
5 bits of grit in my vision of a halcyon river. I learned, without enthusiasm, about the construction of the lock and dam system. Figures began to swim in my head where the dream ought to be. In 1890, 30 million tons of freight had been carried downriver; in 1979, after a long and catastrophic decline in river trade,
10 business was up again to 40 million tons. The Civil War and the coming of the railroads had almost smashed the river as a commercial highway, but the oil crisis of the 1970s had brought the Mississippi back to life. A river barge, I read, 'can move 400 tons of grain a mile on a gallon of fuel, compared with only 200
15 tons for a locomotive'; and a lot of people were now wanting to move a lot of tons of grain because the United States had raised its quota of grain exports to Russia. So the port of New Orleans was busy with ships casting Midwestern wheat and corn and soybeans off to Murmask and Archangel. To someone
20 somewhere, I suppose, this kind of information has the ring of industrial poetry; it didn't to me. It was reassuring to find that the river was important again, a central artery linking north and south in a drifting procession of towboats and barge fleets, but I found the details of its renaissance grindingly dull. They
25 threatened to contaminate that great, wide, open stretch of level water which was far more actual for me than those tawdry scraps of intelligence from the real world.

from *Old Glory* by Jonathan Raban

This isn't easy: it outdistances the Hazlitt extract which I criticized for excessive length. (See pages 51–2.) But I wouldn't make the same criticism here: the paragraph has a unity which the Hazlitt lacked. Moreover, I find the length appropriate to the subject – a 4000+-mile river that has dominated the author's imagination for years.

It opens with a memorable observation, moving elegantly into the controlling topic – the 'real' Mississippi versus Raban's 'dreamed' one. Perhaps you then find the catalogue of facts and figures hard to take in, even annoyingly opaque. Such a reaction supports rather than undermines the writing, for it is Raban's own response. He is 'impatient' at such things, finding them 'grindingly dull' and so many 'bits of grit in my vision of a halcyon river'. But having identified those disappointing realities, he stays with them and puts us as fully in the picture as he can, before returning gracefully to the image of the river with which he began. In effect, he has it both ways. If we find those statistics and commercial phenomena interesting [as I must say that I do], well and good; if not, we share his own instincts, which protects the writing against reader-alienation.

Raban wisely keeps his sentences relatively short. If you're going to tax the reader's stamina with a very long paragraph, it is sensible to ensure that no individual sentence within it gives any trouble. Most readers will contentedly follow you down a long, even arduous road, provided that the way is reasonably clear; if however it's also tangled with weeds, shrouded in mist or pitted with sudden holes and traps, they're going to get fed up.

From unusual length to unusual brevity. The **one-line paragraph** can be a shrewd and dramatic tactic, as these next two passages show. The first I composed myself.

> G. V. Carey published Mind The Stop in 1939. Drawing on his experience as a schoolmaster and in publishing, Carey compiled a no-nonsense guide to clear and accurate punctuation that quickly became a standard work of reference, a 'Bible' to teachers and writers alike. It was not only sensible and readable: it was the most authoritative and comprehensive book yet published on the subject.
>
> Over fifty years on, that is still the case.

The single-line paragraph serves to highlight Carey's achievement, and it does so by **visually isolating** the point. As a result it acquires immediate extra impact.

This second passage is from 'Death', an essay on boxing by Norman Mailer in *The Presidential Papers*.

> Their bodies made a contrast. Liston, only an inch taller than Patterson, weighed 214 pounds to Patterson's 189. But the difference was not just in weight. Liston had a sleek body, fully muscled, but round. It was the body of a strong man, but the muscles looked to have been shaped by pleasure as much as by work. He was obviously a man who had had some very good times.

Whereas Patterson still had poverty in his muscles. He was certainly not weak, there was whipcord in the way he was put together, but it was still the dry, dedicated body of an athlete, a track man, a disciplinarian: it spoke little of pleasure and much of the gym. There was a lack eating at it, some misery.

The bell rang.

Liston looked scared.

Patterson looked grim.

Not one but **three** single-liners: this not only 'breaks the rules' but seems to glory in flouting them! Yet it is a legitimate visual orchestration of a hugely dramatic moment. Set out in this way, the prose causes us to concentrate fiercely on three stark occurrences and to absorb their highly-charged simplicity one at a time. A good sports journalist should try to make readers feel 'they were there'; Mailer brings this off superbly, and a key factor in that success is his daring triple use of the one-line paragraph.

Such audacity must always be accompanied by sober thought. The one-line paragraph should be used sparingly, and you must be convinced it is the right device for your needs. If it is employed as anything other than an occasional powerful 'weapon', your writing can soon lose both rhythm and coherence, at worst degenerating to the point where virtually every sentence is made into a separate paragraph. But if you are sensible and alert about it, such variation can valuably broaden your style and give it added muscular force.

Conclusion

Even the most stunning architecture – physical or verbal – relies on sound foundations, just as the supremely-tuned body of a crack athlete is based on the known properties of bones and muscles. If you are serene about the material covered in Part Two's pages, you should find that your 'skeleton' is in good shape, and that you will write accurately and clearly.

As an 'interim check' on how good your foundations are, please attempt the extensive exercise alongside, which asks you to identify and correct a variety of errors. Some of them are basic, others subtle and/or highly technical; some deal with issues already covered, others with matters still to come. It is up to you whether you try it now or return to it when you've absorbed that subsequent material; however, doing it now might give you a valuable 'fix' on

- How much you've learned so far
- Which later sections are likely to help you most

Whenever you tackle it, as always I hope it will prove as amusing as instructive.

[*]

That concludes for the time being our detailed study of the mechanics and structures of English. We are now ready to consider more sophisticated skills. Later we'll be considering the various tasks your writing may encompass – the essay, the report and so on. First it is time to reflect in depth on how to achieve an individual and supple style – the comely flesh that clothes and gives life to your healthy body.

Exercise 15

There are at least **40** errors here – of spelling, grammar, punctuation, usage, choice of vocabulary and style. Identify and correct as many as you can; answers and explanations can be found in Appendix I, p. 229.

Me and my friend were laying around on the floor when the bell rung. It was the postman, who was in a very stroppy mood, he said that the parcel he was delivering to me was extremely awkward to handle, and that £2–40 was due to be paid because the sender hadn't handed over enough money. I was disinterested in his problems, but his manner was so unpleasantly masterly that I thought I'd better behave judiciously. Undoubtably he'd have been even more unpleasant if I'd stuck to my principals and told him where to get off. After all, he is a public servant and has no business being so officious, it wasn't my fault that the parcel was so tricky for him and its no use blaming the innocent recipient if the sender has been too mean to pay the correct postage. I therefore offered him my condonances on having such a pressurised job, paid the access postage and shut the door on the wicked villain.

When I opened the parcel, I was incredible: it was a priceless diamond that must have cost a pretty penny. The reason it was so bulky was because it was wrapped in yards and yards of paper – tissue paper, newspaper, brown paper, even corrugated cardboard. No wonder the postman had found such a lot of stationary awkward to carry! My friend was fascinated by the jewel and said I could proberly retire for life if I sold it to the right buyer. I told her not to be so venial, it was a treasured present and I would never part with it for no one. Then she asked me who it was from? I scrabbled around in all that paper, looking for a card or a letter, but could find absolutely nothing. I was so upset at not knowing who my benefactor was that I needed an immediate stimulus, and so I dived for the brandy. I poured out a good measure for both of us, but she complained that my half was bigger than hers and inferred that I was greedy. I said she was quite unique in being the nastiest, most grasping little rat-bag I had ever come across and that if she had the intelligence required to find the door, she might like to use it at her earliest convenience. People like that embarass me: their full of criticism for others but never practice what they preach.

Oh, I eventually found out who sent the diamond. There *was* a letter after all, tucked into the outer rapping: it was from a Belgium I met on holiday, whose the most gorgeous man I've ever clapped eyes on. Anyone who doesn't fancy him must be off their head: he's the sort of phenomena that makes me go weak, knees-wise.

Part III

Style

Chapter 6

Introduction

Style versus fashion

> Style is the dress of thoughts; and let them be ever so just, if your style is homely, coarse, and vulgar, they will appear to as much disadvantage.
>
> Lord Chesterfield

> When we see a natural style, we are astonished and delighted: for we expected to see an author, and we find a man.
>
> Pascal

> Fashion condemns us to many follies; the greatest is to make oneself its slave.
>
> Napoleon

Style is not unlike genius: we reckon to know it when we see it, but find it hard to define. And because we confidently recognize style in others, we often assume that to acquire it ourselves we need only copy the original model. That may be the basis of **fashion**; it is not the basis of good **style**.

Fashion is fun; it can also be tyrannical. As I write, just about the quickest way to induce fits of mirth in the street is to appear there wearing flared trousers. Yet thirty years ago they were the height of fashion, and – who knows? – may be again by the time this book is published. That example is trivial; yet isn't it rather sad that someone who feels idiotic wearing Chinos, rejuvenated 'Oxford Bags' or trousers cut straight and narrow[1], should be mocked if he chooses a style that suits him better or in which he feels more comfortable?

A similar constraint can affect one's speech and writing. People often use language in a way that is unnatural – a way they've adopted for reasons which have little to do with how they feel or what they want to say. As with fashion, the process can be insidious. When you buy a certain garment, you may privately feel ridiculous in it, but seeing others wearing similar things will at once make you feel better. As with much else in life, once you get used to it, it soon strikes you as

---

1 In Jasper Carrott's phrase, 'looking like a two-pin plug'.

comfortable and 'right': familiarity breeds serenity. In the same way, the adoption of a linguistic style may at first seem alien, but quickly comes to seem natural.

The trouble about this – and here the analogy with high-street fashion breaks down – is that language is a more complex expression of what you want to 'say' than appearance can ever be. It is also – unlike matters of dress, hair-style and so forth – fundamental. Fashion may create a startling first impression, but language – written or spoken – expresses the 'real you', as this brief excursion into a recent trend might illustrate.

Picture someone with multi-coloured and/or shaved hair, whose face is an alarming amalgam of scrap iron and Druidic war-paint and whose garments suggest a cross between a sadistic jailer and a hob-nailed Geronimo. In short, a Punk stereotype. Now consider how many such blood-curdling figures turn out to be charming, gentle, public-spirited people! Such a 'surprise' is both pleasing and salutary: it teaches us not to judge by appearances, not to (forgive the cliché) 'judge a book by its cover' but to appraise the true man/woman under such essentially superficial 'masks'.

However, the way you talk and write **does** define you in a direct and persistent manner. It is therefore important that your style is not only clear to others but an unsullied reflection of yourself and what you wish to communicate. For true 'style' has nothing to do with fashion or others' usage. Of course there are – as we've seen – certain basic rules you need to obey. It would be crazy to attempt to wear trousers as if they were a shirt, or vice versa; similarly, you need to respect the intrinsic grammatical properties of words and structures. Indeed, just as everyone needs clothes, so must all writers clothe their thoughts in clear and decent forms. Once that is secure, you are free to develop your best method of expressing yourself: it will be all the more effective for being yours and nobody else's.

There are plenty of people in the public eye who are not in the least 'slaves to fashion' but who are indisputably 'stylish': Gary Lineker, Dame Judi Dench, Jeremy Paxman, Tiger Woods and Eddie Izzard come quickly to my mind. They are household names and supreme in their field precisely because they have each obeyed Polonius's advice: 'To thine own self be true'.

In sum: a good style is not imposed from without but emerges from within. It should combine naturalness, flow and pleasure for all; as Somerset Maugham deftly observed,

> A good style should show no sign of effort. What is written should seem a happy accident.

The achievement of such apparent ease is far from easy. In the words of a friend and colleague of mine, 'the art which conceals art is bloody hard work.' I hope to make your progress towards Maugham's ideal less hard and certainly less bloody! And I start by looking at all the things you **don't** need or shouldn't use, which will greatly lighten your way and your burden.

Chapter 7

Fight the flab

All our life is crushed by the weight of words: the weight of the dead.

Luigi Pirandello

When in doubt, strike it out.

Mark Twain

Why begin in such a negative way? Why focus on what **not** to do instead of addressing what is desirable?

Well, bad style and bad writing usually stem from things which should have been jettisoned rather than the absence of things which should have been included. This does not just apply to those times when your writing will improve by being edited and honed down; it also takes in a catalogue of practices which should be avoided on principle and as a matter of course. One of the soundest ways of arriving at your own 'voice' – your individual style – is first to be aware of all the accumulated junk that disfigures our language.

Hamlet speaks of 'the thousand natural shocks / That flesh is heir to.' The afflictions that can impair the 'flesh' of your style may be fewer in number, but they are still considerable. Firstly, a group of ailments characterized by obesity.

7.1 WAFFLE AND PADDING

Waffle: to talk or speak ignorantly or aimlessly. (OED)

We all waffle sometimes – in speech at least. We have all known occasions when we drivel vacuously on, through ignorance, embarrassment or love of the sound of our own voice. It is not something to encourage, naturally; but it will inevitably happen from time to time, especially when we're 'put on the spot' or caught unprepared.

Written waffle is another thing altogether and must always be avoided. The diagnosis is simple and the remedy brutal. Writers waffle when they have nothing to say and/or no control over their material: this is the result of pure ignorance, and the only cure is to stop writing, go back to one's books and do some more preparatory work. If you waffle in an exam, I'm afraid the condition is likely to be terminal. All you can hope for is an indulgent marker!

Padding is a different matter – less obviously ruinous but a major threat to the writer's command. Padding is any word, phrase or structure which does no real work or damages impact and tempo. It can seriously weaken prose which is essentially sound, where the writer does not know what he/she is doing; if the writing is not kept taut, it can reach a stage where muscle and sinew disappear.

There are two kinds of padding to avoid: 'surplus fat' and 'deliberate fleshiness'. The first is the more innocent, arising from clumsiness or ignorance rather than the more sinister desire to hide one's meaning on purpose.

Surplus fat

All bodies need some fat; so does a good style. Lean sentences fashioned like whipcord can be both beautiful and riveting, but few can get away with a style consisting solely of such an approach. **Surplus** fat refers either to words and structures that are superfluous by definition or to once-muscular expressions that have lost sheen and power.

Tautology

A tautology is an expression where at least one of the words is redundant. Two obvious comic examples would be

a dead corpse   **a round circle**

Most tautologies are more subtle, and therefore more dangerous. I've heard or read all these recently, often from highly-educated people:

1   this new innovation
2   at this moment in time
3   whys and wherefores
4   unnecessary fripperies
5   quite unique
6   quite dead

All are illiterate.

1   **Innovation** already includes the idea of newness, so **new** is useless.
2   You cannot have a **moment** in any other dimension but that of **time**. Use **now** instead!
3   **Why** means **wherefore**; it therefore makes as much sense to use the absurd expression **whys and whys**.

4   **Fripperies** are *by definition* unnecessary.
5   **Unique** means 'one of a kind'. Something is either unique or it's not: you cannot have grades of uniqueness. **Quite** is therefore foolishly redundant.
6   Even more obviously, you cannot have **degrees** of death![2]

You can avoid the trap such examples illuminate by sharp attentiveness, and that applies to larger-scale tautologies too. Look at this ludicrously conditional sentence:

If we had some bacon, we could have bacon and eggs, if we had some eggs.

I find that a charming joke; if one were to be more solemnly analytical about it, one would see that its intrinsic idiocy derives from the speaker having no idea where the sentence was going to end up. Such floundering characterizes many inadequate sentences, and poor sentences often start with flabbily thought-out phrases. Here are six in a little exercise.

Exercise 16
Each one of these opening remarks contains at least one redundant word. Can you tighten them up? Answers on page 228.

1   Throughout the whole chapter . . .
2   The final incident with which the chapter ends.
3   These factors combined together to produce . . .
4   It was no more than a mere passing thought . . .
5   But after a while, however, he realized . . .
6   He can do no more than just follow blindly . . .

From the outset I have stressed the need to be constantly on the alert when writing, and that applies as much to spotting little bits of flab as to anything else. Once you train yourself to do that, you will avoid their minor idiocies and also tune up your writing in a healthily active way.

Useless or unwise qualifiers

There are a number of words, in common and forgivable use in speech, which should be deleted from all developing writers' vocabulary. They are at best useless and at worst actively damaging.

---

2   It can be (legitimately) comic to refer to someone as 'very dead' or 'seriously dead': the masterly Raymond Chandler does this several times, as do other good thriller writers. The key is humour or irony: if that's not your intention, stick to strict accuracy.

1 **incredible**   Arguably the single most stupidly used word of all. Its true meaning is **unable to be believed**; its colloquial meanings range from 'mildly surprising' to 'excellent'. Find another word – there are plenty to choose from. Otherwise you risk the kind of inanity perpetrated by Lord Asa Briggs, distinguished historian and Chancellor of Sussex University: we've seen the line before in Part One, but it's worth repeating.

> **We thought this story incredible – very convincing.**

One or the other, please: it cannot be both!

2 **fantastic**   Nowadays used as a vague synonym for 'excellent' or 'supreme'. Avoid that usage in all formal writing. The word means **pertaining to fantasy**; however, the colloquial use of **fantastic** has taken such a hold that you risk being misunderstood even if you use it correctly, so try to use the noun rather than the adjective.

3 **pathetic**   Again, try to stick to the noun – **pathos** – if what you wish to signify is the idea of **evoking pity or sadness**. If you intend the idea of 'ridiculous' or 'contemptible', then use those words, not **pathetic**, which will confuse readers and possibly rebound damagingly on you.

4 **brilliant**   Used far too loosely as a synonym for 'very good'. If you wish to draw attention to qualities that **shine**, well and good; thus it is fine to refer to a hot sunny day or an innings by Viv Richards as **brilliant**, because in each case you capture a central quality. But it is not an appropriate word to describe something impressive which does not also **scintillate**.

5 **definitely**   A curious word: its use often undermines an argument rather than endorses it. If you come out with something like

> **Macbeth is definitely a tragic hero . . .**
> **Time is definitely relative . . .**
> **Nuclear reactors are definitely controllable . . .**

one somehow gets the impression that the matter is in doubt – that Macbeth is neither heroic nor tragic; that time is absolute; that nuclear reactors are frighteningly dangerous. The emphatic tone causes a twinge of suspicion: the reader detects rhetoric, not evidence. Alternatively, it can carry an element of childish triumph – 'Wow! I've made up my mind about that, so there!' In any event, the word is hardly ever used beneficially; leave it alone.[3]

---

3 If you **must** use it, at least spell it right! It's **definitely**.

6 **situation**   This has become an all-purpose suffix that is usually both ugly and redundant. In all five examples below, **situation** is useless:

> **Practice is different from a game situation.**
> **We're in a riot situation here.**
> **Tomorrow you're likely to encounter a rain situation.**
> **And Manchester City have a free kick situation.**
> **Hamlet has an eyeball-to-eyeball confrontation-situation with his mother.**

Above all, avoid the horrible construction based on the words **ongoing . . . situation**. My 'favourite' was this attempt to say that two people were having a love affair:

> **They are in an ongoing carnal knowledge situation.**

7 **no way/in no way**   A recent arrival in yob's English that has infected far too many. It is ugly and dubiously emphatic, like **definitely**, and it often involves needless and unsightly double negatives, as in these charmless structures:

> **No way is Macbeth not a tragic hero.**
> **There is no way you can move an object without expending energy.**

After the World Cup of 1974, the late Billy Bremner, the Scottish captain, defiantly answered criticisms of his team's performance with, 'There is no way I'm not proud of what we did do.' Why didn't he just say, **I'm proud of what we did**, which is simpler, more dignified and clearer? After all, if what you are claiming is that certain, why make such a syntactical big and complex deal of it?

8 **over the top**   A slang expression meaning **excessive, extreme, over-done**. It should be banished from formal writing at all times. Nothing destroys snap and dignity faster than such remarks as

> **Shakespeare goes way over the top here . . .**
> **The Green Party's diagnosis of pollution is over the top.**

The phrase is casual and complacent, and invariably removes the focus from what's being said, putting it firmly and damagingly on who's saying it.

9 **human**   Not much help if what you mean is 'caring', 'sensitive' or 'sympathetic'. Human beings are capable of the noblest responses; they are also capable of cruelty and any number of things that place them below any animal. **Human** is too big, too basic a concept to be a good choice for subtler ideas. Use **kind** or any of the three alternatives mentioned above.

10 **literally** Almost invariably used wrongly. It means **without mysticism, allegory or metaphor**; if incorrectly and emptily used for emphasis, the opposite sense is produced, as in these comical remarks by, respectively, Colin Croft and Prince Edward:

> **The ball came back, literally cutting in him half.**
> **My grand-father, King George VI, was literally catapulted onto the throne.**

Those are the ten 'useless qualifiers' which I come across most often or which most annoy me.[4] There are many others – words that are empty, ugly, unclear, or all three. A little fierce thought should protect you from their harmful use.

Leaden lead-ins

Boastful or arrogant writing is as repellent as a boastful or arrogant person. On the other hand, false modesty or lack of nerve can be just as unattractive. You should always assume that your reader is interested enough in what you're saying to give you a fair hearing, so there's no need to apologize for what you're about to write or to 'wind yourself up' into it. Accordingly, avoid all these:

It is interesting to note that . . .	Kills all interest at once.
It may perhaps be said that . . .	Well, why shouldn't it be?
It is worthy of note that . . .	Ugly, pompous and wasteful.
We can safely say that . . .	If so, why not just say it?
From certain points of view . . .	**Whose** points of view? Looks vague and timid.

These five constructions slow everything down to no purpose. They create a flabby and timorous impression; the attempt to 'cover oneself' either wastes time or is annoyingly unspecific.

Such effects are unfortunate anyway, and can lead to worse problems. Consider this sentence, which appears in the first paragraph of a well-known critical work.

---

4 For literature students only: I'm tempted to add the word 'sincere' to those ten when it is used in aesthetic criticism. If you say a poem or song is 'sincere', you claim a privileged insight into the private motivation and feelings of the composer. That can look conceited; worse, it rarely persuades – unless you document it at length and in dense biographical detail. Even then, your labours may be fruitless or simply inappropriate, as this remark by the poet Liz Lochhead warns: 'poets don't bare their souls: they bare their skills.'

Do not confuse the artist's private [even unconscious] spurs and ideas with their effect on you. The latter is your business and what you wish to communicate: use the word **convincing** instead. If ever tempted to use 'sincere', remember that your prime job as a critic is to say whether and how the writing works, not to pass moral judgments on the writer. Besides, 'sincerity' is not an unambiguously praiseworthy quality anyway: Hitler was sincere, as were Savanorola and Nero. Find a safer compliment!

> We should like to make it impossible for any academic authority . . . to tell us with the familiar easy assurance that Dickens of course was a genius, but that his line was entertainment.

What do you make of the **tone** here?

I find it suspect in its hectoring vagueness. I want to know just who these critics are who insist with 'easy assurance' that Dickens is mere 'entertainment', and I start to wonder if such a mixture of aggression and imprecision indicates a lack of conviction or serenity. In this case, the answer is 'Yes'. The writers are F. R. and Q. D. Leavis, in their *Dickens The Novelist*, published in 1970 and rightly acknowledged as a cogent account. But, as many reviewers pointed out at the time, the only critic who had ever sought to dismiss Dickens as 'a mere entertainer' was one F. R. Leavis himself![5]

I have no wish to pillory a brave and valuable critic; the fact is that such imprecise militancy is as bad a strategy as needless apology. And the two things are curiously related. If you get into the uncorrected habit of writing dully vague 'lead-ins', you may soon find yourself coming on strong in an unspecified and suspect way. That is poor tactics: you must document your argument **at once**. Otherwise, your problem will be graver than flabbiness: it will seem that you've got something to hide.

Unnecessary complexity

Please read these six examples.

1   The poet succeeds in creating an arresting picture . . .
2   Mozart manages to convince us . . .
3   Einstein is trying to put over the point that . . .
4   . . . embodies a representation of . . .
5   . . . the way this is brought to realization is . . .
6   . . . promotes a general level of satisfaction . . .

All are in the first place clumsy, in the second flabby, and in the third disagreeable.

In the first three, the slim-line verbs **creates**, **convinces** and **puts over** are doubly superior. They are clearer, and they avoid the originals' **tonal kick-back**:

1	**succeeds in creating**	suggests that the poor old poet had a hell of a time getting his work up to scratch.
2	**manages to convince**	is patronizing, as if giving a Brownie point – 'Well done, Wolfgang, old chap!'
3	**Einstein is trying to**	Inaccurate, and in a most unfortunate way. It's not

5 In *The Great Tradition*, 1948.

Einstein who's making the effort but **you**. You're struggling to articulate your ideas – something he managed rather well.

At best such structures sound naive; at worst they are condescending. You will benefit in every way if you **keep it simple**.

Similar advice applies to the remaining three examples, which all suffer from pompous timidity.

4	embodies a representation of	= is
5	the way this is brought to realization is	= this happens by
6	promotes a general level of satisfaction	= satisfies everyone

Of course, you want to avoid using the same simple verb time after time, just as you should avoid the Chinese water-torture repetition of **and**, **but** and **then**. But by and large the virtues of simplicity far outweigh its problems; besides, your writing should never be ugly, which 4–6 are. As the American philologist Wilson Follett remarks:

> The writer who fills his pages with ugly dissonances and tells himself that they are not worth the trouble of rectifying, because not one reader in fifty will ever test him **by voice**, is deluding himself. His bad readers may not mind, but his better readers will follow him with pain and inward protest if they are sufficiently interested in his contents, and otherwise not at all.
>
> from *Modern American Usage* (Longman, 1968); my emphasis

Finally in this section, do not clutter up your formal writing with over-use of the first person. **I** itself is not so bad, although it should be watched carefully; but **to me, in my view, in my opinion, it seems to me**, and **I think** should be occasional at most.[6] You're doing the writing; you know you're doing it; the reader knows you're doing it. Regularly to remind everyone of the obvious is tiresome; moreover, there are times when you need to stress that what follows is **your** opinion as opposed to another specified one. In speech, the structure **I think** is very common, but it is only really noticeable when the pronoun is emphasized, as in, **Well, I, think . . .** – i.e. in contrast to anyone else. When writing, if your projected use of **I think** has that force, keep it in; if not, strike it out.

In speech, all of us lapse at times into other 'verbal tics' – **you know, I mean, sort of**, and of course **um** and **er**. I need hardly say that such things must be ruthlessly banned when writing. Even more obviously than over-use of first person phrases, they are forms of 'stuttering': they do no work, and either embarrass or irritate.

---

6 I shall assume you to be incapable of using the appalling **I myself personally**!

Clichés

Clichés are expressions which have lost all charm, power or currency. I know of no better definition than that offered by Clive James:

> On *Nationwide* (BBC1) there was a lady whose cat had recently survived a complete cycle in the washing machine. 'What sort of condition was he in?' asked Frank Bough. The lady answered without smiling: 'My husband said he looked like a drowned rat.'
>
> The essence of a cliché is that words are not misused, but have gone dead. To describe a wet cat as a drowned rat is to use language from which all life has departed, leaving mechanical lips and a vacant stare.
>
> from *Glued To The Box: TV Criticism From The Observer 1979–82*

In a language as rich and globally used as English, there are bound to be plenty of clichés, and the number increases all the time. It is almost impossible to avoid using them altogether; but one should at least try, for two reasons:

1   Clichés are **dull**; no reader enjoys being bored.
2   As Clive James suggests, clichés reflect a mind that is not **thinking**.

No reader will follow for long a writer who traffics in stale, inappropriate and empty-headed expressions.

The stress on thinking is crucial, which is why this defence of the use of clichés is unconvincing:

> **Phrases become clichés because so many people have found them attractive and useful. Furthermore, they're *clear*: everyone knows what you mean by them.**

There is something in the first sentence; the second is decidedly suspect. Many clichés are widely misunderstood and misused, and their effect is anything but clear. Consider these four sadly well-known examples:

nose to the grindstone   **grist to the mill**
hoist with his own petard   **nigger in the woodpile**

These employ metaphors that are obscure and out-of-date, if not positively alien.

Nose to the grindstone is used to express the need for single-minded hard work. It is not much of an image for twenty-first-century life, is it? People who use it invariably have no idea what a grindstone looks like, let alone how it's used. In addition, the phrase strongly suggests discomfort and danger, which are not appropriate to most forms of intellectual work!

Grist to the mill is even more obscure. Hands up all those who are fully aware what **grist** is or visualize the milling process when using the phrase? Not a lot, I'd guess; avoid it.

Hoist with his own petard is fascinating in its useless way. It has a distinguished pedigree for a start [*Hamlet*, III:iv:208], and it has nothing to do with strangulation, which virtually everyone I've heard use it seems to imagine. It means **blown up by his own bomb**, and while therefore appropriate to a gruesome incident in Belfast or Beirut, isn't over-apposite in normal circumstances. The term **own goal** is more in tune with our own society, and it is immeasurably clearer too – though be careful, since it has already become a cliché itself!

Nigger in the woodpile means, I believe, **troublemaker** or *agent provocateur*, but nobody has been able to explain to me why it should mean that. In addition, it is highly offensive: indeed, as a mixture of unpleasantness and imprecision, the phrase takes some beating.

Clichés are not just stale: they are usually woolly. For all their reputed clarity-through-familiarity, they often confuse through laziness and sloppy thinking, characteristics notably evident in the use of proverbs and lifeless similes.

Proverbs

There are two words to say to a young writer on the subject of using proverbs and they are, **forget it**. Proverbs are handy things to **know**: some people still insist on using them, and it helps to have some idea of what they're talking about. But to encounter a proverb in the midst of a vigorous piece of writing is a dreary experience.

There are three things about proverbs that render them a disease. First, nearly all of them seem to go in contradictory pairs:

> Too many cooks spoil the broth / Many hands make light work
>
> Everything comes to him who waits / The early bird catches the worm
>
> Honesty is the best policy / Nice guys come last
>
> Out of sight, out of mind / Absence makes the heart grow fonder[7]

Second, they are rigid and surprisingly abstract. Like other clichés, they had an appropriate and telling power – once. They grew out of a particular situation, and as such had a particular instructiveness. What happens nowadays is the reverse:

---

7 I rather like the 'renegade' version: **Absence makes the heart go wander**. At least it matches its 'twin'.

they are imposed upon a situation as an allegedly perfect summary of it. In fact, most human predicaments are subtle, special, even unique: they require more than some hackneyed formula to do justice to them. And like those pre-industrialization phrases we looked at in the last section, most proverbs are absurdly out of date: when, for example, did you last hear of anyone, anywhere, **crying over spilt milk**? Someone prepared to shed tears over a few drops of UHT dairy produce is a leading candidate for the funny farm, wouldn't you say?

Third, more than a few proverbs are either incomprehensible or simply illiterate. Consider these four:

1 **Fair words butter no parsnips.**
2 **Still waters run deep.**
3 **Don't let the grass grow under your feet.**
4 **You can't teach an old dog new tricks.**

The first proverb manages to be ludicrously self-evident and totally baffling at the same time. Just who, in the entire course of human history, has ever suggested that words ['fair' or otherwise] **can** butter parsnips? But what does it mean anyway? That 'actions speak louder than words'? That 'all this talk won't buy Auntie a new frock'? Those are clichés themselves, of course, but at least they make some kind of sense.

Both 2 and 3 are absurd and/or illiterate. The point about **still waters** is that they don't run at all: that is, funnily enough, why they're still. The broad idea behind this expression is sound enough – that surface appearance can belie a deeper reality. But on the principle that you risk losing your readers if you include incongruous expressions, this is one to avoid and pour gleeful scorn upon.

Proverb 3 is even sillier. How can grass grow if it's blocked off from sun, rain and organic chemicals by around ten stone of human flesh culminating in two shod [and probably smelly] feet? The governing idea, implying ambition, is satisfactory; but it is undermined by the inadequacy of the **literal** image – a definition that encompasses all bad metaphors.

Proverb 4 is, quite simply, incorrect. You **can** teach an old dog new tricks, as I and many other dog-owners will testify. Since this inane proverb is often employed as an excuse for laziness or the refusal to consider another point of view, it's highly satisfying to point out that it serves only to expose the speaker: a 'natural truth' it ain't!

I hope this destructive detour has proved amusing. I stick to the terse point with which I began it: never use proverbs in your writing – unless for humorous or ironic purposes. They are dull, rusty and rarely more than vaguely apt. The same goes for lifeless similes, which I deal with next.

Lifeless similes

When we're very young, learning about not only language but such basic physical things as heat, colour and so on, similes like **as white as a sheet** and **as hard as**

nails are vibrant and valuable. But it really ought not to be beyond the wit of sophisticated students with a five-figure vocabulary to come up with something better than those standard structures, especially as many of them are so much linguistic junk. Here are ten leading candidates for the scrapyard.

1 **As green as grass**. Yawn, yawn. Also astonishingly vague: botanists estimate that the various grasses between them account for over 100 colour shades.
2 **As plain as the nose on your face.** An absurd remark if you're attempting to point something out to someone: it is extremely hard to focus on one's own nose without severe ocular pain.
3 **As thick as two short planks.** Exceptionally boring; and mystifying too: what has the **length** of the planks got to do with it?
4 **As sober as a judge.** Ha ha.
5 **As happy as Larry / As happy as a sandboy.** Meaningless unless you happen to know a cretin named Larry who's always laughing his head off, or number several blissful sandboys – whatever **they** are – among your acquaintances.
6 **As bold as brass.** What does this mean?
7 **As plain as a pikestaff.** What **is** a pikestaff? Is it plain?
8 **As fit as a fiddle.** How many violins do you know that go jogging, or work out regularly in the gym?
9 **As brown as a berry.** Why not 'as red/black/green as a berry'? The berries we eat – and therefore notice most – are those colours.
10 **As right as rain.** Again, what does this mean?

You may have noticed that 6–10 are alliterative – that is, the adjective and noun start with the same letter. Alliteration, though a neat device, should always be used as an **enhancement** of meaning and impact; in these cases the wish to alliterate is for its own sake, and meaning is buried. They may have had a degree of giddy charm when freshly coined; now they are drab as well as nonsensical.

Those ten are a tiny sample: our language abounds with fossilized and opaque similes. Unless you can find a witty variant with which to refresh them, they should be left alone. Make up your own similes: it's more fun, both for the reader and yourself.

Summary

As I remarked earlier, it is almost impossible to avoid **all** clichés: I'm sure you will find at least a few in this book! Clichés are numbered in millions, and each generation produces its own. Recent additions include

> **at the end of the day; acid test; grass roots; stable relationship; nitty-gritty; U-turn; high profile; toy boy; in this day and age; quantum leap; motorway madness; personal organizer; viable alternative**

– all the more insidious because we hear them so often. There may be occasions when you deliberately use a cliché because it really is the best way of getting your meaning across. For all my scorn of proverbs, there is one – **the proof of the pudding is in the eating** – that I do sometimes use, because I haven't come across or invented another expression that so clearly registers what I want to say when I use it. But such moments should be rare. As always, stay alert. Vibrantly idiomatic English is always pleasing; just watch for those idioms that have become stale or obscure and keep them out of your writing.

Redundant qualifiers

An earlier section looked at **useless or unwise qualifiers** – words you should banish from your writing or select only after careful thought. There are other qualifiers that are not suspect in the same way but should nevertheless be used sparingly.

There will be times when you wish to modify your statements with an adverb. But don't do it too often: you must trust your material enough to state it plainly. So be ruthless about the following: **very; quite; extremely; absolutely; utterly; rather; really; somewhat; completely; totally.**

Save them for times when they're essential or make a genuine difference; certain words cannot be qualified, and others need it less often than you might think. For example, all the following phrases are flabby and weak:

1   **quite evil**
2   **rather tragic**
3   **somewhat wicked**
4   **very true**
5   **completely and utterly defeated**
6   **extremely empty**

In 1–3 the adjectives **quite, rather** and **somewhat** modify are so powerful that it seems timid, or indeed plain silly, to 'reduce' them in such a way. The remaining three are further instances of **tautology**, looked at earlier. In 5, **completely** and **utterly** duplicate each other; in 4 and 6 **very** and **extremely** are redundant because the word each one modifies is already an absolute – just like those absurd phrases cited before: **a dead corpse** and **a round circle**.

These are comic because you cannot qualify **corpse** or **circle** in any way that thereby touches on their intrinsically-defined properties. You can however safely say **a rotting corpse** or **a white circle** because these qualifiers **add** information, not duplicate it.

So if your root word is already forceful, make sure that any qualifier does some real work. Thus **a wicked villain** is useless, but **a smiling villain** is additionally powerful. Similarly **a sudden shock** is padding, but **a valuable shock** is intriguing, moving the reader forward rather than wasting his/her time.

In many cases, decisions about **redundant qualifiers** will arise during the editing stage of your work, not in the first flush of composition. It is nevertheless a good idea to be alert to such things as early as possible: if you start your project fully switched-on to how your language sounds and to exactly what you're saying, you will do a more efficient job and your eventual editing will be less arduous. And I must end by confessing that over-use of qualifiers is a fault of mine when I write, which I and others have to edit ruthlessly. You may find some such redundancies even after the thorough going-over this text has had!

Summary

This kind of flab is 'innocent', in two separate ways. First, it is akin to puppy-fat in that it characterizes the young, learning writer. Lapses into tautology, cliché and redundancy, the tendency to be awkward, or taking a long time to get to the point are all symptoms of a writer struggling to acquire mastery. They are not minor: unchecked, they can become a serious threat to healthy style. On the other hand, they can be put right given alert and judicious thought.

Second, the irritation and confusion they cause is not deliberate. Often writers are not aware of their 'surplus fat' and imagine their style to be in fine shape – just as many overweight people think they're 'in the pink'. Pointing out the need to lose that weight may be hurtful; but most such writers are, I find, impressively humble and anxious to improve once the faults have been identified. Most are successful in doing so, too.

But there's another kind of flab – one that the writer is not only aware of but seems positively to revel in. That is my next target.

Deliberate fleshiness

This involves the calculated, even cynical use of complex structures and highly sophisticated vocabulary. Sometimes such a style is employed to impress; at others it is used to intimidate; and on occasion it is designed to conceal, which is worst of all.

It would be incautious to suggest that such intentional flabbiness abounds more than ever before. But there's certainly a lot of it about, and that makes life tough for the learning writer: a good number of the 'models' he/she encounters will be of this sort. So both as an encouragement and as a warning, I offer this observation:

> **An 'adult' style is not necessarily one to emulate. A great deal of adult language is ugly, dull or inept, and it often obscures more than it reveals.**

Certain forms of 'adult' writing indulge three major vices: excessive abstraction; indifference to clarity and the reader's comfort; self-indulgent verbosity.

I The desire to hide

The word **simple** is, paradoxically, a very complex one. For a start it has a host of meanings: *The Shorter Oxford* lists no fewer than twenty-four. The six most relevant to my discussion here are:

1	**straightforward, unelaborate**	a simple sentence; simple diet
2	**absolute**	the simple truth
3	**feeble-minded**	simple Simon; hence simpleton
4	**insignificant, trifling**	simple people
5	**easily done or understood**	give a simple explanation
6	**natural**	a simple heart; simple joys

You will quickly see that these meanings are not only separate: they can be opposites.

One of the most famous questions ever asked was Pontius Pilate's: **What is truth?** That strikes me as 'simple' in senses 1, 2 and 6. It is emphatically not so under the other definitions, especially 5: it is as difficult as anything in human history, and indeed nobody has yet answered it satisfactorily.

When I recommend simplicity, therefore, I do not have meaning 3 in mind, which would be silly; or 2, which is usually impossible. Nor am I suggesting that your efforts will reduce to 4. But you **should** strive for 1 and 6; and if you find the **easily done** part of 5 involves a lot of (hidden) work, you must always try to ensure the **easily understood** part for your readers' sakes.

As your vocabulary and technical skill increase, you will want to make as much use of them as you can. This shows admirable enterprise, but don't let it lead you to ignore the virtues of simplicity and harmfully inflate your writing. This next exercise features a very clever man with plenty to say who has forgotten how to write naturally.

Exercise 17
The following passage is some 120 words long. Can you paraphrase in 40?

In the affluent society, capitalism comes into its own. The two mainsprings of its dynamic – the escalation of commodity production and productive exploitation – join and permeate all dimensions of private and public existence. The available material and intellectual resources [the potential of liberation] have so much outgrown the established institutions that only the systematic increase in waste, destruction and management keeps the system going. The opposition which escapes suppression by the police, the courts, the representatives of the people, and the people themselves, finds expression in the diffused rebellion among the youth and the intelligentsia, and in the daily struggle of the persecuted minorities. The armed class struggle is waged outside: by the wretched of the earth who fight the affluent monster.

Commentary

That is the first paragraph [**first**, mark you!] of *An Essay On Liberation* (1969) by Herbert Marcuse. He was a political philosopher of the first rank, so we should not perhaps expect his work to be easy. But is it efficient or natural writing?

No, surely not. The language is top-heavy, abstract, turgid; above all the passage is **verbose**. As noted, it is 120 words long; have a look at this 33-word paraphrase of mine and compare it to your own.

> Capitalism dominates the affluent society at all levels. By enlarging the range and intensity of its influence, it sucks in and emasculates most potential rebels, leaving only the abjectly poor to fight it.

That is just over one-quarter of the original's length. It may sacrifice the odd nuance, but it captures the essentials of the argument without distortion or omission. And unlike the original it is, I hope, almost immediately comprehensible.

Why do people write like that? Why did Marcuse, an internationally-renowned figure, feel it necessary to use four words where one would do and in general write as if he were almost afraid of making himself clear?

Fear may be the key. Marcuse's subject [the state of the earth and its oppressed poor] may be a large one; his treatment of it is commonplace – orthodox post-Marxist attitudinizing. Since he's addressing a presumably educated and well-informed audience, he seeks to dress up his unremarkable ideas in the most imposing fashion he can find. So he reaches for the grandest 'power terms', hoping they will cow the reader into dutifully accepting that his argument is both important and fresh. In short, the passage tries to bully the reader; bullies are notorious for their underlying insecurity.

All that may strike you as unfair. You might instead feel that Marcuse is an innocent victim of the drift away from the concrete that George Orwell identified half a century ago. Whatever one's view, the fact remains that Marcuse attacks the reader with a string of Latinate words and complex constructions that resist quick understanding. Those 'power terms' – **suppression, escalation of commodity production, potential of liberation** and **persecuted minorities** – fail to prompt any clear physical image. And they surely should: the passage centres on basic physical truths – violence, torture, poverty, mass production and, indeed, how life is lived. Only the phrase **the wretched of the earth** resonates appropriately; and by the time it appears, the damage has already been decisive.

Such writing is dishonest. Once any writer allows a gap to develop between the concrete reality addressed and the language used to express it, muddle and deception result. Intriguingly, that dishonesty does not have to be malicious or sinister: a lot of misleading language can be considerate in intention – which brings me to the topic of **euphemism**.

2   Euphemism

Euphemism: the substitution of a mild or vague or roundabout expression for a harsh or blunt or direct one.

The three commonest causes of euphemism are death, sex and going to the lavatory. If a friend of yours has recently suffered a death in the family, it is sensible and considerate to seek the least painful way of referring to it – 'passed away', 'moved on' or whatever. Similarly, if you're at a formal dinner-party and become aware of the urgent need to relieve yourself, it is just crass to rise abruptly and favour the table with, 'Gotta piss, folks.' Judge your audience!

On such occasions, the roundabout expression is commendably tactful. In most instances, however, euphemisms are cowardly and deceptive rather than courteous. Their dressed-up, inexact nature betrays fearful dislike of unpalatable fact; as such they are enemies of clarity and truth. Furthermore, they are insidious. Shying away from direct linguistic contact with certain ideas and facts can quickly spread to your handling of other ideas and facts; before you know it your language has become woolly and coy. So I believe one should, within reason, be as direct as possible.

For euphemism, whether decorous or deceitful, is everywhere. It permeates all matters of everyday life – not just death, sex and urination but money; serious illness; any kind of mental disturbance; political and business practice; warfare; housing; advertising; education; travel; food and catering; and so on. The more you kow-tow to it, the more your style and its ability to communicate will suffer.

Now to some examples.

The first is from an A Level essay on *Othello*, a play centrally concerned with sexual infatuation and obsession. A good many students get into difficulties when writing on this theme – not because they are adolescently giggly about it, but because it takes a lot of courage to 'go public' in a direct manner about the subject. As a result, they write things like this:

Othello and Desdemona have a huge crush on each other which interferes with their judgment.

The basic idea is sound, but the language diminishes it to a near-comic extent. It is not true that the characters' passion 'interferes with their judgment': it **obliterates** their judgment. And I suspect that such a cripplingly diluted phrase was the inevitable consequence of starting with the feebly coy 'huge crush', which relegates the relationship to a Mills and Boon level.

Appropriateness and 'weight' of vocabulary are all-important. Here the student felt diffident about registering the instinctive ferocity of the lovers' passion, seeking refuge in a phrase that would not embarrass him. But in another way, of course, it **did** embarrass him: the expression is factually inappropriate, and suggests that he has not grasped a point of fundamental significance.

How far you go in a corrective direction is tricky! Perhaps the following is a good compromise between genteel inadequacy and excessive raunchiness:

The sexual delight Othello and Desdemona share in each other bypasses and eventually annihilates their judgment.

That is also an extract from an A Level essay. Both students make essentially the same point; the second, which records the intensity of the pair's sexuality in an accurate and dignified way, has an authority that the first's blushful reticence does not approach.

That first example of euphemism may be gauche, but it is hardly a sinister abuse of language. The next illustration **is** morally disreputable. It is a famous example of the language of war, taken from the *pro forma* letters sent to bereaved relatives of servicemen killed in the Great War (1914–18). The central clauses invariably read:

He died instantly and felt no pain.

In many cases this was simply not true. Most soldiers did not die instantly: a considerable number died in slow agony spread over days, often hanging inaccessibly alive in 'No Man's Land' until they became too weak or infected to survive.

It could be argued that the formula was designed from the best of motives – to cheer the bereaved, to offer them comfort and even some pride in their loss. But it could equally be said that it amounted to flagrant lying, that it cynically blinded the recipients [and thus others] to the lunatic waste and cruelty of a war that political bosses were determined to see carried on. That determination may not have been dishonourable or wrong in itself; it is, however, harder to believe that when such devious methods were used to safeguard its continuation.[8]

'War is hell' may have become the stalest of clichés[9], but the official language of war has shown an increasing fondness for a bland abstraction void of any hint of infernal torment.

The journal *Private Eye* has always been good at 'de-coding' that kind of language. Here is its 'corrective' explanation of the US Air Force's botched 1986 raid on Libya.

---

8 Such tawdry phoneyness is wonderfully satirized in *Catch-22*, where the manically self-seeking Colonel Cathcart sends his own *pro forma* letter to all bereaved relatives without even deleting the unapplicable terms. Thus a Mrs Daneeka's letter of condolence reads:

> Mrs, Mr, Miss, or Mr and Mrs Daneeka: Words cannot express the deep personal grief I experienced when your husband, son, father or brother was killed, wounded or reported missing in action.

9 The remark is attributed to General Sherman of the Union forces in the American Civil War; I imagine a similar idea may have crossed the minds of Julius Caesar, Marlborough, Napoleon and all those involved in the Charge of the Light Brigade.

THAT LIBYAN RAID
Glossary of Terms

What they said	*What they meant*
The mission was 100% successful	We really screwed it up
Surgical precision	All our bombs hit Libya
We only hit selected military targets	Tough luck on all those embassies, schools, kids, hospitals, etc.
We had no intention of assassinating Gadaffi	We missed
We deeply regret any casualties	They're only Arabs
This will teach them once and for all that terrorism doesn't pay	Gadaffi More Popular Than Ever Shock
We have made a major contribution to effectively reducing terrorist capability in the world	Cancel your holiday plans
As a result of what we did Americans can walk a little taller in the world	We're still cancelling our holidays
We've shown that they can't push us around	Did you see Rambo?
We're not contemplating a second strike	Bombs away!

The piece is overstated, naturally, and you may think that measured accuracy would have been more effective than its irreverent anger. You might also think that to attack politicians is itself a cliché: they've been pilloried by satirists for centuries.

I find such debunking scorn healthy and important. When writers aim their vitriol at politicians, it is not things like the shaping of policy, the difficult business of government or even electioneering that prompt their rage: it is bogus conduct. It is the politician as liar that *Private Eye* is attacking – and 'politician' in that derogatory sense means anyone in public life whose task it is to provide the people with information and who fails to tell (or face) a known truth or wraps it up in misleading language.

I stressed earlier that you'll find euphemism everywhere. Here are ten of my 'pet hates' over the years; you might then like to try the similar exercise that follows them.

1 **industrial action**: On strike/doing no work.
2 **strategic labour reserve**: The unemployed.
3 **I've got a cash-flow problem**: I'm broke.
4 **I'm going to South Africa to help break down apartheid in cricket**: They've offered me £100k for two winters' work.
5 **He is suffering from a chemical imbalance in the right hemisphere of the brain**: He's potty.
6 **The site has been rationalized**: All the buildings have been demolished.

7   **The property is in easy reach of good communications**: The house is 100 metres from the M25.
8   **He underachieves on paper and is anonymous in class**: He's a lazy sod and I can't remember what he looks like.
9   **The conditions are not propitious**: We haven't a chance in hell of surviving.
10 **Inexpensive dresses for mature women with the fuller figure**: Nasty cheap frocks for fat old women.

Exercise 18
Now 'decode' these expressions; my versions appear afterwards.

'Nukespeak'[10]
1   strike potential.
2   soft[11] targets

The world of work and business
3   My members' material aspirations have been grossly betrayed.
4   I'm not running a charity, you know.

Medicine
5   The patient is in a stable condition.
6   He is a disturbed personality with schizophrenic and paranoid tendencies.

Housing
7   This property would benefit from a degree of renovation.
8   This attractively idiosyncratic flat is distinguished for the communal friendliness of its adjoining residents.

Catering
9   A pleasant full-bodied red wine that is always in demand.
10 Gratuities at the discretion of the customer.

General
11 I'm sorry about your birthday – I forgot.
12 Eh, lad, you must take us as you find us.

These are my alternatives to the euphemisms of Exercise 18.

1   The ability to kill hundreds of millions of people in a few minutes.
2   Concentrated areas of population.

---

10 i.e. the language of nuclear weaponry.
11 'Hard' targets are military bases and missile sites. Both 1 and 2 are standard expressions in the language of strategic defence [i.e. war] planning.

3   We haven't got the pay rise we asked for.
4   I'm interested only in making as much money as possible.
5   The patient is in very bad shape and will probably die.
6   He is a dangerous lunatic.
7   The place is falling apart and is currently uninhabitable.
8   This flat is decorated in appalling taste and you have to share a bathroom and lavatory with twenty other people.
9   The house plonk.
10 If you don't tip us, you're just a mean sod.
11 I couldn't be bothered to remember your birthday.
12 We're very unpleasant to all strangers and we don't give a toss what you think.

Summary

Not all the euphemisms in my illustrations and that exercise are sinister or devious; one or two even have a certain charm. Nonetheless, use of euphemism should be kept to a minimum. The choice of a roundabout expression nearly always sacrifices clarity, appropriateness or necessary concreteness; sometimes all three. As a concluding guiding principle, therefore:

> **When you've nothing to say, don't say it. And when you *have* got something to say, do so in as unadorned and direct way as is feasible and apposite.**

That will suit best your own purposes of communication, and it will also help preserve the integrity of your style. If you feel that last phrase is pompous, just look back over some of the examples of 'fleshy' writing in this chapter, and note again how ugly they are and how they abuse words as a medium of enlightenment. The more writers there are who do that, the more we risk the shrinking of our language, our judgment and our independent awareness.

In addition, we should all keep a watchful eye on our work and be wary of anything that strikes us as notably pleasing. Each of us then needs to ask a few tough questions:

1   Is it really that good anyway?
2   Does it communicate properly and enlighten?
3   Why have I included it? Does it do any real work, or am I just showing off, disagreeably 'marking time'?
4   What's the lasting effect on the reader going to be?

If any of the answers has a negative tinge, it may be time to follow Dr Johnson's stern command:

> **Read over your compositions and whenever you meet with a passage which you consider particularly fine, *strike it out*.**

'Murder your darlings', in fact. That advice is Noel Coward's, and all writers will benefit from at least considering it.

From the perils of vanity to something more innocent but no less injurious.

7.2 PHONEY RULES AND FAKE FORMALISM

English has surprisingly few hard-and-fast rules. There are certain basic laws of grammar, of course; rules of punctuation are also precise and reliable: the ones outlined in Part Two are watertight. But English spelling cannot claim a single rule to which there are no exceptions; in addition, things like sentence structure, word order and word positioning are largely left up to the individual writer. That is one of the charms, and great strengths, of English; it can also perhaps be a source of uncertainty to the student.

The position isn't helped by the wide currency of counterfeit 'rules' which shackle rather than empower the developing writer. I want to focus on four of these; then I shall look at several flabby and boring structures which many pupils are erroneously taught they must employ.

Phoney rules

1 **It is wrong to begin a sentence with 'and' or indeed any other conjunction.**

Absolute nonsense. Moreover, to believe this prevents you from stressing conjunctions, which we all sometimes wish to do.

In the normal run of things, words like **and, but** and **for**, being both very common and very small, are hardly noticed by the reader: they merely advertise a link or contrast that the brain notes automatically. Supposing, though, you want to stress such a word – just as we often do in speech by placing a heavy emphasis via our voice? The only way to do this is to draw attention to it **visually**, and the only way to do that is to give it a capital letter, advertising its unusual importance. What better method than to start a sentence with it, whereby the capitalization is automatic?

Phoney Rule 1 is believed by an enormous number of people. As with certain other things I've looked at along the way, this is probably because it derives from one's primary school lessons. At that age, we have only a small vocabulary, and we tend to use the same words again and again; it makes a lot of sense, therefore, to find a way to discourage that. By the time we reach our teens, however, our vocabulary has increased a thousandfold: there is no longer any need to follow primary-school advice just for the sake of it. And to repeat, **there is no such rule in English grammar.**

As with any stylistic device, you should not use this technique too often; but if sensibly used for maximum impact, it is not only legitimate but valuable, since it allows your voice to grace your writing.

2 It is wrong to use a preposition at the end of a sentence.

Again, quite untrue.

For a start, there are some constructions where the preposition cannot comfortably go anywhere but the end:

1 **What is the world coming to?**
2 **This bed has not been slept in.**

If you rewrite these to comply with **Phoney Rule 2**, you end up with:

1a **To what is the world coming?**
2a **In this bed no sleep has taken place.**

1a is just about okay, though stiff and pompous compared to 1; 2a is wholly unsatisfactory. It is not only clumsy: it makes the remark nudgingly ambiguous, suggesting that other things may have 'taken place' even if 'sleep' did not!

'It is wrong to use a preposition at the end of a sentence'.

Besides, the 'rule' is daft anyway. As with so much else, you should not make a habit of ending sentences with a preposition; on the other hand, to worry unduly about avoiding the practice can sacrifice voice and flow. Winston Churchill once encountered a civil servant who was pedantically 'accurate' about the matter, rendering his prose ugly and tiresome to read; eventually Churchill drew a line through the man's entire memorandum and wrote at the bottom: **'This is the kind of English up with which I shall not put.'**

His sardonic good sense should be a model to us all. Always remember:

Language does not serve grammar: it is the other way round.

Clarity and easiness on the ear and eye matter most; anyone or any 'rule' that in effect rejects that principle should be regarded with considerable suspicion.

3   In formal writing it is wrong to use contractions.

In other words, you must never use, **it's, they're, doesn't** and so on, but must dutifully write **it is, they are, does not** and the like.

Pure phantom pedantry: no 'rule' is at issue, just formalistic prejudice. It may well be a sensible practice when very young; it even remains sensible a few years later, when pupils begin to be aware of the difference between formal writing and casual conversation. Thereafter it is just silly. The full structure isn't superior to the contraction. It adds nothing in clarity, and its extra 'dignity' is often spurious, as obsessive avoidance of informality can lead to stilted and flabby prose. There may well be times when you feel that the full construction is more appropriate: style is often a matter of 'horses for courses', and indeed Part Four is devoted to that theme. But to argue that contractions in formal writing are intrinsically wrong is just dumb.[12]

4   It is wrong to say 'It's me': it must always be 'It is I.'

Once more, quite untrue.

One reason behind this wrong-headed advice is the dislike of contractions, which we've just been into. The other stems from a technical point of grammar – that it is wrong to use the accusative form with the verb 'to be'. An explanation might go something like this:

It is obviously illiterate to say 'Me am teacher' or 'Him am dead'; in the same way, we should not use the object pronoun (me, him) after 'is' or any other form of the verb.

---

12   It occurs to me that the determined avoidance of contractions may be one reason why so few people know how to use the apostrophe. (See Part Two, pages 42–8.) If you're discouraged from using it in such a way, it's not surprising if you lose all sense of its value and what it's for!

This is correct so far as it goes. However, the point is that it does not go far enough. For **me** is not only the **accusative** (object) form of **I**: it is also the **demonstrative** [= emphatic] pronoun. One uses the expression **It's me** to emphasize that it is oneself as opposed to anyone else that one is talking about. Because of that fact, it could be argued that the expression is not only an acceptable alternative to **It is I** but actually a better one.

Besides, a lot of people who pride themselves on not using **It's me** commit real illiteracies such as **between you and I** and **It's a matter for your mother and I**. The **I** is wrong in both cases: the accusative form must always follow a preposition [**between** and **for**].

Somehow the idea has grown up that it's socially superior to use **I** rather than the 'proletarian' **me**. If words are an army, then **I** is officer class while **me** belongs to the ranks; and all four 'phoney rules' I've discussed contain an element of such disagreeable pretension. The feeling seems to exist that if one avoids contractions, never places a preposition at the end of a sentence or a conjunction at the beginning. and flaunts the 'correct' use of **I** as much as possible, one is more pukka both as a writer and as a person. Mere snobbish drivel, needless to say: all it actually achieves is to cramp your writing and make life needlessly difficult for your readers. If that's 'pukka', you're better off being a pleb!

Take a look at this list, which includes a couple of items considered earlier. It was compiled by the American writer John R. Trimble.[13]

'The Seven Nevers'
- **Never begin a sentence with *and* or *but***
- **Never use contractions**
- **Never refer to the reader as you**
- **Never use the first person pronoun *I***
- **Never end a sentence with a preposition**
- **Never split an infinitive**
- **Never write a single-sentence paragraph**

As he at once points out, not only are all these alleged 'rules' bogus: they are actually harmful. While they may have their place in the early stages of one's education, they quickly become obsolete, shackles rather than sails. Following them will make your writing stiff, clumsy or pompous – possibly all three. The underlying fallacy that *grammar dictates style* will worry you and literally cramp your style, so that you lose all sense of spontaneity and enjoyment; in all, an alarming mix for anyone looking to communicate.

Those 'nevers' rob writing of its natural voice, turning it into something more impersonal and, frankly, boring. That penalty also characterizes certain formal structures that are mistakenly thought to be necessary and good.

---

13 In his fine book *Writing With Style: 143 Conversations On The Art of Writing* (New Jersey: Prentice Hall, 1975; revised edition 1988).

Fake formalism

I have elsewhere[14] commented on the leaden phrases with which many writers open or close their essays – structures like:

> **In order to answer this question, we must first consider . . .**
> **The question is asking us whether . . .**
> **Thus in conclusion we may safely say that . . .**
> **In this essay I have attempted to bear out the title's contention that . . .**

The sad thing about such tedious and useless expressions is that nobody would ever write them down instinctively: they've all been laboriously taught, with a depressing twin emphasis on caution and lack of imagination.

Those examples were taken from sixth-form or undergraduate essays; the trouble starts a lot earlier. There follows a standard type of comprehension question – the kind of thing we regularly encounter from about the age of nine:

> **What three things do you notice about the man's behaviour as described in lines 15–20 of the passage?**

And we are taught to answer in a sentence – which invariably means that we are instructed to begin our answer with the question's wording. Thus:

> **The three things I notice about the man's behaviour as described in lines 15–20 of the passage are . . .**

after which we go on – accurately, let's hope! – to list them.

Now why on earth do we do this? It is irksome, for writer and reader alike; it wastes a lot of time; it has a zombie-esque quality that dulls any possible pleasure.

There is one answer, sensible enough but hardly clinching. That bloated format is encouraged in early years because it ensures that pupils focus on the question and thus increase their chances of answering it accurately. To be sure, this works sometimes – although it should be said that laboriously copying something out does not guarantee an incisive intellect. But the formula becomes almost impossible to defend later on. For every student that really needs it as a 'prop', there will be ten who find such preliminary ritual a valueless drag: they may even make more of a mess of the answer as a result. So what objection can there be to an answer that identifies those three things in this way:

1   **He is nervous.**
2   **He is ashamed of his shabby coat.**
3   **He seems to be drunk.**

---

14   In *Brain Train*[E & FN Spon, 1996], pp. 137–8. See also Part Three above, page 68.

Assuming those answers to be correct, I cannot see anything wrong with that way of presenting them. Indeed, I strongly suspect that the examiner/reader will be delighted to find the information set out in such a crisp unfussy fashion.

If you are an A Level student, an undergraduate or in a profession where you're required to write regularly, you will not, of course, have to do comprehension exercises very often. But their principles – and traps – remain relevant: you too should steer clear of any structure that is no more than an empty block of words. In the first place, these are invariably nondescript clichés; in the second, they cause you to adopt a 'voice' that is not your own. And the practice is contagious: once you feel obliged to observe such 'set-piece' formalisms as

> **Thus it can be seen that . . .**
> **In this essay I shall first consider what the title says and then go on to discuss whether it is a correct statement, and finally attempt some form of summary . . .**

you risk cluttering up your style with further, regular flab. You might even become capable of this kind of thing:

1 **That is not a prerogative we have available to us.**
2 **That information is not to hand at this juncture.**
3 **Post-nutritive substance disposal.**

Those bulbous structures translate into normal English as:

1 **We can't do it.**
2 **I don't know.**
3 **Shit.**

And if you think that these examples have a lot in common with the euphemisms analysed earlier, you're quite right. In every case there is a flabby veering away from directness, from ensuring that one's words do a precise and illuminating job of work.

Now on to positive ways of guaranteeing that you do that.

Chapter 8

Voice

There follow two longish pieces of writing that I admire very much. Their origins are very different – a newspaper article and a film transcript – but they also have something in common. Can you identify it?

Passage A

And now the bloody young man is lifting a young girl from the wreckage and laying her on the verge among the roadworks. She is even bloodier than he is. You've still got one headlamp working, and that is the only light on the scene. You can see the blood quite clearly by the light of that lamp. She is writhing a bit on the verge, in an attitude of complete abandonment and indecency. Then she lies quite still and he covers her. You know she is dead. You wonder about the other car, but the young man is walking over there, and you leave it to him again. Anyway, it's dark over there, and you're such a coward you don't want to go and look. You excuse yourself by thinking that as you know no first aid you could serve no useful purpose. So you stand beside what is left of your car, and you wait, and you don't really think about anything at all. You are not even in very great pain any more, but you know you've got to look at your right leg, because that's where the pain was and you use the headlamp to look, and it's all bloody and unreal-looking. That's **your** leg. It's always been all right in the past. Best not look any more. That blood will just go away if you leave it. Anyway, why stay here? What to do now? If you go away, you'll be in trouble for failing to report an accident. If you stay, you'll just see more horrible things when they uncover whatever is in that other car. You can report the accident tomorrow. Yes, that's right. Walk home now, and report the accident tomorrow. Forget about the car. Don't want that any more. Home is 15 miles away, but it doesn't matter. Just go home, and maybe tomorrow it won't have happened. That's right, down the hill, quite easy going. Leg doesn't really mind being walked on at all. But the thrillers are wrong when they talk of **warm** blood tricking down. It isn't warm; it's cold. Everything is cold. There isn't a footpath to walk on, but it doesn't matter. Just walk in the middle of the road. Walk home. Police car pulling up? Falling to report an accident? It's an offence. You know it is. But they seem to know all about it. They want to know what car you were in, but you can't remember the number. They put you in their own car. Riding in a police car indeed. Proper Z car, with radio. They are using the radio. Hold the ambulance. Fifth casualty found. Leg injuries and shock. Funny, they don't seem to mind that you didn't report the accident. They don't even seem to want a driving licence. Just as well. Left it at home. Then you're in the ambulance. And now you resist. Now you really resist. You're not going anywhere with that lot.

from 'Statistic', *The Guardian*, 1963

Passage B

It's impossible through words to describe what is necessary to those who do not know what 'horror' means: 'horror'. Horror has a face; and you must make a friend of horror – horror and moral terror are your friends. And if they are not, then they are enemies to be feared: they are truly enemies.

I remember when I was with Special Forces – it seems a thousand years ago – we went into a camp to inoculate some children. We'd left the camp after we'd inoculated the children for polio; and this old man came running after us and he was crying - he couldn't say why. And they[1] had come and hacked off every inoculated arm. There they were in a pile: in a pile of little arms.

And I remember, I cried: I wept like . . . like some grandmother. I wanted to tear my teeth out – I didn't know what I wanted to do. And I want to remember; I never want to forget it: I never want to forget. And then I realized – like I was shot, like I was shot with a diamond . . . a diamond bullet right through my forehead – and I thought, 'My God! The genius of that! The genius; the will to do that. Perfect; genuine; complete; crystalline; pure.'

Then I realized that they were stronger than we, because they could stand it. These were not monsters – these were **men**, trained cadres. These men,

1 'They' are the Vietcong, North Vietnamese commandos in the Vietnam war of the 1960s and 70s.

who fought with their hearts, who have families, who have children, who are filled with love; but they have the *strength*, the strength to do that. If I had ten divisions of such men, then our troubles here would be over very quickly. You have to have men who are moral, and at the same time are able to utilize their primordial instincts to kill – to kill without feeling, without passion, without judgment. Without judgment; because it's judgment that defeats us.'

A speech by Colonel Kurtz (played by Marlon Brando),
transcribed from Francis Ford Coppola's Apocalypse Now

To those might be added virtually any passage from J.D. Salinger's *The Catcher in the Rye*; a particularly apposite specimen occurs in Chapter Eighteen, narrator Holden Caulfield's withering account of a movie which he goes to see. If possible, read that in conjunction with the two extracts I've just quoted. What unites them?

Several things may occur to you. For a start, they are of course long extracts – comfortably the longest I've included so far. All are dramatic, too. You will soon see that the Salinger is primarily humorous in intent and effect, but the movie in question contains a fair amount of incident, and his withering account is certainly fast moving. And you will also notice that despite the passages' length, nearly all the sentences within them are punchily short, making focus and concentration relatively easy.

However, the quality I have most in mind is that each passage is distinguished for its sense of **voice**. All three have a 'power of sound', in Conrad's phrase, that doubles the impact of their already-powerful material.

Intriguingly, that clarity of voice enhances our visual awareness and response. I find I can not only 'see' with photographic definition every detail mentioned: I also form a very distinct picture of the person behind the voice. Add to all that the tactile crispness of the writing, and in each case one becomes immersed in it, gripped by its appeal to the senses and intellect alike.

Early on in this book I laid down a fundamental principle:

> **All good writing sounds equally good when read aloud; and all good talking will read well when transcribed.**

The sense of voice is paramount: get that right, and all else should flow from it.

Now to two examples where the voice is deliberately and revealingly disagreeable. I want to stress that the writing is in no sense bad. Each passage spotlights a character whom the author wishes us to criticize or find seriously wanting; we are led in this direction mainly by our sense of the character's voice, which tells us – faster than decoding the actual words – that something is amiss. Both form, in part, an exercise: in each case:

1   Read through the passage silently and carefully.
2   Then read it through again – **aloud**.

3   Make a detailed note of your reactions, especially what effect the 'voice' has
     on you.

Exercise 19

This first passage is taken from early in *Mansfield Park* by Jane Austen. It
chiefly features the odious Mrs Norris, a bitter and spiteful woman who rarely
misses an opportunity to bitch about Fanny, the gentle heroine of the novel.
The discussion concerns an errand that Fanny has been obliged to do even
though she is in frail health.

       Edmund got up and walked around the room, saying, 'And
could nobody be employed on such an errand but Fanny?
– Upon my word, ma'am, it has been a very ill-managed
business.' 'I am sure I do not know how it was to have
5   been done better!' cried Mrs Norris, unable to be longer deaf;
'unless I had gone myself indeed; but I cannot be in two places
at once; and I was talking to Mr Green at that very time about
your mother's dairy-maid, by her desire, and had promised
John Groom to write to Mrs Jefferies about his son, and the
10   poor fellow was waiting for me half an hour. I think nobody
can justly accuse me of sparing myself upon any occasion, but
really I cannot do everything at once. And as for Fanny's just
stepping down to my house for me, it is not much above a
quarter of a mile, I cannot think it was unreasonable to ask
15   it. How often do I pace it three times a day, early and late,
ay and in all weathers too, and say nothing about it?' 'I wish
Fanny had half your strength, ma'am.'
       'If Fanny would be more regular in her exercise, she would
not be knocked up[2] so soon. She has not been out on horseback
20   now this long while, and I am persuaded, that when she does
not ride, she ought to walk. If she had been riding before, I
should not have asked it of her. But I thought it would rather do
her good after stooping among the roses; for there is nothing so
refreshing as a walk after a fatigue of that kind; and though
25   the sun was strong, it was not so very hot. Between ourselves,
Edmund . . . it was cutting the roses, and dawdling about in
the flower-garden, that did the mischief.'

---

2 This phrase means 'made exhausted' and must not be confused with the modern American usage,
   signifying 'made pregnant'. English is a fluid language, and certain expressions dramatically change
   in meaning over the years!

Commentary

I very much hope you dislike Mrs Norris intensely! Austen 'leads' us with an authorial comment just once – the phrase **unable to be longer deaf** (lines 6–7), which suggests eavesdropping and meddling. Otherwise, Mrs Norris is condemned out of her own mouth: her 'voice' is definitively nasty.

Her aggressive prattle is amusing, but it is also most unpleasant. She at once dives into a torrent of self-justification that is as trivial as it is unattractive; then she launches a scarcely-disguised attack on what she sees as Fanny's laziness and own self-indulgence. The suggestion that she believed that **it would do her good**[3] (lines 26–7) is a transparent lie, and her obvious indifference to Fanny's welfare is underlined by the inane **though the sun was strong, it was not so very hot** (lines 29–30). And at the end she behaves like a classroom 'sneak', looking to make Fanny seem a contemptible skiver with only herself to blame for her illness.

When you read it aloud, I'd be surprised if you didn't find yourself adopting a feverish and ugly tone; however you read it, though, I'd be amazed if you liked what you heard. Nor of course were you supposed to: by expert manipulation of voice, Austen has in a few sentences nailed a character who will prompt dislike and contempt throughout the novel.

Exercise 20

The second passage is from Chapter V of *Middlemarch* by George Eliot. It is a letter proposing marriage written to Dorothea Brooke – an ardent but naive young woman – by Mr Casaubon, a middle-aged clergyman who is also a supposedly distinguished scholar. Please follow the same three-part procedure as before.

> My dear Miss Brooke,
>   I have your guardian's permission to address you on a sub-
> ject than which I have none more at heart. I am not, I trust, mis-
> taken in the deeper recognition of some deeper correspondence
> 5 than that of date in the fact that a consciousness of need in my
> own life has arisen contemporaneously with the possibility of
> my becoming, acquainted with you. For in the first hour of
> meeting you, I had an impression of your eminent and perhaps
> exclusive fitness to supply that need (connected, I may say,
> 10 with such activity of the affections as even the preoccupations
> of a work too special to be abdicated could not uninterruptedly

---

3 You may have noticed that this phrase nearly always refers to things that are unpleasant and/or highly tedious, and also that it's invariably used by people who have no interest in you other than getting you to do what they want!

dissimulate); and each succeeding opportunity for observation
has given the impression an added depth by convincing me
more emphatically of that fitness which I had preconceived,
5   and thus evoking more decisively those affections to which I
have but now referred. Our conversations have, I think, made
sufficiently clear to you the tenor of my life and purposes: a
tenor unsuited, I am aware, to the commoner order of minds.
But I have discerned in you an elevation of thought and a
10   capability of devotedness, which I had hitherto not conceived
to be compatible either with the early bloom of youth or
with those graces of sex that may be said at once to win
and confer distinction when combined, as they notably are
in you, with the mental qualities above indicated. It was, I
15   confess, beyond my hope to meet with this rare combination
of elements both solid and attractive, adapted to supply aid in
graver labours and cast a charm over vacant hours; and but for
the event of my introduction to you (which, let me again say,
I trust not to be superficially coincident with foreshadowing
20   needs, but providentially related thereto as stages towards the
completion of a life's plan), I should presumably have gone on
to the last without any attempt to lighten my solitariness by a
matrimonial union . . .

There's a further paragraph before he signs off, but I imagine you've got the
point!

Commentary

If you've never come across the piece before, I would almost guarantee that you
found the first reading not just very difficult but enragingly boring and obscure. I
know I did – and the second reading too. But as with Mrs Norris, the point is that
we're **supposed** to respond in this way. George Eliot's aims are, however, more
complex and ambitious than Jane Austen's, in that she wants our rage and
contempt to be only the beginning.

For how would you feel if you received a 'love letter' like that? Various responses
occur to me: hysterical laughter, vomiting, a feverish lunge for the wastepaper
basket. Or perhaps we might feel great pity for someone who expresses himself in
such a way, together with alarm at the prospect of getting mixed up with him in
any way. And that, I think, is what we go on to experience after that initial head-
aching annoyance has worn off a bit. The prospect of Dorothea marrying a man
who writes and 'sounds' like that fills us with horror. The letter 'places' Casaubon
unimprovably: we really don't need to be told any more about him.

To illustrate just how decisive is the matter of his voice, try this little 'sub-exercise':

1   Read aloud once more the first 14 lines, to 'uninterruptedly dissimulate'.
2   Try and work out what the sentence in brackets means. You will need pen and paper, I assure you!

Tough, is it not? I ended up with two 'translations': first, an attempt to make some sense out of it while staying reasonably close to his style and tone:

I may say that my affections were so stimulated that not even the pre-occupations of my important scholarly work could muffle them.

Second, a translation into direct, suitably emotional language:

I love you so much that I can't work properly.

However, that second version is of course alien to everything that Casaubon has shown himself to be. He is incapable of the warmth and naked affection those simple words communicate: his voice is hopelessly dry, and the impenetrable maze of his style is a basic index of his nature. In addition to the ghastly Latin-soaked flatulence of his phrasing, there are clear indications of smug self-absorption, condescension and delusion: it is no great shock when we later discover that he is not a real scholar at all, just a tired old hack way behind in his field. In short, Casaubon's 'voice' here is the key to everything significant about him.

Now that we've seen how four writers harness voice as a major force in their prose, it's time to look at how the same policy can work for you. I begin by considering the period in which the concept of voice becomes a problem – adolescence.

Voice: the virtues of primitivism

Small children are necessarily limited writers, but their style is appealing and often very funny. Consider this short piece, written by a 7-year-old girl.

Me And My Sickness

First I got a few tummy aches. Not very bad ones, but then in the evening I got a very bad tummy ache. I then started to roll about with my hands on my tummy. Then I did some sick. I kept waking up and doing sick. I did a dreadful thing while I was asleep: I did sick everywhere. Mummy and Daddy took all the bedclothes off and took me out of my bed. Then Mummy took me and put me in the bathroom, where I did sick all over the floor. In the morning I felt much better. Today I have not done any sick so far. I can now have drinks (not food) without getting sick.

This is clear, sharp and – despite the subject matter! – quite delightful. Her natural, vibrant voice is a pleasure to experience, as is her own fresh pleasure in using language. She may not know many words yet, but those she does know have for her a huge charm – almost a touch of magic. In addition, the piece is impressively balanced: there is a strong structure and narrative thrust, but it is also fluent and great fun to read. Our 7-year-old exemplifies a principle I introduced in my first chapter – that the spirit of children's writing offers enduring lessons to writers of every age and every kind.[4]

The fact remains that when I was an adolescent, I wouldn't have been caught dead writing in such a way. It's not just that its obvious limitations would have affronted my 13-year-old's dignity; by then I would have been frightened of its nakedness and spontaneity. And I was **wrong** – and so would be any developing writer who took the same view.

Adolescence: voice change and changing voices

Young children have a **single** voice. They write in the same way as they speak, and they tend to speak in the same way to everyone – parents, friends, other adults, strangers. They have not yet learnt to discriminate; another way of putting it might be that they have not yet learnt to dissimulate or to select the role they think most fitting. Then comes the dawn of self-consciousness, and with it the disappearance of that singleness of voice: adolescence, in short.

Consciousness of self is only part of the rapid expansion of consciousness and knowledge that occurs during these years. This may be a bewildering process, but it is also an exciting and entirely healthy one. Your brain is at its most active and arguably its most efficient. You learn literally tens of millions of things in a wide variety of fields; your grasp and use of linguistic structures accelerate; your vocabulary grows enormously; you start to acquire judgment and intellectual independence. And you begin to be aware of your own nature, its strengths and weaknesses, and what I will call its 'plurality of self'. You come to realize that you have **several** selves – pupil, son/daughter, friend, young citizen and so on.

All those developments are invigorating and positive. But self-consciousness is a two-edged sword: it can be weakening and negative as well. All at once you are acutely aware of how others see you, which can lead to awkwardness, a lack of confidence and a host of 'masks' designed above all to prevent you from looking foolish. These protective layers, or what the German psychologist Wilhelm Reich called 'character armour', are often most evident in your use of language. Where the child is unthinking and spontaneous in giving tongue, the adolescent is more wary. Frequently silence is preferred; otherwise, something non-committal or even

---

4 This composition – one of the girl's first homeworks – later appeared in her school magazine under the by-line 'Anon: Prep 1', and in a way one can see why the writer didn't want to be named! But one would like her identified – in order to congratulate her.

obstructive. And in writing – my chief concern – original freshness can give way to the defensive aping of 'safe' adult models and the gradual denial of all that is most natural and individual. In short, that 'plurality of self' can create a damaging plurality of voice.

Now there is nothing wrong with plurality of voice in itself. For a start it is both unavoidable and often literal in the case of male adolescents, who move from treble or alto to tenor or bass: for many, all four can come into play – sometimes within a single sentence! In addition, to have at your disposal a variety of register, tone and style when speaking or writing adds further to your increased linguistic resources and awareness, and properly harnessed is an unambiguous strength.

The trouble arises if you choose the wrong voice, or [worse] you become so confused that you speak or write in a mish-mash of voices that neither expresses with any clarity what you want to say, nor gives anyone a sense of your true self. As an initial step in preventing such confusion, try the exercise that follows.

Exercise 21

Here I have listed eight kinds of speech encounter which you may experience on any given day. Jot down what you imagine would be each one's most obvious features in terms of tone, the sort of vocabulary you might use, your general demeanour and so on; my commentary follows beneath.

1   Conversations with your family.
2   An exchange with a bus conductor/booking clerk/etc.
3   Conversations with friends, or colleagues whom you like.
4   Conversations with peers/colleagues whom you don't like, or with whom you are neutrally professional.
5   Conversations with your superiors/people in authority over you.
6   A conversation with a complete stranger – e.g. someone requesting directions.
7   A conversation with someone you fancy.
8   Conversations with visitors to your home.

Commentary

1   Likely to be 'informal' most of the time: affectionate, amusing, usually unselfconscious. Such exchanges also feature a good deal of 'code' – the kind of private, intimate language that all families develop.
2   Civil; functional; formal. Your use of language will be business-like and brief – provided you both listen properly.
3   Very similar to 1, although the 'codes' will probably be different. The same kind of ease and informality will be present, however, as will a lack of self-consciousness.

4   Style and behaviour will be markedly different from 3. You will almost certainly be cautious, polite, very self-aware and using a considerable amount of control. Such conversations are as a result very tiring!

5   You will probably display a degree of deference and be anxious for approval, or at least not to offend. If you happen to like and get on well with the superior concerned, your language and manner may be quite relaxed; it would be unusual even so if they matched 1 or 3.

6   Very like 2, except that it may lead to a more involved and complex exchange. In addition, such conversations often occur 'out of the blue', whereas 2 exchanges tend to be planned or expected. Your tone and language may differ as a result.

7   Always different from 3, no matter how much you may like him/her as well! The biggest difference is an extreme – and unique – self-awareness, which can radically alter both what you say and how you say it.

8   The style and register of these conversations will depend on who the visitors are. Atmosphere and behaviour may well be close to 1, and certainly 3, if the visitors are welcome and everyone's relaxed; 2, 6 or even 4 may be nearer the mark if you're less lucky![5]

Those eight are just a sample of the many encounters you could have on an average day. However many I might list, you would find that ultimately they fall into three groups: those where your language and manner are **informal**, those where they are **formal**, and those where **either** possibility exists, according to circumstance. To identify our eight in this manner is simple enough, but it's worth doing, because some important insights and principles can be established as a result.

Informal: 1, 3
Formal: 2, 4, 6
Either: 5, 7, 8

Conclusions

1   We are at our most natural during **informal** exchanges, whether they involve lively banter, the sharing of confidences or just ordinary chatting. The personality is at ease, the voice relaxed; the conversation is a source of pleasure.[6]

---

5   It is a sad truism that relatives – especially in-laws – often make you feel false or awkward, in both speech and general behaviour. You're supposed to feel intimate and relaxed with them, but I know of few families where the kind of language associated with 1 extends to broader family get-togethers. Perhaps that's why Christmas is a strain for so many!

6   Note that this is usually true even when you are unhappy or discontented. Talking informally when 'down' may not solve anything, but it's good therapy, not least because you're being listened to by someone who cares. And sometimes hearing yourself voice your thoughts can lead to a new understanding and perhaps a new mood, which is as pleasing as it is valuable.

2 **Formal** encounters are not so much fun but can be very satisfying: using a different kind of tone and language capably and courteously [which 2, 6 and especially 4 require] carries its own quiet pleasure.

3 The **Either** category is intriguing and instructive. In all three cases cited, the more you are confidently able to be yourself, the more informal [and therefore pleasant] the conversation will be; conversely, the more you feel obliged to be dutiful, cautious and linguistically on your guard, the more the exchanges will become a strain. That kind of formal conversation is wholly unpleasurable: you feel unnatural, under pressure and decidedly uncomfortable.

4 The final and most crucial point concerns your writing. You cannot avoid the occasional conversation that is unpleasant or a matter of joyless effort, where your voice is constrained, dull or even artificial. **But never allow your writing to be similarly corrupted.** If the demands of formal writing reduce the pleasure you take in using words, something is badly wrong: you're using the wrong words, using them in the wrong way, or abandoning your voice. I now move on to further ways of ensuring that your formal writing is no more – and no less – than a pleasurable extension of your natural style.

Words as a window, not a wall

I've been stressing clarity from the first page of the book. If I do so yet again now, it's because a good deal of adult language disguises or hides meaning – sometimes deliberately, more often out of incompetence or a misguided belief that certain phrases sound good. In addition, the onset of self-consciousness can lead to a timidity about saying what you really think. In writing – especially in a task that requires some kind of judgment or decision – don't hide behind others' views. Consult and read them, yes: that is a key constituent of learning. But remember that it's your writing and views that matter. Say what you think and don't 'fudge': you will please and impress your readers far more by doing so than by sheltering behind a wall of received ideas, imprecise opinion and often stodgy prose.

Keep it simple, keep it clear

In a previous section, 'Fight the flab', we looked at the damage deliberate avoidance of simplicity can do. Conversely, a determination to keep things as simple as possible can bring considerable benefits. Appropriately, the guidelines are all easy to understand and should also not be difficult to put into practice.

1 **Never use a long word where a short one will do.**

This was one of George Orwell's six elementary rules of good writing in 1946, and it is just as important now.

2 **Avoid Latinate words and constructions if a simpler alternative is available.**

English is predominantly Latinate, so there will be times when you cannot find a simpler alternative, and others when you (quite rightly) may not wish to do so. But one of English's greatest strengths is that it has a host of simple, basic words to express the simple, basic facts of existence. In all these instances, the simpler word is the clearer and the stronger:

death	rather than	**demise** or **decease**
sex drive	rather than	**libido**
fast	rather than	**exponential**
road	rather than	**thoroughfare**
worsen	rather than	**exacerbate**
show	rather than	**manifest**
yes	rather than	**affirmative**
no	rather than	**negative**

The last two are comical – the kind of Americanism we could all (Americans included) do without. But **all** the right-hand alternatives are faintly absurd: few of us would ever choose them naturally. Nevertheless, there is often a temptation to forgo naturalness and choose expressions which impress. They rarely do: 'Think Simple' wherever possible. Use

meeting	not	**interface**
use	not	**utilize**
illness	not	**malady** or **condition**

That last is particularly stupid in the phrase **heart condition**: everyone has a heart condition because everyone has a heart.

3   **Avoid foreign, scientific or technical words unless they are essential.**

There will be occasions when such words are essential. But they should never be used without good reason: always be sure you fully understand them before committing them to paper.

Inappropriate use of these words looks either pretentious or evasive. Restaurant menus are notorious for both. It is ludicrous to call roast beef 'le boeuf roti' in England, even if the restaurant is devoted to French culinary methods; and virtually every wine-list I've ever read is in urgent need of a ruthless literary editor. If this is admittedly an exaggeration on my part –

This pleasingly rich-bodied Bordeaux has a notably full nose and a sensuous texture that owe their quality to the peculiar eloquence of the grapes of the region, warm-thighed and resonant as they traditionally are.

– you'll probably have encountered something similar if you dine out with any regularity. As with many of the euphemisms we examined previously, the atmosphere of the prose is all wrong. One suspects that the intimidating jargon and forced imagery hide a 'real truth' translation that might go:

> A cringingly average bottle of Gallic red ink that will soon annihilate whatever palate you've got left after eating our over-spiced food, and make your mind too hazy to notice that we're charging the earth for liquid junk.

The only time jargon or imported phrases are justified is when there is no good equivalent in English. Thus it is all right to use **cliché** or **impasse**: they are valuable additions to our language because they pinpoint a concept more exactly than any available English word can. But it is not all right to use **chef d'oeuvre** when the exact alternative **masterpiece** is available. Nor is **modus vivendi** instead of **way of life** anything other than mere posturing.

Scientific and technical words carry the additional danger of inaccuracy as well as pretentiousness. It is now common to see **neurotic** used to mean 'mildly nervous' or **schizophrenic** for 'somewhat inconsistent'. Originally – and properly – both words denote a precise, and very serious, psychic illness: to hijack them for inappropriate everyday use both harms their force as clinical terms and renders one's language vague and unconvincing.

'Intimidating jargon'.

4   Take great care when using slang.

A fair amount of nonsense is talked about the use of slang in formal writing. I believe it is absurd to disapprove of it on principle, which is what more than a few English teachers of my acquaintance do. Good slang – that is, lively and inventive contemporary idiom – is vigorous and concrete; moreover, it is a central index of the healthy fluidity and growth of English (or indeed any language). Those who argue that it has no place in formal writing at any time both overemphasize the resources of 'standard English' and underestimate the fresh precision, wit and energy that slang can achieve, and I am glad to find that no less a figure than George Eliot agrees with me:

> Correct English is the slang of prigs who write history and essays. And the strongest slang of all is the slang of poets.
>
> (*Middlemarch*, Book 2)

I would never suggest, therefore, that you should avoid slang at all times. There will be occasions when it enlivens your writing in a wholly appropriate way, and your readers may well be very grateful for a racy respite from more sedate and sophisticated structures. But the use of slang is dangerous nonetheless, on at least three counts:

- Most slang has a very short life, and nothing seems more dated than yesterday's 'in' phrase.
- Conversely, genuinely current slang is problematic in a different way: your reader may not have heard the phrase yet, and therefore be completely fogged. This is especially likely if you're a young person writing for an older generation!
- Even if a slang phrase is comprehensible and verbally precise, it may be inappropriate in tone.

When writing formally, therefore, and the possibility of using slang arises, ask yourself the following questions about each word or phrase:

1   **Will it be understood?**
2   **Will I be laughed at for using stale slang?**
3   **What is the alternative 'standard English' phrase, and does the slang equivalent do a better job? (N.B.** *not* **equally good, but** *better***.)**
4   **Does it strike the right note, in terms of tone and reader-comfort? Is the 'voice' apt and pleasing?**

And even if all the answers to the above seem to give you the green light, add:

5   **Since the use of slang always carries a slight risk, given certain readers' views, am I really sure that I still want to use it?**

If the answer is 'yes', then go ahead.

Before moving on, I should perhaps stress something I've already made passing reference to: a lot of other teachers, writers and professional guides would offer sharply different advice – and not necessarily because they belong to the 'Slang Is Always Wrong' school of thought. They would probably argue that the potential snags and pitfalls of using slang invariably outweigh its benefits, and that it is wise to avoid it – always.

My own view, while recognizing the soundness of that advice in many respects, is that good and appropriate slang can breathe much-needed freshness into your writing, that it will often sharpen up both your sense of what you're saying and therefore the reader's, and that at its most successful it promotes an immediate sense of voice and individuality. Every major literary artist in history has used – often coined – slang words and phrases to great and memorable advantage; and although the criteria and ethos of 'creative writing' and formal writing are obviously different, I see no reason why they should be entirely cut off from each other. Writers who think only in terms of 'correct English' are not only likely to be priggish, as George Eliot observed: it's highly probable that such inner pedantry leads to their work being impersonal and dull as well.

5   Choose concrete rather than abstract wherever possible.

Human beings are very complex creatures; they are also simple ones. We find nice things nicer than nasty ones, we prefer pleasure to pain, and we have a fondness for clarity over obscurity.

Such fundamental characteristics are relevant to good writing. People think in pictures, not concepts, and unless you regularly stimulate their visual sense you risk losing them. No matter how elegant your sentences or interesting your material, if you fill your prose with abstractions you will not grip. The next exercise starkly demonstrates the contrast.

Exercise 22
The two pieces that follow both address sexual corruption. Which is better?

Passage A

How We Know Sex
The whole movement of 'philosophical anthropology' is opposed to the reductionism implicit in the Galilean-Newtonian-Cartesian approach to knowledge, not least, to knowledge of man, which, in its tendency to objectify, has the effect of reducing life in nature, and man especially, to the status of 'dead' objects. The difference which is being emphasized now is that between what Polyani calls 'attending to' – looking at the outside of things – and 'attending from' – entering into the experience

of the creature observed, by throwing oneself, by imagination and intuition, into the 'inner experience' of the manifestation being studied. It should be obvious that much of the attention to sex in our culture is 'attending to' rather than 'attending from' – and so, lacking imagination, it lacks understanding of the meaning and inwardness of sex. The effect has been a disastrous separation of 'sex' from the personal.

from David Holbrook's contribution to
Pornography: The Longford Report, 1972

Passage B

The Sick Rose

Rose, thou art sick!
The invisible worm
That flies in the night,
In the howling storm

Has found out thy bed
Of crimson joy
And his dark secret love
Does thy life destroy.

William Blake, c. 1792

Commentary

I hope you chose passage B!

I will admit at once that the contrast is hardly fair - on three counts. First, Holbrook's argument is just a paragraph from a lengthy exposition; Blake's poem is complete in itself. Second, to compare discursive prose with the highly concentrated language of a lyric poem is always precarious: the two genres work in different ways and by different criteria. And third, the world is full of writing that would come off second best to *The Sick Rose*, which is arguably one of the greatest short poems ever written.

Nevertheless, some important points and principles emerge. The Holbrook is very difficult to read: it took me three goes before I fully understood its first sentence. It is obviously the work of an intelligent and committed man, but the profusion of commas is distracting and the grandiose references are a further obstacle. Above all, Latinate and abstract language predominates: the potentially valuable distinction between 'attending to' and 'attending from' is, I find, blurred by such accompanying structures as **of the manifestation being studied** and even **the meaning and inwardness of sex**. What do such phrases mean? They conjure up no picture for me, no physical sense of what is being addressed – and that, given that the topic is human sexuality, is surely a serious flaw. Only the last sentence – significantly, also the shortest – achieves immediate impact and clarity; by then, some might think, it's too late.

Blake's language is deceptively simple: there isn't a word in the poem that a bright 8-year-old would not have encountered. [I'm not suggesting that such a person would therefore understand the poem as a whole!] Furthermore, it paints dramatic pictures. Even if one reads the poem on a merely literal level, the evocation of a fragile plant under double attack [the worm and the elements] is gripping; when one adds the symbolic level(s), the effect is overwhelming. Potentially abstract concepts such as **joy** and **love** are made intensely concrete by the addition of **crimson** and **dark secret**, adjectives which 'nail down' guilt, passion, corruption and destruction in a precise, almost tactile way. Intriguingly, Blake demonstrates here exactly the qualities Holbrook associates with 'attending from' – the poem is indeed an immersion in 'inner experience' through 'imagination and intuition', and it achieves this by ensuring that its words have instant physical bite.

Of course, in any substantial and sophisticated writing, it is impossible to avoid the abstract altogether. Nor is it always desirable to even try: a great deal of scientific, philosophical and even literary thinking depends on abstract concepts. The secret is to make sure that they are regularly mixed with, or illustrated by, something more physically immediate. The next piece is a superb example of how to use concrete images to render clear something otherwise unimaginable.

Exercise 23

Please read this passage, which is an edited extract from *The Daily Telegraph's* lead story on Tuesday, August 7, 1945. I find it a splendid piece of reporting, and I hope you concur. Why does it work so well? Which phrases/sentences have the greatest impact on you, and which are the **least** effective? And what, despite its many strengths, is **missing** from the account that perhaps ought to have been included?

ALLIES INVENT ATOMIC BOMB: FIRST DROPPED ON JAPAN

2000 TIMES THE BLAST POWER OF RAF 11-TONNER

ENEMY THREATENED WITH 'RAIN OF RUIN' FROM THE AIR

The Allies have made the greatest discovery in history: the way to use atomic energy. The first atomic bomb has been dropped on Japan. It had:

> Over 2000 times the blast power of the largest bomb ever before used, which was the British 'Grand Slam' weighing about 11 tons; and more power than 20,000 tons of TNT.

Yet the explosive charge is officially described as 'exceedingly small'. A spokesman at the Ministry of Aircraft Production said last night that the bomb was one-tenth the size of a 'block buster', yet its effect would be 'like that of a severe earthquake'.

The first atomic bomb, a single one, was dropped on Hiroshima, a town of 12 square miles, on the Japanese main island of Honshu. Tokyo radio said that the raid was at 8.20 a.m. yesterday, Japanese time, and that the extent of the damage was being investigated.

The official announcement yesterday of the existence of the bomb was made 16 hours after its first use. Late last night no report had been made on the damage done because it had been impossible to see the results through impenetrable clouds of dust and smoke.

EFFECT ON WAR AND PEACE

In a Downing Street statement Mr. Churchill was quoted as saying: 'By God's mercy British and American science outpaced all German efforts. The possession of these powers by the Germans at any time might have altered the result of the war and profound anxiety was felt by those who were informed.'

Mr. Stinison, the United States Secretary of War, said the bomb would prove a tremendous aid in shortening the war against Japan. It had an explosive power that 'staggered the imagination.'

President Truman described the results as the greatest achievement of organised science in history. The Allies had spent the sum of £500,000,000 on the 'greatest scientific gamble in history' and had won.

If the Japanese did not now accept the Allies terms, he said, they might expect a 'rain of ruin from the air the like of which had never been seen on this earth.'

The method of production would be kept secret, while processes were being worked out to protect the world from the danger of sudden destruction. Congress would be asked to investigate how atomic power might be used to maintain the future peace.

Commentary

The most obvious reason for the passage's riveting power is the event itself: nearly fifty years on it still haunts our imagination. If one was in a grudging mood, it might be said that the piece almost wrote itself, so awesome is the topic: you'd have to be a singularly bad writer to render it dull! But that would hardly be just: the reporting is a first-class performances and its key strength is the shrewd explanation of what an atomic bomb can do.

Even today, a large number of highly educated people (myself included) do not fully understand atomic fission. At the time of Hiroshima, the whole thing must have struck all but a handful of readers as science fiction. So the writer at once establishes a frame of reference that can be readily grasped: the bomb's power is explained by comparisons with known, 'ordinary' bombs, starkly and punchily expressed. Particularly effective is the emphasis on the bomb's strange, scary smallness and the instant revelation that its effect resembles that of 'a severe earthquake': these are images that people can at once visualize.

You may have noticed that the report carries no mention of damage to buildings or to human life – one of the 'missing' things I asked you to identify. The reasons for this may be various – security, genuine lack of information [as implied in the mention of 'impenetrable clouds of dust and smoke'], shame or just a shocked unwillingness to spell out the suffering involved. That's a large and separate issue; what strikes me is that the information which is given is presented in such a way as to release our imaginative powers, enabling us to speculate on what the people of Hiroshima would have undergone. That happens of course to be a horrible set of pictures, one which many of us would quickly wish to blot out; the fact remains that no such resonance would occur if the writing was not so vibrantly concrete.

To my mind the least effective moments occur in the various politicians' remarks. With one exception these are generalized and wrapped up in careful phrases designed to reassure rather than resonate. The exception is President Truman's 'rain of ruin' sentence: this has enormous impact, identifying a force that is almost Biblical in its potential anger. Once again, it is the simple concreteness of the phrase that guarantees its power.

Finally, also missing is any attempt to explain the mechanics of the fission process. As the last paragraph reveals, a major reason for this must have been security; but I would also guess that (a) the journalist concerned didn't know how to explain such things, and (b) even if he did, his readers wouldn't have been able to follow him. Even so, the piece gives one a formidably clear sense of what this new weapon can do and of some of the disturbing possibilities its invention opens up, and it does so by recourse to simple, known phenomena and images. Rooted in the concrete, it brings the inexplicable and the unimaginable within reach.

6   Within reason, be as simple and direct as possible

I have already cited this principle (see page 77ff), and I've also stressed that you have to be careful about it. There are people to whom you should probably not in answer to an enquiry after your health, reply, 'God, I'm knackered!' But provided you pay proper attention to courtesy and appropriateness, you should be as direct as possible, and that means being as simple and concrete as possible.

This short extract from P. G. Wodehouse's story *Jeeves And The Song Of Songs* illustrates the point beautifully, along with most of the other 'guidelines' I've offered in this section. The speakers are Bertie Wooster [the narrator], his Aunt Dahlia and, first, his incomparable manservant Jeeves. In addition to everything else, notice how masterly is Wodehouse's capturing of the three distinct voices.

> 'In affairs of this description, madam, the first essential is to study the psychology of the individual.'
> 'The what of the individual?'
> 'The psychology, madam.'
> 'He means the psychology,' I said. 'And by psychology, Jeeves, you imply –?'
> 'The natures and dispositions of the individuals in the matter, sir.'
> 'You mean, what they're like?'
> 'Precisely, sir.'
> 'Does he always talk like this to you when you're alone, Bertie?' asked Aunt Dahlia.

This is comic writing of a high order, and the humour resides in the radical difference between the register and vocabulary of Bertie and his aunt and those used by Jeeves. In the context, therefore, both registers are essential and appropriate. But if we take Jeeves's language **out** of context, it seems needlessly elaborate in normal circumstances. Bertie's simple **You mean, what they're like** is **precisely** what Jeeves has taken many words to say. One could further argue that Jeeves's remarks are not only lengthy: they are difficult, semi-scientific, Latinate and abstract – a combination that makes him hard to follow. No wonder Aunt Dahlia asks about their private conversations!

Punch once observed that to criticize Wodehouse was 'like taking a spade to a soufflé', and to subject that passage to my kind of analysis is doubtless equally clumsy. Nevertheless, I think the extract shows – through its wit, not despite it – that neither meaning nor impact need be lost by choosing the simple concrete approach. Indeed, both will often thereby be strengthened.

Conclusion: voice – friend or foe?

My stress on the primacy of voice may seem to contradict the kind of advice most 11- or 12-year-olds [and sometimes their seniors] receive from their teachers:

It's time you stopped writing in the way you speak.

In that extract from *Apocalypse Now*, Kurtz spoke of making 'horror' and 'moral terror' one's friends, lest they become 'truly enemies'. Less dramatically, we can say that there seem to be conflicting views about whether speech and writing are 'friends' or 'enemies'. Which should it be?

The answer is **both**. As adolescence takes hold, a difference should be emerging, yes, between the spontaneity of speech and the more considered use of words necessary for effective writing. But if that division becomes absolute, leading the student to regard speech and writing as mutually exclusive, great damage to both can result. It is essential not to regard your conversational rhythms and your written style as enemies or as separate activities that have little to do with each other. Keep your 'voice' present all the time. You need also to make your language appropriate – for example, a thank-you letter to a great-aunt will require a different vocabulary and tone from the 'friendly-rude' style you adopt with friends and peers. But that great-aunt should still be aware of you – your personality, your individual voice. Indeed, if she cares about you, a stiffly impersonal letter will hurt and disappoint her. As a final principle, keep in mind that

> **Adult, formal writing does not require self-obliteration, nor is 'politeness' the same as 'impersonality'.**

Good adult writing is properly aware of circumstance, and respects self and audience equally. As William Hazlitt implies in one of the epigraphs to this section, the art of conversation involves good listening as well as good speaking. The same is true of the art of writing: once you stop listening to your voice – the essential 'you' defined in childhood – you're in trouble.

Interlude

Writing and computers

The four biggest world industries are automobiles; energy production; illegal drugs; computers.

John Naughton[1]

Introduction

Revising *Write In Style* for twenty-first century use has led me to make a number of significant changes, but this section is the only entirely new one. Maybe the original edition should have included some such chapter; after all, I wrote that on a word-processor, and it is a fair bet that amongst my likely readers there were plenty who were struggling, like me, to come fully to terms with the new technology and whose baptism was similarly characterized by delight and frustration in roughly equal amounts. I may therefore have missed a trick; if so, silly me. What is beyond dispute is that ten years on any *Guide to Good English* which does not address the use of computers cannot be considered complete or even credible. The number of writers – of all kinds – who use a PC as a matter of course has increased out of all proportion; to ignore that would be worse than silly. And to put that extraordinary development into a context both appropriate and illuminating, I want first to glance at a diverting little survey published in 1997.

In that year Collins Dictionaries boldly claimed to have encapsulated the twentieth century via a chronological list of words and phrases coined from 1897 to 1997. Many indeed remain eloquent of the way we live now – *aspirin* (1897), *jazz* (1909), *bikini* (1946), *miniskirt* (1965); others have proved as durable if less than universally understood – *schizophrenia* (1912), *robotics* (1942), *pulsar* (1967), *butterfly effect* (1970); more than a few have become all but archaic – *talkie* (1927), *Angry Young Man* (1956), *Fosbury flop* (1968); *SDP* (1981). And then there are those few which transcend mere neologism: *radioactivity* (1896); *Labour Party* (1900), *television* (1926) and *rock 'n' roll* (1954) could each be put forward as the century's most significant innovation. The consensus at the

---

1 *The Observer*, 14 April, 1996.

time was to give **television** the nod ahead of those other three, and for what it's worth I think that was right.[2]

Collins's initiative was both amusing and instructive, and it is perhaps faintly churlish to suggest that its most remarkable feature was an omission. **Television** may qualify as the definitive phenomenon of the last hundred years, but if one narrows the focus to the last twenty-five and considers also the start of the new millennium, then a term which that list didn't even mention has an overwhelming claim to analogous status: the **personal computer**. Every generation brings any number of momentous changes, but since (say) 1970 nothing – not the mobile phone, the obsession with 'healthy eating' and all other outbreaks of political correctness, not even the credit card – has had such a seismic influence as the PC. It can be seen as the symbol of our age – which is why this chapter had to be written, however belatedly.

It is nevertheless a shortish chapter, chiefly because I have no pretensions to expertise. I've moved on a bit in ten years: this edition has been prepared on a much more sophisticated word-processor than I owned when composing its predecessor;[3] I have become more confident and wide-ranging – and faster – in using PC facilities; I am familiar with several systems and a fair number of software packages; I even teach ICT.[4] But in all conscience that's about it. Like many of my generation I've dragged myself into computer semi-literacy, but I shall never approach anything one could call professional mastery. And quite apart from my 'eternal amateur' status, there are now several hundred books that offer expert (and usually good!) advice on how to get the best out of your PC, so it might be wondered why I'm bothering to add my twopennyworth.

My answer centres on the fact that a considerable number of writers somehow contrive to get the *worst* out of their PC. Computers are no different from anything else in having the vices of their own virtues. To put it starkly:

> **Like every single technological 'advance' from the discovery of fire to nuclear fission and beyond, computers are excellent servants but *appalling* masters.**

Anyone not properly aware of that will soon find that using a PC more easily spells 'trouble' than 'blessing', and although my ultimate aim is to accentuate the latter, that is best done by looking first at some of the dangers inherent in using a PC.

---

2 If (as I hope) this brief sample has whetted your appetite, you might like to know that the complete list, with an explanatory introduction written by Philip Howard, was published in the *Times* of Monday, 3 November, 1997. Howard also provided a witty and scholarly commentary on each of the 101 selections.

3 It would be untrue – not to say libellous – to tell you that my first wordprocessor ran on *gas*, but to someone now Microsoft-comfortable it seems in retrospect to have been quite awesomely primitive. And in fact I suppose it was: if 'a week is a long time in politics' (Harold Wilson), then a decade is an *eon* in computer-technology.

4 (1) On an occasional basis only; (2) in a purely secondary, 'staff-support' role.

TROUBLE SPOTS AND TROUBLE-SHOOTING

Computers pose a triple threat to the unwary:

They are sexy
They encourage laziness
They are bossy

Those may seem unrelated and even contradictory claims. In fact they interlock to a considerable extent, chiefly because

Each one tempts you to surrender your most precious commodity: your own mind.

The undoubted and multiple powers of computers can blind even the most intelligent person to the fact that they are just machines and, indeed, that

Even the most magical-seeming, awesome new model is utterly inferior to the living brain between your ears.

Once that is forgotten, you are in double jeopardy – on the one hand forsaking your greatest asset, on the other expecting its replacement to do your work successfully on its own, without your control or judgment. In their different ways those three properties are equally dangerous in this respect, and they need a separate and detailed look.

- **PCs are dangerously sexy!**

A PC's appeal is as obvious as multi-faceted. It is a thoroughly glamorous object whose seductive charm can reduce one's understanding of its status and functions to a perilously simplistic level. Yes, its an amazingly compact resource, storing masses of information and offering any number of valuable facilities; it is also

1   a toy;
2   a high-*performance* machine.

There's nothing wrong with either feature, naturally. In writing as in all things, pleasure is preferable to tedium, and in that respect 1 is a plus, not an objection. But while toys are, obviously, fun, they are also things we play with, things we turn to when bored or at a loose end. Nothing wrong with that either – unless and until it leads you to *confuse* work and play. There are times when working elsewhere and/or in different 'mode' would be far more productive. However, these toys have a formidable charisma. I know from costly experience that the mere presence of a PC on your desk generates a kind of force-field: it *drafts* you to it. And the magnetism doesn't stop there: the dazzling array of facilities on offer can seem its own justification, allowing you to con yourself into the belief that you're making effective progress when all you're doing is fooling around.

On the surface 2 is so self-evident as to be hardly worth saying. Even the most computer-illiterate person has a vague grasp of a PC's power, precision of micro-engineering and sheer speed of activity. But like its toy/fun status, those properties can work *against* the writer: they can give you delusions of adequacy. No matter how dazzling its facilities, a PC cannot in and by itself create any of your material, nor can it make you ready to write when you're not. That is why I italicized the word 'performance', which in turn leads me to a crucial distinction.

Product 'versus' process

Reading that sub-title might prompt a response on the lines of

> **What's this 'versus' nonsense? You can't have one without the other. The final stage of any writing task, the performance, creates the product: the rest is process. Far from being in opposition, they're complementary, even symbiotic.**

I hope that *is* your reaction, for it is entirely correct. But such is a PC's allure that it is all too easy to jettison **process** and switch to **product** long before you are in any shape to do so. **Process** is essentially a private and internal activity, hinging on necessary reading, unhurriedly thinking over what you wish to do and say, planning some sort of structure.

Whether you're a student tackling a major written assignment, a professional compiling a report, or someone writing a detailed and important letter, most of your time will be expended on that kind of preparation and exploration. Only when you're sure of what you want to say will you wish to commit yourself to print – and getting to that stage is often more quickly and clearly achieved by using an old-fashioned sheet of lined A4 paper than by reaching for the mouse. It is often better to keep the latter (literally) at arm's length.

Moreover, not only must you resist the temptation to perform too early and in haste; when you *do* get to the product stage, you must not be seduced by the blandishments on offer. Your PC can furnish instantly any number of features that will enhance your presentation, but never forget that

> **Enhancing is the PC's job; writing what is to be enhanced is *yours*.**

Speaking both as a teacher and an ordinary reader, if I had a fiver for every time I've encountered a word-processed document that looks superficially beautiful but (a) turns out to be awash with errors and as a result (b) is barely coherent . . . well, I'd be so flush that I could cheerfully donate all my royalties from this book to a deserving cause. The galaxy of choice open to you regarding fonts, print sizes, shading, borders, spreadsheets and all the rest of it does not reduce by one iota the need to make your basic prose accurate, clear and comfortable to read. The PC will help you in all those things, but only if you keep your own brain fully in charge. And while we're on that subject, try always to bear in mind that excellent acronym

GIGO.

As many of you will know, that stands for **Garbage In, Garbage Out**, and it is a telling reminder that it's no use blaming the computer if things get fouled up or come out badly: it's *your* fault! And that leads me to Danger number two.

- **PCs encourage laziness**

That may strike you as

- **A peculiar thing to say anyway: surely the PC epitomizes concentrated efficiency?**
- **At odds with the notion of computers as alluring: how can something which impels you to work simultaneously induce indolence?**

Nevertheless, it's true. The kind of laziness I'm talking about is far removed from couch-potato slobbery: it resides in not caring quite enough, not thinking quite straight enough, or a combination of the two. As implied in the previous section, getting into sloppy habits isn't difficult: all that is required is for you to mortgage the unique powers of your own brain and in effect 'pass the buck' elsewhere – in this case to the PC.

Problem	Alleged Solution
Don't feel like checking your spelling?	Never mind: the PC will do it for you.
Wondering if your punctuation and grammar are okay?	No problem: the PC's software has just given them a clean bill of health.
Sure your argument is as clear and persuasive as it needs to be?	Not to worry: it *looks* terrific.

I exaggerate, naturally; yet while I am sure you would be incapable of such crudely dismissive responses, there's a lesson in them for even the most conscientious writer. I shall be shortly addressing the whole question of spell-checkers and other such packages in a separate section, but for now it might be useful to remember two things:

All software is made by human beings, all of whom are fallible.
You are in charge at all times; you are also responsible at all times.

There's no need to be too hard on yourself – just tough enough to be on your guard against those little lapses that can make all the difference. For the most part laziness is a subtle vice, and it can infect even those who are normally diligent.

On to that third threat.

- **PCs are bossy**

On the surface this notion is an odd one, coming hot on the heels of the claim that your PC can make you lazy: how can it do that and also boss you about? One (semi-facetious) answer might be that since everybody dislikes being nagged and will often in consequence refuse on principle to carry out the nagger's wishes, a machine that peremptorily issues orders or advice is likely to cause you to rebel, thus promoting laziness in the form of inaction. A more serious explanation returns us to that governing need to **stay in charge**. To assume that your PC will automatically safeguard accuracy and clarity may be different in *kind* from craven obedience of its every suggestion, but there is no difference at all in degree or in outcome: you surrender control and judgment in each case.

Actually, a computer's bossiness overlaps with its allure. I have already commented on how a PC can magnetize you: there it sits on your desk – imposing, important, demanding your immediate attention. Once at work it is easy to feel a similar deference when it alerts you to excessive use of the passive voice, squiggles a red line here and a green one there; and when it informs you that you did not shut it down properly last time and that (sigh) it now needs to run a check for you, it is difficult not to feel guilty even when you know that you only shut it down improperly because the damn thing suddenly 'froze' and your only recourse[5] was to start all over again.

Well, such craven behaviour is as understandable as frequent, but it must be resisted every bit as doughtily as the other two traps. To paraphrase an earlier observation:

You are the master, the PC the servant.

You tell *it* what to do, not the other way round. Of course, like any good servant it will have valuable advice and suggestions to offer; but these need to be mulled over, not kowtowed to. If you find the coloured squiggles I've just mentioned valuable, fine: they will not only help to ensure that your spelling and/or grammar are right in this particular case but also, through the very act of concentrating on the material at issue, help you commit it to memory, thus increasing your future mastery. On the other hand, you may be like me in being driven crazy by such nasty doodles: I could just about put up with their bullying manner, but they

---

5   Having failed (if your experience matches mine on every single occasion that I've tried it) to create any effect whatever by pressing **Ctrl, Alt** & **Del.**

disrupt thought-flow, sometimes destroying it altogether. If that's how you feel too, then cancel them![6]

If the PC is indeed the symbol of our age, then I suppose its hectoring properties are only to be expected. There's a lot of bossiness about these days, from your car nagging you about anything the manufacturer thought you should be aware of,[7] to every conceivable announcement in an airport, railway terminus, bank, post office and the London Underground,[8] not to mention those accursed traffic reports which interrupt your in-car entertainment whether you like it not and never seem to have anything to do with where you happen to be driving.[9]

Those remarks may seem frivolously self-indulgent, but their chief purpose is to set up my last, entirely serious and very important point:

Bossy people don't just want you to obey them: they want you to obey them *now*.

A PC can seem to demand a similar urgency: don't let it. Two central guarantors of good writing are the unhurried preparation of what you want to say and the equally unhurried final edit. Thanks to its many amazing properties, your computer will help you to accomplish the latter more speedily, and that's good; as in all other PC matters, however, make the rate of speed your decision, not the machine's.

In the normal run of things, **sexiness, laziness** and **bossiness** are far from all bad. Sexiness is almost always delightful, laziness can often be so, and even bossiness has its virtues and value. But for the PC user they are fraught with danger. Each one threatens your independence and control; succumb to all three and you are almost *bound* to get the worst out of your PC. It will be akin to something you repeatedly bang your head against (damaging brain and work alike) rather than a facility which clarifies and stimulates: in short, a wall not a window.

So much for trouble and trouble-shooting. Now it's time to accentuate the positive.

---

6 This should not prove difficult; however, different systems and packages have different methods of effecting such changes, so you'll need briefly to consult your PC manual.

7 This trend was beautifully spoofed in one of the more recent James Bond movies, *Tomorrow Never Dies*, in which Bond's state-of-the-art BMW issues a string of 'for your own good' warnings and rebukes during a hair-raising car chase in a multi-storey carpark.

8 The capital's tube system now boasts (if that's the right word) well over a dozen lines. Virtually every one of them seems to think that passengers require a running commentary on where they are, what the next stop is, what the ultimate destination is, and the need to keep all parts of their anatomy clear of the closing doors. The London Underground represents a triumph of style over content, or rather shows what happens when politically correct bossiness and inane PR initiatives take over completely from efficiency, comfort and any desire for anything to be any good.

9 Unless of course it's to tell you, after you've been stuck in a gridlock-jam for an hour, that you *risk* being stuck in a gridlock-jam if you go that way.

COUNTING YOUR BLESSINGS – AND HOW TO *USE* THEM

I admitted at the outset that I am a computer-amateur, and that has probably become increasingly clear as this chapter has unfolded. So my account of the 'blessings' which a PC offers is going to be decidedly selective. If you want advice on spreadsheets, Powerpoint, Microsoft Excel and many other sophisticated facilities, there are many first-rate guides on the market. Any attempt on my part to compete with them would be silly, especially as I have little of value to say about such things anyway. Instead I offer some writer-centred observations on three specific facilities – checker-software; email; the internet – and a brief enquiry into the twenty-first century status of handwritten work.

Spell-checkers – friend or foe?

As I write, the jury appears to be still out on this question. Amongst English/ Humanities teachers of my acquaintance, about half swear *at* them, the other half swear at them, and I can identify with both points of view. Insofar as they focus students' minds on the importance of getting things right and supply them with the means to do so, they can only be applauded. As noted, computers are fun, and if a student finds SpellCheck more enjoyable to use than a dictionary or teacher-provided spelling list, fine. As with so many things, the proof of the pudding is in the eating, and if electronic gadgetry produces results that pulped trees don't or can't, you won't find this teacher complaining. Indeed, I'll go further: I am now convinced that such software is a real boon, potentially a major aid for all writers. But – and I cannot stress this enough –

> **Spell-checkers and all related packages have to be *used*, not just relied on, and you need to *learn* how to use them.**

In pursuit of that principle, let us consider some of the ways in which *mere reliance* can undo you.

First and foremost, these valuable aids instantly become destructive viruses once you imagine that they can *think*. Correct spelling is not just a matter of getting the right letters in the right order: it's a question of getting the right word for the context as well. Even with the benefits of the very latest software, you can slip up in any number of instances. There are now programmes which can distinguish between homophones – that is, words which sound the same but have different spellings and meanings.[10] But you still need to be in charge: one such package of my acquaintance alerts you to the problem but does not – cannot – solve it: it

---

10   For example, **bread / bred, cede / seed, curb / kerb** and those old favourites **there, their** and **they're**.

merely *asks* which one of (say) ***whether*** and ***weather*** you require. Moreover, there is no software that I'm aware of that provides definitions alongside the words concerned, and if you're not sure what the word which you're about to write *means*, you run a high risk of being wrong. In view of that

Keep a good dictionary alongside you at all times.

Chambers or the *Concise Oxford* will do nicely; if your work-surface has room for it, the *Shorter Oxford* is even better. Whichever you opt for, look on it as a valuable partner to your PC software. And on those occasions when you can't find what you need, ask someone else. That's what teachers/parents/friends are for, and if they don't know the answer themselves, they will almost certainly 'know a man who can'.

Before I move on to an even trickier area, I can happily dispose of one alleged spell-checker problem – 'the American English trap'. It is often argued that since a great deal of computer software is made in America, the UK writer can be misled into using US spelling. That may have been so in the past, but nowadays all such packages allow you to *set* them for English or American use: cancelling potential misguidance should take you no more than thirty seconds. However, while that particular divergence is simply dealt with, there are other 'confusibles' which require constant vigilance.

Let's take as an example a spelling that I see used wrongly every day – and not just by students but journalists and other professionals too. If you run **dependant** through a spell-checker, it will (or should!) confirm its authenticity. What it won't tell you is that the word is only used as a noun, meaning 'one who depends on another for support', and that the other form, with an **e**, is the ordinary adjective, as in

His entry for the race is dependent upon his fitness.

Furthermore, all other forms based on the root **depend-** also take an **e: dependence, independent, dependency,** and so on. Your spell-checker will have them too, of course; the point is that only a human brain can decide which one is needed. That goes for every 'confusible' other than homophones – and there are hundreds of them.[11]

Using a dictionary in conjunction with your PC will prove especially productive in this area. Nevertheless, I recognize that such double-handling is both physically awkward and time-consuming, and many otherwise conscientious writers are tempted to give it up as being more trouble than it's worth. That is a serious mistake – or it would be were there not an alternative, one which returns us to the fundamental need to ***use*** your spell-checker.

---

11 You will find a selection of these in Chapter 18, pp. 215–221, but even that tolerably substantial list is far from comprehensive.

I've already pointed out that a spell-checker has been compiled by human beings. It is most unlikely that they were illiterate, stupid or anything other than thoroughly competent; nevertheless, their original task was dramatically narrower than attends the making of any dictionary. The vocabulary of a spell-checker is specialist and limited; if it fails to recognize a word, that does not mean it doesn't exist or that you've spelt it wrong. Those limitations are particularly noticeable when it comes to proper names, of which a spell-checker has no knowledge: it cannot tell Kingsley Amis from King Charles, nor will it grant either name any currency.

In these cases you need to expand your spell-checker. It is easy to do – analogous to up-dating your email 'address book' or your internet 'favourites' column – but it needs care: if you type in an entry wrongly, that's the false oracle you'll be trusting in all future checks. Proper names need special care: as noted, a spell-checker doesn't know Bill Gates from Gateshead or Shakespeare from Shagsby, so get them right!

This facility is why I consider checker software to be such an exciting advance. If used **actively** in such a fashion, it will quickly improve your spelling rather than just protect you from mistakes. It is *fun* to up-date your PC's armoury in this way (much more so than writing words out in a small dog-eared notebook[12]) and you will soon find that the fierce concentration required to do so accurately helps log the word in your brain anyway. This is the best kind of aid to successful study and good writing practice – a wonderfully fast and durable asset that truly *serves* you, since you are not only in charge but regularly emending it.

My last point returns us to that crucial fact:

spell-checkers cannot *think*.

They are able to recognize any number of words at a speed which dazzles; they can alert you to things they've been programmed to question; used creatively, they can even make a much more rapid difference to your accuracy and confidence than any dictionary could effect. But just as they cannot distinguish between 'confusibles', so they aren't much help with typographical errors, universally known as 'typos'. If (as we all occasionally do) you place, say, a maverick **d** in *obvioudsly* or a ditto **v** in *macvhine*, they will pick it up via those bossy squiggly lines I complained about earlier. But if you write

bitch	instead of	batch
gaol	instead of	goal
snag	instead of	sang
commuter	instead of	computer
appraise	instead of	apprise

---

12 That old-fashioned method nevertheless continues to be a sensible and time-effective way of logging new vocabulary; I still give my students note-books for such use.

then I'm afraid you're on your own. All the words in the left-hand column are perfectly correct in themselves, but they aren't what you intended or what you want, and only you can put that right. And at the risk of sounding pompous, I must emphasize that a typo is just as much a mistake as one born of ignorance, and that both are your responsibility: as always, the onus is on you to stay in charge.

Summary

A spell-check is a kind of sorcerer's apprentice which will create havoc if you uncritically accept all its suggestions.

Judith Woolf

That is the best metaphor I've ever encountered on the subject. In the immortal story to which Ms Woolf refers, the sorcerer's apprentice is constitutionally lazy: he thinks a touch of magic can save him hours of hard labour and accompanying tedium. His problem – which strikes with terrifying swiftness – is that he has no *control*: having started the process he has no idea how to stop it. The magicked buckets go on and on discharging water, threatening a Noah-esque finale until the sorcerer himself arrives back just in time, and his 'antidote abracadabra' at once restores order and dryness.

For 'touch of magic' read 'technology'; for 'sorcerer's apprentice' read 'the lazy writer'. Spell-checkers will damage your work and make you look ridiculous if you fail to understand what they're like, what they can do (and can't do) and above all if you surrender the initiative to them. However, once equipped with all that requisite awareness and clear-headedly in charge of its properties, there is every chance that you'll be more like the sorcerer himself than his apprentice: a true master of spelling.[13]

Overleaf we move on to other things; you might find the spoof-verse below a diverting and confirmatory postscript.

To Spellcheck Or Not To Spellcheck

A Sine of the Thymes

This is a mix 'n' match compendium of verses kindly provided by several friends who work in ICT. Amusing in its very remorselessness and exaggeration, it nevertheless illustrates very effectively the dangers of trusting a spell-checker exclusively.

---

13   I feel compelled to apologize for this pun, which was as intentional as it is grotesque.

That's awl rite

Eye have a spelling chequer:
It came with my pea sea.
It plainly marques for my revue
Mistakes I cannot see.

Eye strike a quay and type a word,
And weight four it to say
Weather eye am wrong oar write:
It shows me strait a weigh.

I've run this poem threw it,
I'm sure your plea's two no;
It's letter-perfect all the whey –
My chequer tolled me sew!

Internet and email: the new orthodoxy

Use of the internet and email has increased to a staggering extent in the last decade. Such a development hardly requires my approval, but it has it: I use email more and more, while the internet strikes me as having a potential analogous to Caxton's invention of the printing-press over five hundred years ago. And so if most of what now follows concentrates once more on traps and dangers, that does not in the least imply a negative attitude towards such facilities. However, just as there are any number of expert guides on how to get the best out of your PC, good advice on the most effective use of these electronic marvels is hardly thin on the ground, and the most telling contribution a *non*-expert can make is to look at some of the ways in which the new technology can hamper rather than enable or cause delusion rather than enlightenment.

The internet: boon or doom?

The internet is a young phenomenon still, but it has already prompted wildly exaggerated reactions, many of which – whether for or against – are simply preposterous. Accusations include such claims that the medium offers unrestricted opportunity for the peddling of filth (sexual, political and otherwise) or that it transforms the user into a credulous moron ripe for exploitation and even brain-washing. Just as bad are those hysterical apostles who proclaim the imminent internet-induced deaths of traditional shopping and the pulped-tree book.[14] It is somewhat unnerving to reflect that technology seems to have had no impact on superstition, confirming rather than obliterating that most ignorant and destructive of human characteristics. In both camps Superstition Rules OK.

The real point about the internet is that, just like the PC itself, it is a marvellous *tool* – no more, no less – which for the purposes of this book boils down to a research aid.[15] And it is essential to remember that

Anyone can publish on the internet

On balance I think this a good thing, as is the fact that anyone can create a web-site: it has a democratic potential that I find heartening. But it also has obvious dangers – perhaps to the student in particular, but to writers of any other kind as well. During my time as a teacher I have often been astonished by how deferential people can be to the printed word, and that same unquestioning reverence seems to attend many internet users. Well, in one respect the old and the new media *are* identical:

A great deal of what is printed or available on-line is either transient or of marginal value, and much of it is unalloyed rubbish.

Whoever you are and whatever you're doing, your own judgment is crucial. An essay or article on the internet is not necessarily any better than those dire Study Aids that still infest our leading bookshops; trusting any such work on a blithe or lazy basis is a recipe for disaster. Indeed, internet-material can be even more of a poisoned chalice to the unwary than are lousy or mediocre books: the latter are only available because somebody else thought them worth publishing, whereas internet writers are their own bosses and sole courts of appeal.[16] Great care is required, otherwise doom beckons.

On the other hand, if you use the internet in a discerning and critical way, it is without question a boon. The speed with which search-engines can put you precisely in touch with the topic you need is wonderful – and the same goes for the many illuminating items you will then go on to find. Just make sure that, as in all other PC facilities, you stay firmly **in charge.**

14   For a magesterial demolition of the latter inanity, see Simon Jenkins, 'No Plug, No Wires, No Rivals', *The Times*, Saturday, 4 January, 1997, whose last paragraph reads: 'The Internet will strut an hour upon the stage, and then take its place in the ranks of lesser media. It needs no subsidy. If we want to splash public money on culture, splash it on books.'

15   Even if I had anything illuminating to say on the subject of on-line banking, shopping and so forth, this would not be the place.

16   It is true that all but the most honourable houses publish stuff for cynical or purely mercenary reasons: they need their best-sellers and their regular sellers, and sometimes they aren't too fussy about quality. But there are several English Literature efforts available on the internet which I know were rejected by every publisher in the land.

Email: a letter is still a letter

I am aware that email – especially in America, but increasingly so elsewhere too – is now a formidable sub-culture, attended by all kinds of hierarchical and operational considerations against which matters of royal protocol pale in comparison. That to my mind is as comic as perplexing; in fact – let's be honest – it is *barmy*. At bottom, email has no more glamour or *mana* than Ceefax or an unsolicited New Labour or Pizza-Palace circular: all are just means of communication.

That waspish introduction, in keeping with the rest of this Interlude, is designed to make you alert to the pitfalls of this otherwise splendid innovation. You don't have to be a grumbling curmudgeon to look on email as both faster and more reliable than the Royal Mail. A first-class letter *may* arrive the next day, but you can read, ingest and respond to thirty (or more) emails within a seven-hour span, whether you're in the office or at home. That is excellent – provided you use that boon with the same single-minded conscientiousness you would apply to a handwritten or word-processed letter.

For an email-letter has unique dangers. Even if they aren't *your* funds you're spending while on-line, the pressures of that notorious equation 'time = money' can make you careless. The temptation is twofold:

1   To compose before you are truly ready or clear.
2   To hit 'send' before you've either reflected or checked.

Both strands are regrettable, but 1 is probably the worse. If the letter is poorly organized and peppered with errors (2), that will irritate and reduce your impact; but if *you* are less than sure about what you want to say, the chances of your recipient having much idea are slim.

I am as surprised as distressed by how many otherwise diligent writers think that in some ways the 'rules' are suspended when writing emails – that decent spelling, paragraphing and punctuation somehow don't matter. This is nonsense. Even if your readers are as sloppy (or ignorant) in such matters of accuracy and presentation as you have just been, your message will still be hard to decode; and if they are more punctilious, it will annoy them even further. As my sub-title pronounces, a letter is a letter no matter what its medium of transmission, and bad letters aren't made any better simply by virtue of electricity.

Indeed email is *more* vulnerable in that respect. Most 'ordinary' letters are directed at one reader, or an intimate equivalent.[17] Very often, emails are sent to a significantly plural audience, all of whom have different skills, different agendas, different ways. Any eccentricity in your letter, let alone a profusion of errors or misleading signals (including 'stops') and your work will be severely

---

17   Apart from those excruciating Christmas round-robin jobs that even stylish and sensitive people seem to consider the done thing these days.

diluted. Your various readers will invariably need clarification on this or that point, this or that sentence, maybe the whole thing. I don't have to tell you that in addition to any embarrassment such a response may cause you, it costs valuable time to put matters right. And since saving time is the chief *raison d'etre* for email, that isn't too smart.

Handwriting: an obsolete art?

To my mind clear and fluent handwriting is and always will be a virtue. That may date me badly as a decrepit phogey whose time is about to pass; in addition, it could nail me as something of a hypocrite, since I am now so accustomed to doing nearly all my composition via some sort of machine that I find writing at any length by hand physically arduous: the fingers and wrist don't seem to obey as they once did. In that latter respect I am a child of our age, albeit a middle-aged one. The use of the PC has become so widespread that handwriting has a much lower profile than it did a generation ago; there are indeed quite a lot of influential people who wonder if the skills involved are any longer essential.

This sub-section's first sentence will give you an idea of what I think about that last view. But it *is* an issue – and one whose trendiness is underscored by something much more traditional, not to say timeless. Writing any kind of formal letter, especially to someone whom we don't know and/or who is in authority over us, is a daunting task: doubly so if anything important hinges on it. In those circumstances it is a common experience to 'freeze', to wonder if in addition to everything else we want to risk the recipient's derision at our nasty spidery hand. I am not being facetious: most people privately think their handwriting is ugly or inferior. Not the least stressful aspect of submitting a piece of work at school or college is that one's writing is under scrutiny as well as one's content: for many of us that is as embarrassing as hearing our voice on tape or watching ourselves on video.

All that is both natural and rather charming; it is also usually uncalled-for and therefore a potential impediment. The key here is to be

Sensible and honest about your handwriting – *both* ways.

Very often one's handwriting is a great deal better than one imagines. Provided it is clear, fluent and controlled, it will not only satisfy but give pleasure. You don't have to go along with graphology – the alleged 'science' of determining character and personality through handwriting – to appreciate that something written in an individual hand is always going to be more interesting than typescript, and provided that hand is not too eccentric or difficult, it is therefore likely to be a 'plus'. If on the other hand your writing is clumsy, ugly or lacks any kind of 'style' – and if that is the case you will almost certainly have been told about it! – then it's probably wisest to use typescript whenever and wherever you can.

Sometimes you don't have a choice. Quite a number of application forms I've seen can't be typed upon or word-processed: there simply isn't enough room, even if you choose the most miniscule font. You can squeeze up handwriting more than type, and as long as your words are clear and neat, they will look fine. One major warning, though:

Don't use block capitals!

A lot of 'official' forms require or request you to do this, and I've never understood why. Block capitals are no clearer than ordinary printed letters; surely crucial also is the fact that

They are *immensely* tiring to read

One short sentence in such a format is about all I can take before things start getting blurry and oppressive. And even if not everyone will be as hypochondriac as I am on the matter, you would be wise to bear in mind that such an unnatural form (nobody writes like that normally) is likely to cause mild irritation at least; that can cause problems of concentration, which is not what you want if the thing being concentrated on is you!

The use of block capitals carries a further danger: the reader may decide that either your ordinary writing is horrible or that you haven't yet learned 'joined-up writing'. Again, I'm not being facetious: first impressions always count, and I cannot think of any way in which a remorseless chunk of block-capitalled prose will help you in that regard.

So, in sum:

Don't be frightened of your handwriting or undervalue it.

I mentioned graphology just now, and you ought to know that during the 1980s there was a trend amongst some firms to bring in a graphologist to help judge and sift applications, both internal and external. So far as I know, this practice is now on the decline, as are the equally marginal – and often bogus – 'personality tests' that used to be all the rage with certain large corporations. Nevertheless, your handwriting *will* be assessed – naturally and automatically. There is no reason why that should be bad news for you, something that will decrease your chances. On the contrary, a clear and confident hand may say all kinds of positive things about you that mere typescript can never achieve.

Conclusion

Most of this chapter has focused on the pitfalls of PC use. But I hope it is clear that I am not a Luddite, that I indeed glory in the opportunities, legitimate short-cuts and countless benefits that these compact powerhouses offer. And in case that is *not* clear, let me alert every reader to this undoubted fact:

Not only are computers here to stay: their influence and use can only increase as the next few years go by, and anyone whose life and work involves writing will need to be thoroughly computer-literate.

John Naughton's summary which forms the epigraph to this **Interlude** demonstrates those truths with startling economy. A generation ago the likelihood is that the first three enterprises he identifies – automobiles, energy, illegal drugs – held a similar if not identical place in that 'industry league table'; it is equally probable that computing was not even in the top hundred. Now it would seem its potential is, if not infinite, immeasurable. To take two examples from my own world: within the next ten years it is distinctly possible that examinations will be written on lap-tops rather than headed A4 paper,[19] or even that some examinations will be taken on-line, to a specification unique to each candidate.

I end with a quotation from a play – *Julius Caesar*. The speaker is Cassius, and although he was not talking about computers (not even Shakespeare was that prescient) his words help nail a fundamental truth: insofar as PCs are problematic and dangerous

The fault . . . is in ourselves

It is grotesque to blame the computer if you lose sight of distinctions between product and process or its 'brain' and your mind. You are in charge, and if our culture's present emphasis on hi-tech presentation, vast databases/data-banks, and above all sheer speed of access makes it hard for you to maintain such control, it can – and must – be done.

---

19 I imagine by then someone will have worked out what to do about the distracting noise 150+ keyboards are going to make, each one used by an operator working at his/her personalized speed and weight of touch.

Part IV

Tailor-made

Chapter 9

Introduction

The previous sections on style have, I hope, shown you how to maintain a clear sense of voice in all that you write. I have stressed the twin needs: listen to what you write and keep your reader in mind at all times.

If you take care of those tasks, you will quickly find that your judgment becomes sound –judgment of tone, of circumstance, of what the most appropriate register might be.

You will also come quickly to realize that different kinds of writing require different approaches. This section looks at a variety of specific tasks, all of which have their own conventions and criteria.

Chapter 10

Essays

An essayist is a lucky person who has found a way to discourse without being interrupted.

Charles Poore

Argument seldom convinces anyone contrary to his inclinations.

Thomas Fuller

An essay is a formal, coherent and usually quite lengthy piece of informative and/or argumentative writing, as are its 'cousins', the article and the report, to which I devote my main attention in the two chapters following this one.

All essays develop an argument and seek to persuade. The argument may be pre-provided, as in a student answering a title set by a teacher and an executive producing a study requested by the board of directors, or it may be the writer's own idea. Whichever one applies, the activity ought to be fun, bringing pleasure to writer and reader alike. As Charles Poore suggests, writing an essay is an arguably unique opportunity to hold forth for as long as you like on a topic that interests you and about which you have plenty to say.

If those remarks strike you as wildly idealistic, I can assure you that you're in good and large company. For while I stand by what I've just said, the fact remains that most people find essay-writing the hardest, most elusive and most frustrating skill to acquire, and that it takes a long time for them to look on it as remotely pleasurable; indeed, some never do.

Writing a good letter undoubtedly requires you to make an effort, and often puts you under a certain amount of pressure, especially if an important matter of business or finance is at stake. However, that seems very pale stuff when faced with writing an essay. Weeks of preparation, discovery and sheer hard work now require a product: it's 'crunch time', and you are aware of being under a glaring spotlight both intimate and very public. If it is true that the single most frequent phobia is that of speaking in public [more often cited than death, apparently!], then many would admit that the fear of writing in public is hardly less formidable. Moreover, the problem seems to have little to do with ability: in my experience the very bright student encounters just as many difficulties as does the moderate one.

If you're suffering from any or all of these symptoms, what can you do to ease matters, even cure them for good?

Writing essays: some preliminary points

1 Trust your voice

I've been stressing this matter throughout the book, but I make no apology for raising it again. For the majority of people who are required to write regularly, the essay is the longest, most complex and most ambitious genre they will use, and it is all the more important to stay as natural and individual as possible when writing it. Just because it is a formal, public and intellectually demanding task does not mean you need to adopt a disguise or hide behind others' views and style. On the contrary: a successful essay reveals something of the writer as well as an argument. It is ultimately a very personal form: you should bear that centrally in mind, and take advantage of it. Naturally, you need to make your language appropriate; but if you follow the many guidelines earlier in this book, there is no reason why your essay style should not be both pleasing and telling.

2 Try to start the essay in plenty of time, and on no account leave it till the last minute

Part of the pressure attending the writing of an essay or a report is *compulsion*. Students are formally required to write essays, or they risk being thrown off the course, and any rising executive who refuses to submit an important report to his or her board of directors will soon be collecting a P45. As a result, only a handful default; but many shy away from the task for too long, perhaps because shelving it gives them the illusion of a freedom that the sudden arrival of a deadline brutally explodes. As a psychological ploy, this is readily understandable: we've all done it. And we therefore also know that **as a strategy, it's very bad indeed, if not disastrous.**

If you leave an essay to the last moment, you've got no choice: you've got to do it however tired, stupid, stale or resistant you are. It is all too probable that such negative states will show through in your writing. And even if you're lucky enough to be feeling fresh and vigorous at such a time, you've still got to rush things. There's unlikely to be time for any editing or a period of careful thought to ensure that you get something just right.

All this is obvious enough, I know; nevertheless a sizable proportion of students continue wilfully to ignore such obvious facts. As a result, they put themselves under an extra and severe pressure that a little sensible planning would render unnecessary. Furthermore, there's a positive side to it: if you do start early, you'll feel much more confident about being in control, and that will increase both your pleasure and your quality of performance.

3 Pay full attention to mechanical accuracy, sentence structure and paragraphing

I am constantly struck by how many students whom I know at root to be mechanically sound seem to jettison half their competence in this respect when they write essays. [The same is true for many younger pupils when they write 'compositions'.] The reason for this is not hard to find. If one gives students an exercise on punctuation, parts of speech or whatever, they concentrate specifically on such things. There is, after all, nothing else to do; consequently, they perform very well as a rule.

But writing an essay is a multiple activity. You've got to:

(a) decode/understand the question/title;
(b) work out what you chiefly wish to say;
(c) figure out how to start;
(d) decide on how best to deploy your material;
(e) ensure you regularly substantiate your points with detailed illustration, quotation or reference;
(f) effect a satisfying conclusion

and several other things.[1] It is therefore not surprising if you fail to pay ordinary attention to mundane matters like spelling and grammatical accuracy. Not surprising – but very unwise and probably highly damaging. Careless errors reflect badly on you and undermine any authority your arguments may have; moreover, there is a bigger danger still.

> **If you don't pay enough attention to how to spell words and structure individual sentences and paragraphs properly, the chances of your essay having a clear and persuasive *overall* structure are very slim.**

Good large structures consist of well-engineered and flawlessly connected small structures: that goes for essays as well as buildings, cars and domestic machinery.

4 Always pause before embarking on a fresh argument or theme

There are two good reasons for this. First, it allows you time to check that you've got all you can out of your previous focus. Very often, a few moments' reflection will lead you on to further points that lift the material from the merely satisfactory to the truly authoritative.

Second, the slight rest or change of activity will do you good, and should ensure that when you do turn to your fresh argument, you yourself are fresh and ready to tackle it with real vigour. If this does not happen, the chances are that you've become tired and should stop for a while. Note, incidentally, that this provides

---

1 All these matters, the six cited and the 'several other things', are covered shortly.

'Read as many essays/articles as you can'

another reason for not leaving the essay until the last minute, when you won't be able to afford such valuable rests!

5 Read as many essays/articles as you can

You cannot become a good essayist simply by osmosis, but reading others' work will quickly make you more alert to matters of style, structure and so on. You will learn from their strengths, but equally from their weaknesses and flaws: when you come across something that is unclear or badly expressed, the chances are high that it will help you not to make the same mistake. There are many extracts from essays [good and bad] throughout this book: you could do worse than start with them.

So much for preliminaries; it is time to consider problems. And judging from my own students' experience and requests for advice, most of these hinge on how to structure an essay. The matter is large and complex, best introduced by looking at some of the more obvious areas where difficulty arises.

Essay structure: traps and troubleshooting

1 **You cannot begin to write a decent essay until you have a good command of the material concerned.**

That is such a banal observation that I almost blush to include it. Nevertheless it is remarkable how often students' alleged problems with 'structure' boil down to the much more mundane – and unflattering – fact that they do not 'know their stuff' well enough yet. And I'm not just referring to the lazy or dilettante student who thinks a quick perusal of the source material plus recourse to some tawdry 'Study Aid' is enough of a platform for an adequate essay; conscientious and meticulous students can suffer from this flaw too.

An essay is like a good meal: it takes a lot of careful preparation and preliminary time. It makes about as much sense to attempt an essay without a clear grasp of the relevant information and ideas as it does to get out a plate and sit in front of it expecting food to materialize on it as if by magic.

If basic ignorance or incomplete knowledge isn't the problem, you may still be very low on confidence, and there can be several reasons for that.

2a **What does the question/title ask you to do?**
2b **Do you know what you chiefly wish to say?**
2c **How are you going to start?**

I've listed these together because ultimately they intertwine – all exert a fundamental influence on how you deploy and structure your material. But each one also addresses a specific matter, and they're worth considering separately first.

Whether you're engaged on a 'weekly essay' or the much more pressured task of performing in an examination, your first job, before even picking up your pen, is to 'decode' the question.

Be absolutely sure that you've understood any concepts or 'targets' stated; above all, look at the instructional verbs and obey them. As an example, try this little exercise.

Exercise 24
What is the difference between these two questions?

1   **Describe the rise of Hitler.**
2   **Explain the rise of Hitler.**

Commentary

An incautious student might think there is little or no difference, and would as a result be flirting with disaster, no matter how knowledgeable and confident he or she may be. For there is a **big** difference. The first question calls for an 'objective' historiographical account, listing stages, events and what we will call 'facts'. The second question, by contrast, is much more a matter of interpretation, possibly involving a consideration of mass psychology, of the emotional appeal of Fascism, and an understanding of how mania can take hold of a nation. Of course, certain things may well emerge as common to both questions, but 1 demands an account that is essentially external, whereas 2 requires a more intuitive or internal approach. To confuse them in the heat of the moment may be understandable in a way, but it would prove a very expensive mistake.

To reinforce this important consideration and to give you a near-comprehensive awareness of the different instructional verbs you will come across and what they require you to do, try the exercise that follows. It is a demanding one, undoubtedly: I first encountered it years ago, have used it in many and various classes, and it *still* gives me trouble whenever I am confronted with it in virgin, unannotated form!

Exercise 25 What does the question mean?
Below follow fourteen instructional verbs and alongside them fourteen definitions of those verbs. Not one of them forms a match: can you pair them off accurately? The answers are in Appendix I, p. 232.

Verb	Definition
Account for	Give reasons; say 'why' rather than just define
Analyse	Write down the information in the right order
Comment on	Item-by-item consideration of the topic, usually presented one under the other
Compare	Point out differences only and present result in orderly fashion
Contrast	Estimate the value of, looking at positive and negative attributes
Describe	Elect features according to the question
Discuss	Present arguments for and against the topic in question; you can also give your opinion
Evaluate	Explain the cause of
Explain	Make critical or explanatory notes/observations
Identify	State the main features of an argument, omitting all that is only partially relevant
List	Give the main features or general features of a subject, omitting minor details and stressing structure
Outline	Make a survey of the subject, examining it critically
Review	Point out the differences and similarities
Summarize	Separate down into component parts and show how they interrelate with each other

---

Do not be downhearted if that taxed you: it should have done! And even if you found it a major ordeal, you ought now to be much better-versed in the kind of questions you'll be set, how to decode them and thus how to present your material and arguments to their best advantage. However, the last observation I want to make about Point 2a is this: the prime need to work out what you've got to *do* must not, in any circumstances, be taken to mean 'What do they want me to *say?*' That leads us to 2b.

If you don't yet know what you chiefly want to say, two possible explanations arise.

1   You haven't done enough preparatory reading, thinking, or both.
2   You're unsure about what 'line' to follow. You may have some ideas that clash with those of your teacher, or other opinions/interpretations you've read, and you're doubtful about whether to include them or 'play safe' instead.

I've covered 1 already, of course: if this applies, you're not yet ready to contemplate doing an essay, and should go back to your books at once!

The second reason is a much more sympathetic problem; it is nonetheless wrong-headed. In exams especially, but also in more leisurely contexts, students often imagine that their essay must be 'the right answer', that it must match what the marker thinks. **This is an absurd and extremely harmful delusion.**

It is absurd because in many cases (virtually all exams included) you will have no idea who the marker is, and therefore no knowledge of his or her beliefs, prejudices and so on. Trying to second-guess an unknown and invisible assessor is just crazy! More subtle – and also more important – is the harm done by sacrificing your biggest asset: **you.** The quest for 'the right answer' ignores the fact that it's your essay, nobody else's, and that its quality will depend on your ideas, your intellect, your prose. Provided your 'information base' and knowledge are sound, your reader/marker will be interested in what you have to say – and that will be all the stronger if it really is what you want to say, and not what you think the reader wants to hear.

I admit that you may, from time to time, be unlucky: there are teachers around who want their own views more or less reproduced in their students' essays and who penalize or are very snooty about attempted departures from them. There may also be a few such examiners at any given time – although I can assure you that they do not last long in the post if they are doctrinaire in their marking. But by and large it makes the best and most profitable sense to stick to your guns and argue the case you've worked out to your own satisfaction. And that brings us to the crucial matter of how to start.

Even to an experienced writer, a blank sheet of paper is a uniquely frightening thing. It seems to stare at you in a sneering or threatening way [possibly both], as if taunting you to get something down, however feeble! All of us succumb, at least occasionally, to such temptation, and I cannot stress too strongly that **we are *always* wrong to do so.**

There is no single good way of beginning an essay: we'll look at some of the options in a moment. Conversely, however, there are also several bad ways in which to start, and they need listing at once.

'A blank sheet of paper is a uniquely frightening thing'

1   **Never allow your first sentence to be a mere paraphrase of the title/ question.**

This should be obvious enough: few things are more boring than to read a [usually wordy] repetition of something already established. Yet thousands do it, time and again! It's invariably based on fear, on that intolerable need to make your mark on that blank sheet. But don't do it: it will make only a negative mark on your reader.

2   **Always ensure that your first sentence does some real work.**

I'll be going into positive ways of achieving this in a little while; but as I've implied, more than half the battle is knowing the kind of thing to avoid.

A   **Don't waste time with vacuous 'general' introductions.**

These may seem to read quite well, but they will usually be flabby, however pleasantly written. [An example follows shortly.] As always, keep your readers centrally in mind: they may not object all that much if you gradually 'wind yourself up' into action, rather like an athlete warming up, but they will much prefer it if you give them something that immediately engages their full attention.

B   **Beware of confusing 'private' thinking with 'public' performing and arguing.**

That is not an easy instruction to understand, and I hope an analogy will help.

I would imagine that all of you have been to a theatre at some time. The opening moments of any production are always fascinating. One has so much to absorb: the set, the costumes, the make-up, the voices and of course the spoken lines. This heady assault on the senses is central to the unique appeal of live theatre, and it is the expectation of such imminent pleasure that accounts for the 'buzz' in the air just before the performance begins.

However, let us suppose that during those expectant minutes you not only have your chocolates, programme and the lively chatter of friends to beguile you, but also access to a closed-circuit television network that shows you what's going on backstage. You now have the opportunity to watch step by step the intricate make-up an actor needs to apply to play *King Lear*, *Othello*, *The Phantom of the Opera* or even the tramps in *Waiting for Godot*. Alternatively, you can 'tune in' to the special effects technicians and see them preparing their tricks. Or you may just see cast and stage crew chaffing desultorily as they await the cue to begin. And my question is: would you make use of this new facility?

My own answer would be: yes, but almost certainly only the first time. If such a thing became available to every member of the audience, I think we all would have our curiosity too much aroused to ignore it. But I am almost sure it would diminish our overall pleasure in the performance, however initially interesting those extra insights might be. When the actors appear in role, or those special effects occur, our most likely reaction would be one of anti-climax, a loss of 'magic' or at least a reduction in excitement. On our next theatre visit, we'd firmly keep our set turned off.

Writing an essay is no less of a 'performance' than appearing in a play, albeit a less glamorous one. Just as an actor's initial impact might be seriously impaired if we had witnessed his private preparation, your impact as an essayist will be much reduced if you subject the reader to a lot of private thinking before making your first 'public' point. So I would strongly advise you not to write down this kind of thing:

Exercise 26

There follow three essay introductions. What's wrong with them?

(a) In this essay I am going to look at both sides of the proposition at issue, make a number of points about each side, and then move towards what I hope is a satisfactory and balanced conclusion.

(b) Question: Was Henry VIII a good and successful king?
I find it difficult to answer this question. It all depends on what you mean by 'good' and 'successful'. My definitions might be different from other people's, which would obviously cause confusion.

(c) Question: Are the terms 'recession', 'depression' and 'slump' synonymous?
In order to answer this question, it is first necessary to decide what is meant by the three terms 'recession', 'depression' and 'slump' cited in

the title. For although they are closely linked, they are also precisely separate, and they must be distinguished between if one wishes to understand how an economic crisis can arise.

Commentary

All are quite elegantly written; none is a wise or effective way to begin.

The first is distinctly poor: indeed, it's useless. It tells the reader nothing not already implicit in the title; it is blandly vague; and it is has no 'voice'. Anyone could have written it, in answer to virtually any question. That's why I didn't in this case cite the question: it wouldn't have made any difference. The introduction spells out what one would expect as a matter of course from any answer to a two-sided proposition – and there is an almost infinite number of such questions.

So, (a) is a classic example of the vacuous first paragraph that confuses preliminary private thinking with public impact. It is very sensible to work out the structure and strategy of your essay, but it is unnecessary and boring to call public attention to them. Let your ideas speak for themselves at once and without such featureless advertising.

The second is less dull, but it still won't do. It is superficially engaging in its modesty, and a clear 'voice' is present. But it is too defensive, quickly collapsing into vagueness as a result. Sadly, the writer's instincts are sound: the words 'good' and 'successful' are indeed problematic, or at least need defining. Instead of doing just that, the introduction slides away into something uncomfortably close to a whine. I strongly suspect the root of the trouble is that 'quest for the right answer': a worry about 'other people' prevails at the expense of the writer's own views.

The third has a vigour and implicit independence of mind absent in the other examples; it also echoes the flaws of both. As I remarked in an earlier section (see page 68), the structure 'In order to answer this question, it is first necessary to . . .' falls dully on the eye and does no real work; moreover, it can frequently decline further into a wordy paraphrase of the title, which is essentially what happens here. You might think me a little unfair, and argue that the first sentence implies that the three terms are not 'synonymous' and therefore has already begun to answer the question in a clear fashion. I wouldn't altogether disagree, but would add that the writer would have been better advised to launch into the separate definitions straightaway, which would have been much punchier. Alternatively, he could begin with his pleasingly cogent second sentence. As it is, his introduction is somewhat wordy and also not fully confident, even if it is the best of the three examples, signalling genuine promise.

So much, then, for the dangers of vacuity and confusing private thinking with public performance. These are, I hope, obvious flaws; other 'starting traps' are a little more subtle.

C   Long introductions are rarely advisable.

If essay structure worries you, it is best to keep your introductions short for the time being. Even if they are not vacuous, long introductions can be arduous to read, and your first aim should be to grab your readers' attention as attractively as possible.

Long introductions can be very impressive, I admit. I have read many good ones from students engaged upon a large task who conscientiously establish the full context and 'ground rules' of what they go on to explore. But you need a lot of confidence and a certain amount of practice to bring this off; in addition, it can tempt you into generalizations that are best left until after you've put together a detailed argument. If in any doubt, therefore, go for a short, snappy start.

D   Don't launch an attack on a question in your opening remarks.

I've already suggested you shouldn't be over-dutiful or craven when considering a title, and that you should stick to what you feel and want to say. But instant aggression is equally unwise. I don't simply mean that you should avoid openings like 'This proposition is a load of rubbish'. That kind of remark, unattractively combining stale slang and naive arrogance, nearly always bounces back on the writer, and should not be used at any time. Even if your attack is a good deal more sophisticated and elegant, however, you still risk alienating the reader if you come on too strong too early:

Question: Despite its horrors, the action of *King Lear* persuades us that 'The gods are just'.
One really doesn't know whether to laugh or cry at this proposition. The world of *King Lear* is so full of horror, especially at the end, when even the traditional grim comfort of tragic resolution is denied us, that any idea of divine benevolent control is just obscene. The most we can conclude is that even if the gods exist, they are indifferent to human suffering; many would argue that they seem positively to glory in it.

This was a written by a highly intelligent student of mine a number of years ago. For what it's worth, I agree with his underlying case; but I pointed out to him that some of his phrasing was at best incautious anyway, and **especially at the start of his answer.** I also suggested, prompted by his use of conclude, that his remarks (suitably toned-down) would be far more effective as his conclusion, when his undoubted knowledge and intelligence would have 'earned' him the right to quarrel fiercely with the title.

The point here is not that you should never attack a question, but that you should be sensible about doing so. The following guidelines are worth bearing in mind.

1   **You will very seldom encounter a title or question that is truly stupid or nonsensical.**

You may quite frequently come across a proposition that you disagree with, even fundamentally so; that is quite a different matter. It is a truism that there are two sides to virtually every question: academics and examiners are especially aware of this, and are chiefly interested in why and how you argue your particular case. That's why they won't set you anything obviously idiotic, and why you'll almost certainly harm yourself if you accuse them of having done so.

2   **It is best to establish your credentials before going on the attack.**

In all writing, you need to take your readers with you. If you know that you are going to ask them to consider a case to which they may be hostile, you should first establish a 'base' that persuades them that you know what you're talking about and have carefully considered a lot of evidence. If you do this well, some of your later controversial points may be gently implicit already, creating a unity and flow that will satisfy even a reader who disagrees with you.

3   **Never allow your disagreement to degenerate into name-calling.**

It is usually possible to respect, or at least understand, views different from your own, and that should be your strategy.[2] By all means attempt to demolish the opposite case, but this should be done with dignity, even courtesy. Indeed, you can often make your case more effective by praising an opposing point before demonstrating that yours is even better!

4   **Be *especially* careful to demonstrate your points.**

Naturally, you need to do this in any essay. But it's particularly important when arguing a contrary or controversial case: any mere assertions unaccompanied by evidence or illustration will be dismissed by those whom, perhaps against their will, you're trying to persuade.

My final **'don't'** to bear in mind when seeking to ensure that your first remarks do some real work may seem puzzling at first, but it opens up a more positive approach.

E   **Do not assume that an introduction is automatically necessary.**

---

2   There are exceptions to this. My first sentence in Part One identifies destructive criticism as 'one of life's great pleasures', and I hold to that, as several sections and exercises in this book make abundantly clear. And if you do come across a question or view that you genuinely despise, then I think you should say so. My point here, however, is that such occasions will be very rare in the writing of academic essays, and that it's poor policy to anticipate the need for ridicule.

Sometimes your best policy will be to make the first 'scoring' point that occurs to you, and to move straight on from there. Indeed, it is worth developing this into a principle that applies to both the beginning and the end of an essay:

There is no virtue in having an introduction or a conclusion *for the sake of it*. It can be better to just start or just stop.

I must urge caution about this: there is probably nothing better than a stylishly argued essay which has been vigorously set up and satisfyingly rounded off. But as is doubtless clear by now, writing a good introduction is a difficult skill, and to agonize about its structure can cost you valuable time, energy and confidence. Since you will be most crisp and to the point when you arrive at what you know best, it can make a lot of sense to start with that material.

Even so, having an introduction may make you feel more comfortable, or your teachers may insist on one. In that case, this next principle, which in a way is a variant of the previous one, may be valuable.

The best time to write your introduction is last thing of all – even after the conclusion.

This is not as crazy as it looks. It has a number of strengths that may well improve an adequate essay and render a good one really impressive.

1   It will almost certainly prevent your introduction and conclusion from virtually duplicating each other – a very common flaw in essays that I read.
2   By this time you will be aware of what you have argued and why. This knowledge should allow you to write an introductory paragraph which sets up that argument in an assured and muscular way, increasing the reader's pleasure and attention.
3   As a corollary to 2, your introduction will impress by its lack of flab, uncertainty and defensiveness. You will now have filled several sides, and the shaping of your opening remarks should carry none of the normal 'blank sheet terror' syndrome!
4   Your confidence will receive a double boost. First, to start with material you're secure rather than anxious about should ensure that you write vigorously from the beginning – and you'll be beneficially aware that you're doing so, which will help to sustain your performance. Second, when you do write that introduction, you'll be sure of what you're doing and confidently aware of exactly how much to write. Furthermore . . .
5   . . . The long-term advantages of such a strategy may also be considerable. Success in any extended course hinges on confidence almost as much as on talent and industry; if this method causes you to feel less frightened about structuring your essays, and therefore confidently able to enjoy writing them more, the progress you make should be rapid and substantial.

Finally, an apparently paradoxical advantage:

6   It will no doubt have occurred to you that writing your introduction last is
    almost impossible in an exam, unless you can guess with uncanny accuracy
    how many lines to leave blank! But this shouldn't prove as much of a problem
    as you might imagine.

Exams usually occur at the end of a year, or not until a good deal of the course
has been covered: there isn't much point in them otherwise. By then, you will
have written a number of essays, and if you've adopted good habits in doing so,
you should find that you've developed a practised 'feel' for how to structure and
deploy an argument. In short, by the time you sit your exams, you should be
experienced enough to write your introduction first and be confident about its
quality.

Summary

At the outset I listed three things that should come into play as soon as you sit
down to begin an essay:

What does the question ask you to do?
Do you know what you chiefly wish to say?
How are you going to start?

We've spent a number of pages considering these separately. But as I said earlier,
they are closely related in the fundamental influence they exert on your performance. Indeed, they are almost symbiotic, as these two formulae illustrate:

- **Solve the first 'problem' properly, and the second will be easier; solve that,
  and the third one will be.**
- **Ignore or make a mess of one of them, and the other two will suffer as well.**

Essay writing as a performance

So far I've looked at ways of ensuring that your essays are sound. If you follow the
'preliminary points' and stay mindful of 'potential 'traps', you should do a very
satisfactory job. The only remaining thing to do is to consider ways of making your
essays impressive rather than just solid, and I want to look at six 'advanced' skills
which characterize the work of a truly authoritative writer giving a performance.

1   Keeping to the point.
2   Drawing on a proper *range* of evidence and focus.
3   Linking, digging and polishing.
4   More on introductions and conclusions.

5   Quotation and reference.
6   The strengths and limitations of 'argument'.

1   Keeping to the point

This may seem an elementary skill, and so it is in terms of obeying basic relevance and the need to answer the question. But 'advanced' writers are vulnerable to a phenomenon that rarely if ever affects their less sophisticated counterparts – that of becoming temporarily 'lost in thought'. What starts as an unremarkable idea may suddenly open up a new avenue of enquiry – a gratifying experience but also a perilous one. In your excited determination to milk this sudden inspiration to the full, you can easily make a major detour from your planned route without realizing it; sometimes it proves to be not just a detour but an elaborate dead-end.

There are times when this is entirely useful – during an 'exploratory' essay early in your course, when your essay work is as much a learning experience as a performance. But when the latter is your chief or sole aim, you need to be ruthless. Fortunately, there is a simple way of ensuring you do not get lost in this beguiling but wasteful way: keep your title and main targets in mind at all times.

How you do this is up to you. You can make regular visual checks of your first page; you can write title and targets in bold capitals on a piece of paper kept in front of you; or you can just train yourself to issue regular mental reminders. But however you go about it, make sure that your material is not just interesting in its own right but achieves an overall unity and unbroken pertinence.

2   Drawing on a proper range of evidence and focus

Most of your essays will address topics that are quite large and broad, although from time to time you will be asked to do something narrow and specific – e.g. the analysis of a scene in a play, a particular scientific reaction, or an historical document. And if the question is wide-ranging, make sure your essay is too. If you're asked to write about, say:

A   The development of a character during a large novel
B   X's foreign policy during a ten-year period
C   The strengths and limitations of Utilitarianism

you cannot afford to have a narrow or thin 'data base'. If you look at only two episodes for A, a couple of incidents for B or one example per 'side' for C, the essay is unlikely to satisfy even if the analysis you do offer is brilliant.

Good prior planning will more or less guarantee that your scope of example and detail is suitably broad. But stay alert to this while writing: as I've just pointed out during 1, it's all too easy to become so engrossed in a particular issue that earlier resolutions and schemes get forgotten.

There is a complementary danger that should be mentioned here:

Ensure a good range of evidence, yes; but don't go to the opposite extreme and sacrifice depth for quantity.

Sometimes an essay title can seem forbiddingly broad, prompting you to think that you must try to cover absolutely every relevant incident or detail. Unless you're intending to make your essay the size of a small book, you can't hope to achieve such comprehensiveness without becoming damagingly thin in your treatment of each point. Go for a muscular compromise: in a 4–5-side essay, you can focus on several key pieces of evidence and deal with them in sufficient depth to persuade the reader of their satisfying representativeness.

3 Linking, digging and polishing

Earlier I advised you to beware of boring your readers by taking them through over-obvious, unnecessary steps in the basic logic of your essay's structure. But as a writer of sophisticated essays, you must also be careful not to omit steps in the logic of your argument. It is one thing to assume that the reader knows without needing to be told that you're starting the essay, moving on to another point, finishing: such omissions are sensible and indeed essential if you don't want to irritate. But it's quite a different matter if you leave out an important link between two points, leaving the reader to do the work: that is equally annoying. As an ideal compromise:

Spare the reader a dull, unfruitful survey of your essay's architecture, but don't overdo it by insisting that he/she supply the bridges between your ideas.

Make sure your argument progresses clearly and comfortably. It is not quite enough to put down two related points without showing that they are linked, and why. Very often you will need nothing more than a simple conjunction [which means 'linking with'], such as **so**, **thus** or even **and**.

Essays whose material is not adequately linked acquire a bland, almost unfinished quality; the same is true of essays where the writer doesn't 'dig' into the material with quite enough penetration. As a result, the points lie on the surface, as if waiting for the reader to mine them properly. So explore and develop your points as far as you can – don't, as many do, settle for the first and second useful ideas that occur to you. If you're talented enough to think of those, then a little vigorous turning over the ground is very likely to lead to a third, and a fourth – and that's one of the surest ways of transforming quite a good essay into a very good one. 'Linking' and 'digging' are closely related, in that writers who concentrate fiercely on making their points flow lucidly from one to the other will very probably find that such a clarity of focus sponsors further telling ideas.

Finally, you should read your essays over critically – that is, in the position of the reader rather than you the writer. Look them over closely: have you really said what you thought you said? Any uncertainty in your reaction, and you should clarify your material. For something to be 'more or less there' or implicit in your writing won't do: it's got to be unambiguously out in the open. Look, too, for any 'flab' or emptiness, thus ensuring that the style is as taut as you can currently achieve. To 'polish' essays in this way is a pleasant experience, and one which can make a lot of difference to their final impact and quality. Moreover, to get into the habit of 'polishing' will prove highly profitable in an exam.

4 More on introductions and conclusions

As is clear from my previous remarks on this matter, I believe that knowing how **not** to write an introduction is most of the battle. But two positive things need to be said as well.

> 1 **If you think the title requires you to define the terms it cites, then do so at once as your first paragraph.**

There is no need to be apologetic or diffident about this: you should not 'pussyfoot'. By all means spend some careful time composing your definition and confirming that it will sustain your argument; once you're satisfied, write it out clearly and confidently and then move onto your first point.

> 2 **The art of writing crisp and stylish introductions takes a lot of time and trouble to acquire, but it's worth it.**

If you can guarantee that your first few sentences will have real impact and get the reader anxious to read on, you are already well on the way to writing a successful essay. As I've said, there are times when your best policy is to leap straight in with your first detailed point; but an introduction that serves as a clear platform and is also invigorating to read will give your work that touch of class that always impresses. And as a perhaps faintly scary index of that, a friend of mine who regularly marks Finals papers for London University tells me that

> **In at least 80% of cases, he can guess (accurately) what overall grade the script will get by the time he's read the first page.**

Taking extra care over that first page will not **automatically** ensure that the rest of the essay is good, naturally; but such good habits and sharp performance tend to be self-sustaining.

So far, I've said rather less about conclusions than introductions. The chief reason is that in several respects exactly the same points apply: if you side-step the various traps and flaws that characterize poor introductions, the likelihood is that you'll also avoid ending your essay in a lame or vacuous way. However, some separate guidelines may be valuable.

1   Before closing your essay, always look back at your introduction and then make sure that you say something fresh and/or express yourself in a different way.

I don't of course mean you should contradict yourself! What I'm concerned about is ensuring that your introduction and conclusion are not mere duplicates, which tarnishes a good number of essays that I read. You want to achieve unity, but that does not mean the essay should be circular.

2   Short conclusions are usually preferable to long ones.

Your ideal is a snappy tying-together of the main points and discussion you've recorded, leaving the reader impressed by your clarity and authority and perhaps interested in 'talking back'.

3   If possible, conclude your argument in a way that makes explicit insights that have been implicit along the way.

The conclusion is often the best place to register your overall reaction to the proposition at issue – better, in most cases, than at the start, when you haven't yet 'earned' your right to pass a considered judgment.

4   As with introductions, try to avoid self-evident phrases.

I've touched on these elsewhere, and will not weary you with a lengthy repetition. But if you observe guideline 2, it's then worth remembering that it will usually be obvious to the reader that you've reached your conclusion, because the writing stops a few lines down! You therefore don't even need the phrase **In conclusion**, let alone anything more bloated.

5 Quotation and reference

Note: if in doubt about how to punctuate quotation, please consult Chapter 17, which covers that skill in full.

Layout and stylistic conventions

There are six chief procedures you need to follow.

1   The noun is **quotation**, not **quote**, which is a verb. The use of **quote** as a noun is becoming ever more widespread among educated people and media pundits. But don't do it: it's illiterate. And if you think that to worry about such minor confusion is tiresomely pedantic (and I can see your point), let me just say this: virtually every academic examiner I've met, dealt with or read finds the

use of **quote** as a noun intensely annoying. Silly of them/me, very possibly; but if as a student you're subject to such pedantic whims, it's best to play safe!

2   There is no need to include the absurd phrase **and I quote.** All that is required is a colon after your introduction or 'set up', and to open quotation marks. (Don't forget to close them, either!)

3   Quotations shorter than two full lines may be incorporated into ordinary text. However, if quoting say 1½ lines of **verse**, you should signify with an oblique stroke (/) where the break occurs in the original's lines.

4   Longer quotations should be isolated – i.e. treated as if they were self-contained paragraphs. In addition, they should be *block-indented* to add visual emphasis and thus impact.

5   If these longer quotations are in **verse**, always write them out in their original form – that is, in blocked lines. The oblique stroke usage identified in 3 is not appropriate in 'isolated' quotation.

6   When dealing with eponymous works [where the title of book is the same as the protagonist's name], be sure to distinguish between book and character. Underlining the former is probably the best way; thus **Macbeth** would refer to the man, <u>**Macbeth**</u> to the play.

You can use quotation marks instead – **'Macbeth'** is perfectly in order. But since one tends to use quotation marks quite a lot in many academic essays, to underline may strike many as the clearer, better option.

Now for two examples that illustrate all those points. Both happen to be taken from a student assignment on *Macbeth*, but the principles they enact apply to all academic usage, not just the writing of literary essays. Numbers in brackets refer to the convention at issue in the above list.

Passage A

Macbeth [6] never enjoys a single moment of ease throughout the play. Whether considering the murder of Duncan, hallucinating just after he has 'done the deed' [3] or bitterly reflecting on his sterile and joyless life as king, a quotation [1] from Act III, 'O, full of scorpions is my mind, dear wife!' [3] could be said to define his mental state at <u>all</u> times.

The two quotations are short enough to fit into the essayist's text while retaining their necessary punch. But in this second extract the 'isolated', block-indented quotation becomes necessary.

Passage B

. . . The next exchange between Macbeth [6] and his wife is crucial: among other things it shows us that killing Duncan was <u>his</u> idea originally, not hers. Here he argues that such an act would be sub-human: [2]

'Prithee, peace!
I dare do all that may become a man;
Who dares do more is none.' [4, 5]

To which she retorts: [2]

'What beast was 't then
That made you break this enterprise to me?
When you durst do it, then you were a man . . .' [4, 5]

She witheringly makes him responsible for the plan, but also tempts him lovingly. The last line of that quotation [1] is full of implicit admiration, even sexual invitation – a hint that is fully developed in her next remarks designed to arouse him further: 'to be more than what you were, you would / Be so much more the man.' [3]

That is elegantly set out and easy to follow. Isolating the two longer quotations ensures their impact – partly because the reader's ease has been considered. The third, shorter quotation can fit into the ordinary text, as before, though notice the oblique stroke this time.

Following those six procedures will sharpen and clarify your presentation, which should usually have a beneficial knock-on effect on your overall organization and style. If and when you come to write articles for journals and so on, you may find that certain publications have a set 'house style' that may differ at times from what I've outlined; however, I'd be very surprised if such variance is anything other than slight.

So much for the mechanics of **how** to quote; now let's look at **when** to quote, and **why**.

Quotation: choice and timing

'Help! I've been writing this essay for half an hour, and I still haven't quoted anything. I'd better bung one down, pronto!'

That kind of attitude or procedure characterizes an alarming number of even good essays. As I write these words, I've just finished marking nearly 200 International Baccaulaureate Literature scripts. They ranged, as such papers do, from awful to excitingly impressive, but only the very best displayed an authoritative use of quotation. This is not in fact surprising: the ability to quote with telling assurance and apposite timing is a highly sophisticated skill, one which usually takes quite a time to acquire. As with many other writing skills, knowing what not to do is a great help, so let's start with a few **don'ts**.

1   **Don't quote for the sake of it.** Any quotation that does not illuminate a point just made or one about to be made is useless. Especially avoid the 'bung

it down' approach our panicking student above seems to think advisable! Furthermore . . .

2 . . . **Don't quote in a vacuum.** Quotations hardly ever speak for themselves, and it is a great mistake to think that a quotation will automatically make your point without any further contribution from you. You need to show **why** you've chosen it and **how** it illustrates your argument.

3 **Don't quote too often.** Too many essays resemble a Jumbo Quotation-Sandwich whose 'filling' consists of increasingly indigestible extracts from other sources. It is very irritating to have an argument constantly interrupted (or indeed suspended) in such a way: be selective.

4 **Don't quote at great length** – or keep occasions when you do so to a minimum. Quoting a substantial extract can be justified sometimes, when the material is crucial to an argument or establishes several issues that are to be explored. But I find that most students who quote at length do not use such extracts well, providing only a cursory gloss before moving on. Such practice is an elaborate extension of the flaw cited in 1, similarly reducing quotation to a feat of memory, or simple copying!

5 **Don't make your quotations mere *duplicates* of the points they accompany.** It's important that quotation and point match, as observed in 1 and 2; but this kind of thing is feeble:

> . . . Lady Macbeth cannot bring herself to kill Duncan, because he looks like her father:

> > 'Had he not resembled
> > My father as he slept, I had done 't.'

The quotation adds nothing to the point already made, other than proving that the writer has read the play. Good quotation always does some real **work**.

Similarly or conversely:

6 **Don't just *paraphrase* quotations that you use.** Look at this extract from a sixth-form essay on Keats's *Ode To Autumn*:

> . . . The second stanza's last two lines are notably successful:

> > 'Or by a cider-press, with patient look,
> > Thou watchest the last oozings hours by hours.'

Here Keats imagines Autumn as a spectator serenely observing the gradual fermentation of the cider, not concerned by the slowness of the process.

These comments are attractively written, but they don't **say** anything. Having cited the lines as 'notably successful', the writer tells us merely what they mean, not how and why they work. We might have expected a gloss on 'hours by hours', where the unusual use of the plural emphasizes the drowsy, long-drawn-out process, or some mention of the profusion of 's' sounds, which have a similar effect. As it stands, however, we have no idea why the writer thinks these lines successful or indeed why they were quoted.

Sometimes, admittedly, you will feel it is necessary to 'explain' the lines you quote, because they are difficult or ambiguous; if you're sure this applies, go ahead – it is sensible and helpful (see page 154ff). But make sure you analyse or comment upon such quotations as well as clarifying their meaning.

As may be evident, most of those **don'ts** include or imply more positive principles, which can now be listed.

1   Always ensure that your quotation matches your point.
2   Use your quotations: comment on them, show why you've chosen them.
3   Quotations are fine servants but bad masters: they should assist your essay, not run it! Stay in charge, so that it's your thinking and writing that chiefly register.
4   Your quotation must be grammatically complete in its own right and it must also fit in grammatically with whatever point of yours it accompanies.
5   Before writing out a quotation, ask yourself if it's really necessary. Is it going to do any useful work? If in doubt, leave it out. It only takes a few such 'dubious' quotations to blur or dilute your argument, or even to convince the reader that you're emptily showing off your textual knowledge to no other purpose.

In addition, or as a summary:

6   **Think** before you quote, while you quote, and after you've quoted. If you stay alert in this way, the chances are excellent that your quotation will be apt and fully integrated into your argument.

Bearing those six points in mind will make your use of quotation illuminating and pertinent. This will apply to 'ordinary' essays – those you compose in your own time – but also the 'extraordinary' ones written under pressure in exams, about which I offer this final don't:

Don't imagine there is any special or 'secret' formula concerning quotation in an examination. Success depends on good knowledge and alert thinking, not on 'tricks' or any model craftily designed beforehand. You should rid your thinking of any dependence on these false props, and treat with extreme caution any teacher who advocates them.

Quotation: when to explain

Usually it is a waste of time and space to cite a quotation if all you then do with it is paraphrase its meaning. This is known in some circles as 'telling the story', and those who do it are nearly always guilty of underestimating the reader's intelligence and knowledge.

There are occasions, however, when meaning is ambiguous, difficult or obscure. Such instances are worth brief elucidation on your part; sometimes, as in the example that follows, the way a particular word or phrase is interpreted can be crucial.

A good example is A *Study of Reading Habits* by Philip Larkin, published in 1960. It is a deceptively provocative poem – and the adverb 'deceptively' is pivotal. For the last line became instantly famous and is still much-quoted – often for absolutely the wrong reasons. I have been astonished at how many readers (including more than a few professional critics) take that line at face value. They assume that Larkin is dismissing books as enragingly useless, that in middle age he has sourly come to regard literature as a futile con-trick.[3]

Citing references

So far my examples have been literary ones. In a way this is only to be expected: I teach English, and most of the work I encounter has a literary focus, where the ability to quote aptly from a text and make significant deductions thereby is an important skill. On the other hand, I am of course aware that the writing of history or economics essays brings other things into play. In such work you will probably make less use of quotation as such: it will be more a question of citing sources, theories and known arguments.

In fact, most of the principles and guidelines I've outlined are relevant to all subjects, especially those on pages 151–3. It makes no real difference whether you're citing an actual quotation, acknowledging a source or referring to a particular theory: you need to be sure that

1   It's necessary and relevant.
2   It does some real work, moving your essay forward.
3   It's accurate and correctly set out.
4   You're not doing it too often.
5   It is not merely a time-wasting paraphrase.

3 Or to put it a different way, as Clive James has done: 'To believe Larkin really meant that "Books are a load of crap" you yourself have to believe that books are a load of crap. The arts pages are nowadays stiff with people who do believe that ... [and with] people reviewing books, even reviewing poetry, who can read only with difficulty, and begrudge the effort.' From his *2001 Postscript* to 'Four Essays on Philip Larkin', *Reliable Essays* (London: Picador, 2001), pp. 70–71.

This last point is especially important when referring to a well-known source or argument, and needs a paragraph of its own.

You must of course acknowledge major sources if mobilizing them in your own argument. But it is invariably a mistake to reproduce them in detail if they're seminal or even just renowned. Let us take two examples – Elton's work on the Tudors and Friedman's monetarist theories. Any competent historian will be fully conversant with the former, and any competent economist with the latter. You may therefore take such readers' knowledge for granted, and concentrate on showing how **your** knowledge of this work influences your own thinking. Reference to such sources can and should be crisp and brief: if you know what you're talking about, there is no need to prove it with a lot of laborious 'story telling', just as there's never any need in a literary essay to recite the plot.

The mechanics of citing references are fairly straightforward – more so than the rather intricate conventions affecting quotation. A reference, whether it be the name of a writer, a well-known theory or the title of a book, can be worked into your text within brackets, or as a footnote. However:

> **Be careful about footnotes. While they are a useful device and suggest scholarly devotion, too many of them can clutter up an essay and start to irritate the reader.**

If your essay is going to contain a lot of references – and you should be aware of this before you start writing – it is probably better to use a numbering system and collate all of them at the end of the essay. Alternatively, if your use of others' work is more general, functioning as overall influence rather than the detailed citing of specific points, you can just provide an extensive Bibliography of sources used.

As a summarizing piece of advice, remember that

> **It's *your* essay. The ability to provide illuminating references and apposite quotation is a valuable part of any good writer's armoury, but such things should always be ancillary to your work and thinking. To rely too frequently on others will seriously damage your impact, no matter how superficially learned it may make you seem.**

6 The strengths and limitations of 'argument'

In this brief closing section, all I want to do is emphasize the wisdom of Thomas Fuller's remark that forms an epigraph to this chapter: your essays are unlikely to cause a major change of mind in someone with firmly established views of his or her own. That is not to say you will never do so: I have found that one of the delights of being a teacher is that I constantly learn from my students; sometimes I have significantly changed my view or interpretation of a work in the light of their insights. But on the whole I would advise you to look on your essays as a pleasurable discourse rather than a battle for supremacy, as these two admirable remarks propose:

The aim of argument, or of discussion, should not be victory, but progress.
Joseph Joubert

True disputants are like true sportsmen; their whole delight is in the pursuit.
Alexander Pope

If you adopt such an attitude, you will find essays more fun to write; moreover, it will stop you from using embattled or aggressive language, which can often mar an otherwise impressive case. Consider this paragraph from an essay written by a sixteen-year-old girl:

To a much greater extent than most of us realize and any of us wish to believe, we have become 'programmed' like computing machines to handle incoming data according to prescribed instructions. Anyone who denies this is either naive or wilfully stupid; there is nothing more dangerous than the illusion of freedom, as Orwell demonstrated with such terrifying wisdom in 1984.

She is clearly intelligent, and her confident tackling of a huge subject inspires admiration. But her hectoring tone is a serious flaw. Her technique of labelling anyone who does not agree with her is a decrepitly stale rhetorical trick: the idea is that readers will not want to think themselves stupid, so will meekly go along with the proposed case. In all likelihood, however, they will instead resent this approach and dissociate themselves from the argument. In addition, she offers no 'proof': she just asserts. The use of Orwell is an arresting analogy, but is less effective than intended because no attempt is made to demonstrate that Orwell's vision was accurate.

The writer's youth makes it easy to forgive her tonal misjudgments, but they offer an important warning. If you really want to persuade people of your case, courtesy and dignity are crucial ingredients; readers will follow you much more readily if you treat them as likely friends rather than probable enemies. Don't make any concessions in your material and the points you believe in, naturally; but you can stay true to yourself without being aggressive.

Always argue as if you mean it, and by all means look to persuade people to your way of thinking – it is a good ambition to have even if it is not always realized. Perhaps your ideal response from your reader should be something on the lines of 'Yes, but . . .', signifying a committed interest in what you've said but a certain degree of respectful departure from it and the desire to discuss things further with you. That is a great compliment that should satisfy most writers. What you cannot afford is a reaction on the lines of 'No, and . . .'! You may feel you're in the right, you may even **be** in the right, but all you will have achieved to convince the reader that you match perfectly this definition:

Positive, adj. Mistaken at the top of one's voice.

Ambrose Bierce

[*]

Addendum 2001

We shall shortly move on to consider the essay's 'cousins' – the article, the review and the report. Yet so much has happened in and to education in the last decade that some up-dated comment and further advice are necessary. That is not to suggest any of the preceding material is now obsolete or of tenuous value: if I thought that, I'd have jettisoned or ruthlessly emended it.[4] But students are now tested more often and more stringently than ever before, and in an increasing variety of ways; there have also been signal alterations to the way syllabuses at 16+ and tertiary levels are designed, administered and assessed.

If interested in my views on all those matters and a detailed account of how they influenced the revision of this book, you are cordially referred to the new Preface. All I need say here is that since a student's working life is more complicated and demanding than when I wrote the first edition ten years ago (in addition to being examined more frequently they are, almost paradoxically, required to do more coursework than ever before) this pivotal chapter on **Essays** needs to address those changes. All the material which follows is newly written, and while there are times when it confirms points and principles explored above, it never merely duplicates them.

Coursework assignments: a checklist

Most students seem to regard *any* kind of non-timed assignment as preferable to a two-to-three hour examination. They aren't necessarily deluded in this belief: the great majority of my own students enjoy and prosper in their coursework, and although in all conscience a deal of nonsense is talked and written about 'the tyranny of exams', it can often be true that students do their very best work when able to take advantage of a more leisurely time scale.

---

4 You might be interested to learn that <u>emended</u> is not an editorial slip. A surprising number of highly educated people think, on encountering **emend**, that it is a misspelling of **amend**; in fact, the two words are equally authentic, denoting two separate things. **Amend** means (merely) *to change*; **emend** means *to improve*. This subtle but important distinction is also logged below in Chapter 22, 'Spelling and Confusibles', *Spelling List 2* (page 215).

However, the welcome absence of intense time-pressure does not mean you can afford to relax much. Non-exam assignments tend (rightly) to be marked more strictly; there is invariably a word limit that must not only be obeyed when it comes to the finished product but borne in mind from the earliest planning stages; recent years have seen the need for a bibliography, detailed footnotes and a summarizing abstract become similarly binding. In short, the requisite level of professionalism and thoroughness makes such assignments just as demanding in their own way as examination answers are in theirs – hence the detailed checklist provided below.

One thing before we start. In more than a few of the points which follow the verb 're-read' either appears or is strongly implicit, and it's important to be clear what I mean by that and what it involves for you. Nowadays programmes of study are so intensive and compressed that even the most dedicated student is going to find it very difficult to re-read in its entirety Middlemarch or something analogously hefty, whether the material be literary or otherwise. Besides, it isn't necessary. The last thing I would ever want to do is encourage laziness or skimpy work, but it's important to be

- **realistic**
  There may be a student or two out there who will gladly undertake a comprehensive re-consideration of source material, but it would be unwise to base any programme or advice on there being very many of them. Moreover, such remorseless diligence is not very . . .
- **practical.**
  The smart student knows how important it is to be energy-efficient and s/he will be aware that this re-reading time can be spent more profitably. No assignment on *Middlemarch* – or on Stalin, monetarism, the US Presidential system or anything comparably large – can be other than highly selective: you're going to be asked to consider these or those *aspects*, not the whole thing. That is what you should concentrate on when preparing your submission.[5]

On, then, to a stage-by-stage countdown. Your first task features some terminology that I don't like any more than you do; however, we're all stuck with such stuff for the time being and I'm afraid it matters.

1 Are you properly familiar with the *assessment criteria* for this assignment? Do you understand the *descriptors* and what they require you to do?
If you're in the least bit unsure about any of these things, check with your teacher at once, who may also be able to remind you of any particular 'weighting' that characterizes this or that criterion in the assignment at issue.

---

5 I am of course assuming that you have done the full *first* read of the material in question. If you haven't, doing even a decent job will be impossible.

2 Have you carefully re-read the relevant texts or material recently, with a fresh eye and mind?

You shouldn't begin to write if you haven't done this. It is clearly unwise to attempt an assignment with a knowledge-base that is stale or rusty. Moreover, re-considering your sources will re-invigorate your ideas, leading to new insights and/or 'angles'.

3 Have you selected a topic that truly interests you and that you can explore profitably? And is it relevant and clearly titled?

In an exam, of course, you cannot nominate your own titles: the most you can hope for is a choice of questions. But in all other circumstances your options are almost unlimited[6] – and that, like all things seductive, has pitfalls as well as pleasures. Do not pick something because you think it looks good or impressively 'different'; that's fine if it's really what you want to do, but if your heart isn't in it, you will do a progressively disappointing job. And make sure your title is precise and enables you to zero in on the material from the outset. Vagueness in coursework assignments is penalized even more stringently than in exam answers.

4 How many sessions is your assignment going to need?

Items 1–3 are essential preliminary checks; no less important is a sound sense of how much *time* writing the assignment is going to take. Unless you have unusual stamina or happen upon a remarkable burst of academic energy, you are unlikely to be able to wrap it all up in one go, and you may decide you'll need three sessions or more. On completion, you should then plan an *extra* session, preferably a day or so later. You may be very pleased with the finished product, but it is highly probable that you'll be tired by then – not the best state in which to do your final edit. Walking away from it and coming back refreshed will make you more efficient; it may also be that some profitable new ideas, or at any rate some better turns of phrase, will occur to you now.[7]

5 Is your essay effectively structured?

I've discussed this in some detail already. All I want to repeat here is that you need to decide whether you need an introduction (sometimes it's better to pitch straight in) and that your conclusion should be an invigorating finale, not just a re-iteration of points already logged. In addition, ensure that your argument progresses as clearly as possible. There is no need to spell things out on a cat-sat-on-the-mat basis – your reader expects to do some work – but what you're doing and where you're going should always be evident.

---

6 Partly to reduce opportunities for plagiarism, the International Baccalaureate insists on a centre's every candidate choosing a different title.

7 This is also the best time to devote yourself to matters of presentation. See above, **Interlude: Writing & Computers.**

6 Are your main ideas and points properly supported?

In a literary essay, that means the use of quotation and/or textual reference; in other subjects it involves allusion to data and evidence of whatever kind. You don't have to be obsessive about this: too much quotation or evidence-citing can harm the tempo of your work and also cause your own personality and mind to become damagingly nebulous. But you do need to show that you know what you're talking about, especially if the argument you are advancing is in any way contentious.

7 Have you consulted secondary sources?

This is permissible, naturally, and indeed often advisable. But all such sources must be *attributed*. These days any suspicion of plagiarism is ruthlessly investigated (in some programmes of study it can summarily cost you your diploma) and even if your 'crime' is laziness as opposed to theft, not to acknowledge authors you've used is a serious flaw.[8]

8 Is your essay properly *analytical* or merely *descriptive*?

The distinction is all the more crucial for being often difficult to spot when you're writing. You may think you're 'saying' something when all you're doing is trotting out things that your (expert) reader knows already. Whatever your subject

never just 'tell the story'

---

8 Quite apart from being amateurish at best and a felony at worst, plagiarism is often so *unnecessary* – i.e. the student has no need to fall back on others' work in such a tawdry fashion. To illustrate that, here's a true story – one which also, incidentally, draws attention to how those thrice-accursed Study Aid publications can infect the intelligent but pressured student.

A Lower Sixth former chose to write on Philip Larkin for his first official coursework essay. Bright and enthusiastic about Larkin though he was, he apparently couldn't trust his own ideas, his own prose, his own choice of poems or his response to them. Instead

He copied out, virtually word for word, an essay on Larkin that he'd found in a Study Aid.

When it came to be marked, the colleague assigned to the task recognized the essay and its source. It was amongst the better fare that Study Aids tend to produce, but that did not make any difference, of course: the assignment was declared 'void', the student felt humiliated, and a great deal of time – his in particular – had been used to no decent effect whatever.

Distressing and wasteful – except that he re-did the essay later (his own this time!) and all four of us who eventually marked/read it agreed that

It was better than the original 'cribbed' version.

It wasn't as stylish in some ways, maybe: after all, the student was only 17 and still learning, not a middle-aged critic who'd been churning out such stuff for ages. But it was fresh, sharp and above all *his* – a direct and incisive response to poems that had captured his imagination and intellect.

There's a lesson there for anybody tempted to plagiarize: it's not just moral considerations that make it a very poor strategy.

– be it the plot of a novel/play or in non-literary assignments anything that is common ground between you and the reader. All good academic essays deal primarily with what the reader *cannot* yet know – i.e. what's in your head and what *you* make of the material in question.

9 Are you within the word limit?
Nowhere to hide here. I have known students who think they can get away with exceeding the word-limit by 'forgetting' to provide a word-count or, worse, lying about it. Either course of action is simply an elaborate way to commit academic suicide.

While it is true that the examiner has yet to be born who will painstakingly compute the wordage of every essay s/he is sent, that tedious task isn't necessary: it is always obvious to even a newish examiner (let alone an experienced one) that an essay is too long, simply because of the time it is taking to read it! So

When it comes to word-limits, don't ever play games.

At best you'll be marked down; at worst the examiner will just stop reading at the stipulated point and assess your work on that basis alone. Since you're unlikely by then to have fashioned your case in any decisive way, your fate may be a grim one.

Those nine considerations should prove germane to most assignments, regardless of subject. Finally, two more that apply mainly to literary tasks, although the principles they address may prove useful for work in other disciplines too.

10 Does your essay reflect awareness of the time the works were written in?
Although this was always an interesting consideration and worthy of inclusion, nowadays it is more or less compulsory. You need to be aware of what the authors were trying to achieve in their works; if you're writing on drama, you need to show you're conversant with the theatrical conventions of the time. In addition, you must exercise both caution and imagination. There is, for example, limited value in using the term 'sexism' – a very recent coinage – when discussing the literature of Ancient Greece, the Renaissance or Victorian times; even if you argue well, the chances are you'll reveal more about your attitudes and those of contemporary society than illuminate the texts in question.

11 What if your assignment is a *comparison*?
Your planning here needs to be especially careful. It is all too easy for your essay to evolve into two separate mini-essays; while such work may contain much quality, it will inevitably lack the impact and insight that characterize a thorough exploration of similarities and differences. Conversely, you should avoid the 'tennis-rally' approach – one sentence on text A, one on text B, another on A, a second on B, so forth – which quickly becomes tedious for the reader and (more important still) often causes the writer to lose focus and a sense of the bigger picture. Sensible thinking beforehand should effect a good compromise, one where the works are treated both discretely and in tandem.

Chapter 11

Articles

This is a short chapter, because most of what you need to consider when writing an article has already been covered under **Essays**. An article is an essay, obviously enough; however, the circumstances in which it is written and a number of technical matters make it worth investigating as a genre in its own right.

Unlike the majority of essays, articles are written for publication. They are also different from essays in that the dimension of compulsion is absent. People who write articles do so because they want to, because they're being paid for it, or both. Naturally, once you've accepted a commission or decided that you want to write a piece for submission somewhere, the pressure to get on with it is considerable; nevertheless, the original choice is yours, not imposed on you by teachers or superiors. And the choice of subject and title is also yours, which should mean that some of the agony that attends essay writing – do I know what I'm talking about yet? Do I know what I want to say? – is also absent. If it makes little sense to begin an essay before you're sufficiently knowledgeable to deal with the subject at issue, it makes no sense at all to contemplate being published on something you're not yet competent on, and I can't imagine any would-be serious writer being that foolish.

So far, so very cheering: you want to write your article because the subject matters to you, you know plenty about it, and you want to share your views with a lot of readers. These are major positives, and together with the technical strengths that I hope the previous chapter has vouchsafed, they should ensure that you do an essentially sound and vigorous job. But there are one or two constraints or special considerations when engaged on an article that do not always apply to ordinary essays.

11.1 WORD LIMITS

I have yet to meet or hear of an editor for whom space is not a permanent problem. Any magazine that survives for even a few weeks will normally have more material 'in house' than it can currently use, and the stuff it does use is always under threat of being cut, sometimes savagely. You need to bear this in mind from the start, and act on it:

A **If the article has been commissioned, or if you're offering it to an editor you already know, establish the word limit before you do anything else.**

B **If you're planning to send it to an editor you don't know, try to determine the apparent standard length of the pieces published and use that as your target.**

And stick to it. You often risk being cut even if you obey the word limit originally proposed; if you exceed it, the risk is very high – and you might find that something very important to your argument disappears in the carnage.

Word limits can be maddening, but on the whole they work to the writer's advantage. The discipline they impose strengthens one's work: every sentence, every word even, has to be thought about with ruthless clarity: is it really necessary? Can it be said more economically? There are times, it's true, when to keep your piece within bounds an idea or an illustration that you like very much has to go, and that can be painful. More often, however, such strict attention will render your writing more muscular and easier to read – and that should increase your chances of being published.

11.2 HOUSE STYLE

There are two separate things you need to consider here.

A **The publication's mechanical conventions.**

Magazines and journals tend to have their own preferences as to layout, punctuation conventions, abbreviations and so on. Most of them provide their writers, actual or hopeful, with a sheet explaining all these things, and although getting to know them can be an intricate business, it is essentially trouble-free.

B **The tone and register of its written style.**

This is a subtler matter – and also more fundamental. Any successful periodical quickly develops a 'voice' – and that voice is intimately connected with the kind of reader it imagines it is speaking to and for. It is vital that you pay at least some attention to this. I've argued throughout that you should allow **your** voice to ring clearly through all your writing, and I'm not about to go back on that. But if writing for an established publication that has a clear sense of its market and readership, you must be sure that your style is reasonably appropriate. If you can't achieve this, or feel that the change is injurious to all that is most natural and effective in your writing, it's very likely that this particular publication is not for you, and that you need to seek out one with which you're more in tune.

In addition, take careful note of the favoured length of its sentences and paragraphs, and work to that approximate model. Also, work out how often sub-headings appear. You don't usually have to provide the latter – the editorial staff will do it for you. But to be aware of the frequency of such 'trailers' will help you to organize your material accordingly.

11.3 EDITING

It is always important to read your work through carefully, but the need to do so is intense when you've completed an article. It goes without saying that you must check everything fiercely – facts and mechanical accuracy – and make sure that your work is 'clean'. In addition, you now need to do a careful word count. I can virtually guarantee that it will not match the word limit you're been given, especially if you're a comparative newcomer! If you've gone over the limit (the more common flaw), you'll need to delete certain words or phrases – perhaps whole sections if you're wildly out; if you've fallen short, you can consider inserting ideas that you originally thought must be left out.[1]

Your edit will also be the time when you make final decisions about the number and length of your paragraphs, the quality and cohesion of your introduction and conclusion, and (if applicable) where you'd ideally like photographs or illustrations to be placed. In short, this is when you shape your work to perfection, paying equal attention to what you most want to achieve and the likely desires of editor and readers.

There is a particular kind of article that calls into play one or two additional considerations, so before I move on to the writing of Reports, I take a look at **Reviews.**

---

1 If you can't think of anything else to say, on no account fill out your piece for the sake of it: that is an unhappily certain recipe for the worst kind of **flab**. (See Chapter 7.)

Chapter 12

Reviews

A review is an essay that draws attention to and passes comment on a topical matter – the publication of a book, the release of a record, the opening of a stage play or film, and so on. Reviews are usually quite short, mainly because a sizable number of things need reviewing each week, and space is at a premium in all journals and newspapers. So even if you're given a generous word allowance for a review, you need to be as concise as possible.[1]

Any review must do these three things:

1 **Tell the reader broadly what the book/play/film/etc. is about and what it's like.**
2 **Give a clear sense of what the reviewer thinks of it.**
3 **Say whether it's worth spending money on.**

That seems straightforward enough, but a lot of reviews fail to do one or more of these things.

The worst kind of review is that which indulges a frenzy of self-advertisement on the reviewer's part, offering little or no information about what he or she is allegedly assessing. Hardly less bad, albeit more humble, is the reviewer who is either too scared to venture a clear opinion or not interested enough in the work to care about doing so. And there is an additional complication that can threaten the quality and integrity of even well-written reviews.

Quite simply, reviewing is an **industry**, and an ever-growing one. A single, non-specialist organ like *The Sunday Times* carries thirty pages of reviews every week, on everything from books to restaurants, cars to compact discs, holidays to TV programmes. The chances of any reader experiencing all these things is nil; consequently, the review can easily become a substitute for experience rather than an inducement to it. That is a large issue, and this book is not the place to explore

---

1 If being concise causes you problems [it does for all of us at times!], you may find it helpful to consult Chapter 15, Précis and Summary, where the skills involved in writing with maximum economy are analysed in detail.

'Give a clear idea of what the reviewer thinks of it'.

it fully. What I must say, however, is that because reviewing is an industry, it is not ultimately concerned with aesthetic judgments or anything so pure: at root, it is part of a commercial process, and every reviewer forgets that at his or her peril.

That is why 3 above is so important. I am lucky enough to review records and books regularly for monthly periodicals. Every time I write a review, I try to have uppermost in my mind that I received the goods free but that readers will have to shell out a lot of money for them – £10 and upwards for most compact discs, double that or more for a hardback book. Those are not negligible sums even for well-off readers; a reviewer who blithely recommends this, that and the other as 'essential' not only does readers a disservice by ignoring the cost involved, but as a result is likely to be guilty of inflated, unreliable judgments.

One last injunction: when reviewing something, be sure that you've taken full account of it. To put it more baldly: listen to **all** the record, read the **entire** book, stay for the **whole** of the show. The reviewing world is fairly well-populated by people who don't do this; this is not only immoral in its abuse of privilege (sorry to be pompous) but, more mercenarily, carries the high risk of being exposed as a lazy fool or a charlatan – the last stigma that any writer wants.

Chapter 13

Reports

Prelude 2001

In the 1993 edition, the chapter on Reports ran to just over three pages. That was not because I regarded the writing of reports a minor or straightforward activity: far from it. However, at the time I believed that 'most of what you need to consider when submitting a report is covered under Essays' and for all that there were 'a few additional points to make and others that need particular emphasis', I felt the task could be properly accomplished within that modest span.

I may have been wrong even then; be that as it may, there are three main reasons for the radical change of mind underscoring this major 2001 expansion. One was my NatWest engagements discussed in the Preface: virtually all the students I advised during seven successive courses thought report writing their most pressing requirement. Another is that the secondary students in a specifically academic environment need such skills far more than pertained ten years ago. Indeed, it is becoming apparent that they need them as much as or even more than they need the 'traditional' essay-writing skills addressed in Chapter 10. More than a few academic subjects no longer require students to submit 'standard' essays; the use of the bullet-point and such computer-generated conventions is as common as the paragraph.

A third is that the last decade has seen – in education and everywhere else – an obsession with tabulating information and reporting as often and as thoroughly as possible. As I've argued already, I am far from sure if this is a welcome development. In any organization of any kind, valuable things take place which cannot be measured, cannot be reported on; indeed, some of the most important are in effect invisible. The impulse towards 'accountability' (aka blame) refuses to recognize this: the prevailing orthodoxy is that if it isn't on paper it doesn't exist – and if it *is* on paper, it is by definition authoritative and binding. Beyond a certain point this is not only nonsense but pernicious, for it implicitly elevates propaganda to the level of absolute fact.

That can and will be debated: what is certain is that, like it or not, the various skills and issues of report writing are central to all writers regardless of their particular context and duties. I still adhere to that 1993 contention that most of the criteria you need to address when writing a report also characterize the writing of essays. But it is also clear to me that report writing is sufficiently different to warrant a much more detailed consideration than I originally gave it. That explains why this section is (a) the biggest single alteration to the original edition; (b) almost completely re-written; and (c) four times longer than its 1993 'parent'. All the original material is incorporated in what follows, and I begin now as I did then with matters of **attitude**.

Introduction

As noted in preceding pages, essay writing is a stressful business, especially early on in a student's career, and I've yet to encounter anyone who has not at some time regarded the activity with fear and dislike. Yet a great many come genuinely to enjoy it, deriving pleasure and profit from something that once inspired only anxious hostility. I have, however, met very few people who actively enjoy writing reports.

That is hardly astonishing. Even those who are good at writing reports tend to approach the task as a matter of duty, of 'taking care of business'; they may be quietly satisfied with the result, but little or no sense of fun is present. Others are more negative still: the most prevalent attitudes are those of The Cynic and The Sceptic. The Cynic's view may be typified thus:

> So 'few people actively enjoy writing reports', eh? Well, *there's* a surprise! Reports are by definition boring, to writer and reader alike, and a lot of them are simply unnecessary, better left in their original rain-forest form.

The Sceptic, less withering but also more troubled, might argue:

> Reports are essentially a matter of protocol. They are expected, traditional and must 'be seen to have been done'; even though we connive at such practice, it is invariably joyless and often futile.

Both views will doubtless have their supporters; all the same, they are equally dangerous. I will admit to a certain sympathy with The Cynic's words, but they clearly won't do. That dismissal – like a lot of cynicism – lays claim to a worldliness that is entirely bogus: it is instead shallow and counter-productive, and it is not hard to imagine what a poor job such an attitude will produce.

The Sceptic's case may be more reasonable, but it is characterized by a grudging indifference that can be just as damaging. If you need to write a report, the only safe attitude is to believe that it **does** matter and that you need to devote your best energies to it. The sad fact that a lot of reports are poorly written should never become an excuse for doing likewise; rather it should increase your determination to do an admirable job.

In pursuit of that goal, a degree of scepticism can nevertheless be very valuable, especially when addressing matters of **Length**, whether **Quality or Quantity** is more important and to what extent **Substance** and sheer **Effort** should dominate. If you are at all anxious about any of those, it may comfort you to learn that you are in good company: they are concerns regularly voiced by any number of practitioners. In the hope that my 'answers' will comfort you further, they are worth investigating at once.

Length

It does not seem to make any difference what reports are about or whether they run to five pages, fifty or three hundred: the unanimous feeling is that they are **invariably too long**. Now that may be a subjective judgment, but it implies an important lesson for **writers**. One can almost always reduce the wordage, however 'important' all the points addressed may be. Time is a major constraint, naturally; that said, even ten minutes' ruthless editing will prove beneficial.

Quality 'versus' quantity

Many feel that submissions are judged on sheer size rather than what they actually have to say. It is a feeling I've often experienced myself, and it is insidious. The good news is that it's almost certainly wrong: if they've got any sense at all, readers and bosses will always put intelligence before word-count. However . . .

Substance and effort as 'self-justifying strengths'

Sometimes the *public ideology* of a firm or institution runs counter to what everyone *privately* feels or wants. In the UK there is a publicly accepted belief that effort alone is a good thing and its own reward. That is not true: in fact, taken beyond a certain point it is rubbish. Quality should always be the main aim. Talent, including the ability to say what you want as clearly and concisely as possible, is always going to be superior to sheer slog. Needless to say, that does not mean that you should be lazy or uncaring about what you write: nothing of any value is achieved without effort and work.[1]

[*]

For all that they are related activities, there are two major differences between writing a report and writing an essay. I did not emphasize them sufficiently in the original edition, and it is to their thorough investigation that I devote the rest of this introduction.

---

1 'Hard work will always beat talent if talent doesn't work hard.' Ann Brentall, physiotherapist to Derbyshire County Cricket Club, pinned that maxim onto her office door, and there is a lot of truth in it.

Every essay argues a case that is unique. The tone can be cautious or unashamedly polemical, the substance can be well-worn or startlingly original, the effect can be anything from thrilling to enraging; essays are as various as the people that write them. Of course, the harsh fact remains that good essays persuade, or at least engage one's full attention and respect, whereas bad essays do none of those things and cause irritation or depression into the bargain; that means that amongst all else essays need to be well-informed and illuminating. Nevertheless, every essay is ultimately a personal testament – a rather grandiose definition, perhaps, but one which properly acknowledges the *subjectivity* of the genre.

Some of those observations could be applied to report writing too: an interesting report will always be superior to a tedious one, and there is no need for reporting to be utterly impersonal. But there is a decisive difference in **priorities**, of which the most pressing is that

the chief purpose of any report is to *inform*.

The genre covers anything from a few lines to thousands of pages. It makes no difference whether it's a brief comment from a subject teacher on a school report or a massive document collating the findings of a major public enquiry: a report is useful only insofar as it is illuminating. Above all things, therefore, you need to

present your information as clearly and concisely as you can.

That 'umbrella' principle governs all the individual points that follow in a moment. It may seem obvious advice by now (it has after all underscored this entire book) but it deserves renewed emphasis here. A report is often a highly technical and intricate document, and one can easily get so absorbed in its sophisticated subject matter that ordinary writing skills suffer, making life very uncomfortable for readers. And that leads me to the other important difference between writing an essay and composing a report.

All essayists' primary duty is to themselves. They seek to entertain, stimulate and persuade, yes, but they are unlikely to achieve any of that if their work does not first please *them*. That aspect of the Pleasure Principle does not apply to report writers. While nobody would suggest that they would ever be happy submitting work that *dis*pleased them, their paramount aim is to inform and satisfy their readers. In short, the matter of **audience and readership** is crucial. Many essays are written with no real knowledge of who the reader(s) will be.[2] In sharp

---

2 That does not, on the surface, apply to a student-essay set and marked by a particular teacher. Yet as I noted in the Essays section above (pp. 138) it is always bad practice for such a writer to kowtow to what s/he thinks that marker's tastes and prejudices may be. Not only are the chances of being wrong in such guesswork very high: slavish canvassing of that kind is likely to wrench the writer away from what s/he truly thinks and wants to say.

contrast, the majority of reports are written for a defined and known audience – which means that what I will term the **psychology** of writing a report is almost as important as its **substance**. As I now turn to specific issues and techniques, I have both concepts simultaneously in mind.

1   Where and how to start

This is no less a problem for the report writer than it is for the essayist: a blank piece of paper or PC screen is extremely intimidating, and the temptation is to get something logged as soon as you can. The trouble is that 'something' can easily mean 'anything' – which will be not only not much use but actively damaging, in that a poor start creates further problems as well. So your first tasks are to ensure that

1a   You know for whom you are writing and why
1b   You know what information you are going to use and present

It is always important to have a sense of your audience when writing, but especially so when fashioning a report. Are you writing for experts, for intelligent non-specialists, or beginners? You need to address that question – and its answer – in every sentence you write. Experienced and knowledgeable readers will quickly tire of having elementary points spelled out; conversely, an non-expert audience will soon become lost if you go too fast or fail to explain crucial things. There will also be times when your audience will be a mixture, describing a considerable range of knowledge, intelligence, opinion and so on. That is a very tricky matter, and I won't pretend I've got any easy or foolproof remedies. But you'll be far likelier to bring off even this delicate balance if you're firmly aware at all times of who's going to read what you've written.

Incidentally, if you have the chance to find out *when* and *where* your report will be read and/or discussed, do so. Is it likely to be item 9 on a twelve-point Agenda? Will it be considered early in the working day or towards the end of a hot afternoon? For whatever reasons, is the report likely to be welcomed or resisted? These questions cannot always be answered, but just considering them will increase your sense of psychological context and thus sharpen your impact.

When it comes to *what* to write, you will need to do some preliminary thinking about what is essential, what is secondary and what is marginal. You may decide to include all those items, but some idea of what can be side-lined or included in an Appendix will be useful; while the process may not involve much writing as such, it will clarify your mind, and without that you are unlikely to achieve clarity of presentation and argument. And then . . .

1c   It is probably best to start with your new information

A great number of reports form part of a sequence: it is quite likely that the one you're writing is amongst all else an 'up-dating' exercise. The temptation is to begin with a resumé, a careful chronological review of previous work or thinking; although this is an understandable and apparently logical strategy, I would say it's tactically weak on two counts. First, and crudely, you risk boring those readers who are thoroughly familiar with 'the story so far'; to make their first experience one of tedium is not a good idea.

Second, such an approach does not allow *you* to enter into it all that obviously. It's your report: it's therefore a mistake to spend its vital first pages operating as a largely anonymous scribe. And there is a positive counterpart to those two negative reasons: to start with new information gives your report immediate impact and personality. So now you should be properly aware of three vital things – your audience, your core material and your starting point. The next step is to

2 Make an overall plan

Some people scoff at this – 'Why waste time planning what you know you're going to do anyway?' But they are usually wrong: non-planners waste more time than they save, through mental blockages and sudden crises of sequencing and structure.

It's entirely up to the individual how the plan is done and what it looks like at the end. The only person who needs to understand it is you, so use whatever methods you like – shorthand, 'spidergrams', index cards etc. But make sure it's as comprehensive as possible: go through your notes and double-check that everything you want or need to include is there in some form, if only implicitly.

A decent plan, let alone a good one, accomplishes two things. One, it dramatizes your decision about the ordering of the main sections and the individual points within them; two, doing it refreshes your memory about all the details you're going to be concerned with, so that you are indeed 'fresh' and ready to write. Before you do, however . . .

3 Make – and discuss – a synopsis

Interestingly, I've never done this for any lecture I've given, nor do I normally advise my students to include it in their preparation of essays.[3] But I propose it here because a report is invariably a public document whose readership is going to be *plural*; it therefore makes sense to furnish and talk over your projected ideas with others, especially as they may well be part of the readership.

Making the synopsis is straightforward. You simply write out your plan, being careful this time that all 'codes' and abbreviations are fully and clearly explained. Then ask some colleagues and friends to look over and comment on it, with this mandatory proviso:

You must encourage absolute honesty in them.

The whole exercise is rendered useless if these readers feel they can make no criticisms beyond the most cosmetic. Of course, if the plan really *is* a masterpiece, then it's always nice to hear as much! But such a likelihood at this early stage in

---

3 It could be valuable in those fields, and I intend to adopt it.

the composition is virtually zero, however able you are. So make sure they are as tough as you need them to be – especially in the matter of clarity. One of the most subtle traps in writing is to confuse what you *think* you've said with what you've *actually ended up saying*. A quick synopsis-critique of this kind will probably ensure that you avoid that trap later.

If possible, contact your manager or whoever commissioned the report and ask him/her to peruse your synopsis. This will reassure you both: the manager will see that work is progressing and that you're being suitably conscientious in the way you're going about things; you will feel good that s/he is impressed, and it is most unlikely that you will leave such a meeting without further valuable advice and clarification.

4 Draft the text

This is the fourth of seven stages: in other words, you are over half-way through the task as a whole, and only now are you embarking on substantial writing. I stress this point because too many writers – whether of reports, essays, articles or occasionally (God help us) *books* – start writing before they're properly ready. You can't write well unless you are clear about what you think and what you want to say; that's why the planning and discussion sessions outlined above are so important.

Let me also emphasize something I too often disobey myself:

Don't be too perfectionist too early.

Wanting to get things right is an estimable professional quality, but in writing there's a time for worrying at the exact choice of word or the nuance of punctuation required, and during the first draft isn't it. Get as much down as you can, as fluently as you can, and above all with damage-proof basic clarity. Once that is in place, the stylistic improvements and precise adjustments will follow much more easily: indeed, they will come naturally and be much more pleasurable.

The mention of style leads me to four interlocking considerations.

4a Do you really *need* jargon? Will 'plain English' do?

A great many reports address technical or specialized matters, and it's inevitable that some of the language used will reflect that. You need to be careful, however. As always, remember who your audience is, and be prepared to explain technical terms and other jargon. If writing for experts, don't be any less watchful: frequent jargon is tiresome even for readers who fully understand it. As much of your prose as possible should be 'en clair': readers forced to decode every second sentence will rapidly become tired and fed up. Conversely, however . . .

4b Try to avoid chattiness and trendiness

The admirable desire to keep jargon to a minimum can lead the writer astray in an opposite direction. Nobody wants you to be boring or pompous, but slang and conversational idiom are rarely appropriate to a report. Above all exclude trendy phrases: they are often as impenetrable to the 'outsider' as the severest jargon, and they tend to make the writer look like a show-off.

4c Be especially diligent about accuracy and pleasing lay-out
Self-evident – yet many reports do not take enough trouble over such basic matters. Good reports are always dignified, and errors in spelling and presentation seriously undermine dignity. Arrange your sections, sub-sections and paragraphs with the reader's flow and convenience chiefly in mind. If a particular section is long and involved, it is both profitable and courteous to provide a short summary.

4d There is no need to be wooden or anonymous
I've just suggested avoiding both excessive jargon and over-familiarity, and that may seem to restrict your range a great deal. In fact, you have plenty of scope left. Like a successful essay or article, a good report will be a subtle blend of the soundly impersonal and the stimulatingly personal. Yes, it must be clear and logical, professional in its knowledge and dignified in its deployment of material; on the other hand, it needs a discernible **voice**, some kind of individuality. Nothing is more tedious than an extended piece of prose that appears to have been written by a robot – the reading equivalent of a telephone answering machine.

5 Walk away
This next stage is another aspect of planning and time-management, all the more important for being often ignored. You want to allow yourself enough time before submission is due to leave your draft alone – overnight or, preferably, for a day or so. There are two main reasons for this.

The first hinges on **fatigue.** By the time you've finished that first draft, you will be pretty tired; if the text is at all hefty, you'll be *very* tired. You're not going to be in optimum condition when you read it over, and although it is inevitable that you *will* read it over then, if only to look for mistakes and typos, you also need to re-appraise it when fresh – ideally after a good sleep and when you're healthily fed and watered.

A major fringe benefit comes into play if you wait for the 'real' reread in this way. Towards the end of your draft – just as can attend the end of any concentrated session of writing or study – you may have experienced blockages, the frustrating search for the right word or phrase, and so on. When you return, it is highly probable that these will come to you quickly and naturally; subconsciously the brain will have been chewing things over while you're 'away from it all'. This is a nice development anyway; moreover, it gives you a significant confidence boost right at the outset of your final editing session, which in turn will sharpen you up and give you added energy for the task.

The second reason returns me to that distinction between what you think you've said and what your words actually say. When you return, you will have forgotten the precise circumstances of the piece's composition – i.e. what exactly was going through your head, what you were aiming for and so on; instead, you will in effect be reading it as another person, not the absorbed creator of the day before. That may cause you some embarrassment, but such a *critical* response is crucial to the penultimate stage . . .

6 The final edit
This is best done in stages.

- First, look for any and all errors; doubtful spellings; sloppy, imprecise or irritating punctuation (including its absence); facts and names which need checking.
- Next, read it as critically as possible, especially those bits that trouble you or don't seem quite right yet. [By now you will be well aware which they are.] Think these through before picking up the pen or hitting the keyboard: a little reflection is superior to immediate feverish composition. As always, when in doubt go for clarity – which normally means simplicity rather than sophistication.
- Last of all, peruse it again, with two governing questions in mind:

> **Is the style accurate, readable and consistent?**
> **Is the report structured to your liking?**

If you've followed the above strategies, the chances are high that the answer to both will be a pleasingly firm 'yes' and that your report will be a very good one – concise, clear and above all suitably informative.
Finally:

7 Compile a single-sheet summary of your major points, and affix it to the front
This is good public relations: it eases the reader into the task, providing a clear and welcome map for what may be a very substantial journey. You benefit also: composing the summary will automatically involve you in a close check of the material and its organization, and you may well find you can improve them.[4]

Conclusion

Writing reports need not be drudgery. Within the limits outlined, stay natural as well as properly alert, and you should find that your prose is crisp, appropriate and quite pleasurable to write. If you still think report writing and fun are irreconcilable opposites, have a look at the list below, adapted slightly from a piece that appeared a few years ago in *The New York Sunday Times*. It is both valuably instructive and

---

4 Incidentally, this practice is an intriguing variant of the idea discussed in Essays – the value of writing your introduction **last.**

genuinely entertaining – a combination that characterizes the ideal report. After that there is a final exercise which you might also find diverting.

REPORT WRITING
Some Rules of Grammar

1 Remember to never split an infinitive.
2 The passive voice should never be used.
3 Punctuate run-on sentences properly they are hard to read otherwise.
4 Don't use no double negatives.
5 Use the semi-colon properly, always use it where it is appropriate; and never where it isn't.
6 Reserve the apostrophe for it's proper use and omit it when its not needed.
7 Verbs has to agree with their subjects.
8 No sentence fragments.
9 Proofread carefully to see if you any words out.
10 Avoid commas, that are not necessary.
11 If you reread your work, you will find on rereading that a lot of repetition can be avoided by rereading and editing.
12 A writer must not shift your point of view.
13 Give slang the elbow.
14 Conversely, it is incumbent upon us to avoid archaisms.
15 Don't overuse exclamation marks!!!!
16 Place pronouns as close as possible, especially in long sentences, as of 10 words or more, to their antecedents.
17 Hyphenate between sy-llables; avoid un-necessary hyphens.
18 Write all adverbial forms correct.
19 Writing carefully: dangling participles must be avoided.
20 Steer clear of incorrect forms of verbs that have snuck in the language.
21 Take the bull by the hand: always pick on the correct idiom and avoid mixed metaphors.
22 Avoid trendy locutions that sound flaky.
23 Never, ever use repetitive redundancies.
24 Everyone should be careful to use a singular pronoun with singular nouns in their writing.
25 If I've told you once, I've told you a thousand times, resist hyperbole.
26 Also, avoid awkward or affected alliteration.
27 Don't string together too many prepositional phrases unless you are walking through the valley of the shadow of death.
28 ""Avoid overuse of quotation marks.""""
29 For Christ's sake don't offend your readers' sensibilities.
30 Last but not least, avoid cliches like the plague; seek viable alternatives.

Adapted from The New York Sunday Times

Afterword: specialist reporting and composing instructions

I have not attempted to offer advice on scientific or technological writing. That is partly because I believe good writing is good writing is good writing; it is often a mistake to imagine that a particular subject requires a wholly different style, approach and set of 'rules'. But it's also because I have done very little such work myself, and advice on those specific considerations that are important would be presumptuous. There are several relevant books cited in my Bibliography; here I would like especially to recommend *Effective Writing* by Christopher Turk and John Kirkman – and not just because we are all published by the same firm! It is comprehensive, practical and authoritative, and its elegant prose is a model embodiment of what it encourages. As a sample of its quality, and as a final exercise, look overleaf at the 'compendium of ambiguities' they assemble on advice that might be offered to a learner driver.

I am particularly grateful to the authors for granting permission to reprint this passage, because it dramatizes just how difficult it is to compose foolproof instructions.[5] Such a task is a special *kind* of report writing, and the exercise is therefore an illuminating way in which to end this section, as well as I hope an amusing and beneficial one. You should know that the authors indicated that the results were 'not all from one writer', and they also left it to their readers 'to work out in how many ways these instructions can be misunderstood'. I have not done that: as before, I offer a few introductory pointers and afterwards my own observations, which you might like to compare with your findings.

Exercise 27

What is wrong here? In how many ways could these instructions be misunderstood? Be as picky and exhaustive as you can, and in addition to the shortcomings of the fourteen items listed, how many important considerations can you think of which *aren't* mentioned or even implicit?

Instructions For Driving A Car*
1   Sit behind the steering wheel.
2   Adjust mirror for best rear view.
3   Ensure handbrake is on.
4   Put gear lever into neutral.
5   Pull choke knob right out.

---

5   It bears more than a passing resemblance to the very first passage in this book, which centres on baby-feeding; see page 3.

6 Turn key to right.
7 Rotate engine until it fires.
8 Depress accelerator until engine can be heard running fast.
9 Select first gear.
10 Allow clutch pedal to gently rise while depressing accelerator still further.
11 Take off handbrake.
12 Wink in the direction you are going.
13 Grip steering wheel at ten to two.
14 If you need to brake read the following instructions . . .

> *From *Effective Writing*, Turk and Kirkman (E & FN Spon, 1989).
> Reproduced with permission from Taylor & Francis.

Analysis and comment

Although I trust you found this exercise an entertaining experience, it may also have proved a salutary one. Writing even the most elementary instructions is strewn with pitfalls; indeed, some might say it is the fiercest task that can confront any writer, especially if catering for the absolute beginner, which I assume to be the case here. Your writing needs to be spotlessly clear; you cannot afford the remotest ambiguity or anything that might confuse; above all you must take nothing for granted, nothing at all. It is an unremitting task, and it is perhaps unsurprising so many instructions are flawed.[6]

My observations follow the chronology of the original instructions, and they begin with two items that should have been there but aren't:

- Might it be a good idea to say something about how to get into the car?

and

- Why is the binding legal requirement to engage the seat-belt not mentioned?

---

6 Sometimes tragically so. In *Effective Writing* Turk & Kirkman furnish this grim instance:

> An aircraft fitter was instructed, during an undercarriage overhaul, to:
>
>> 'Check undercarriage locking pin. If bent, replace.'
>
> He took out the pin and examined it. It was indeed bent, so he carefully put it back into the mechanism. The aircraft subsequently crashed.

As the authors then point out, the (fatal) problem here is that **replace** can mean *either* 'put back' *or* 'substitute with a new one'; the latter was of course what was required. The subsequent disaster wasn't the fitter's fault but that of whoever wrote the manual he was dependent upon.

An inauspicious start; things get worse.

I'll pass item 1, despite the diverting picture that comes into my mind of the bemused learner sitting in the back seat or attempting to get between the steering wheel and the windscreen. But 2 is damagingly incomplete: 'best rear view' of *what*? The back-seat passengers? The two girls currently walking down the pavement? You may think I'm just being facetious, but to repeat: when instructing the uninitiated, nothing can be left to chance or taken for granted, however pedantic the requisite spelling-out may seem.

Item 3 is fair enough – except that it appears too late: if the handbrake were to be *off*, there's a fair chance that the momentum caused by two people getting into the car would cause it to move forward, freewheeling into the car in front or the open road. Number 4 looks all right, but it is a technical term, however rudimentary: the student might not understand it or (more probably) not know how to accomplish the manoeuvre.

Number 5 manages to be both arcane and hilarious. The action in question is becoming increasingly obsolete: cars built in recent years invariably sport an automatic choke and therefore do not have a 'choke knob'. That said, the prospect of our learner pulling the object 'right out' – i.e. divorcing it completely from the dashboard – is beguiling in its vandalistic way! Number 6 suffers from the fact that no mention has yet been made of inserting the 'key' into the ignition-slot – a vital and by no means simple manoeuvre which needs full and early explanation.

Item 7 is awful. Puzzling even to experienced car-users, it would simply bewilder a newcomer. The phrase is ridiculously antiquated anyway, taking us back to the days of vintage cars, which could only be started via an external crank-handle. (Who knows, our learner might imagine that's what needs to be done now!) And while 8 seems okay, I have two criticisms: it should be clearly 'accelerator' is[7], and the 'running fast' bit will become dangerously problematic if and when the driver executes stage 10.

Number 9 is seriously deficient. I still remember what my very first attempts at gear-selection were like, even though I'd been carefully instructed in the use of the clutch. There is no mention of that device here, and the mind boggles as to what the learner will get up to as a result. In the same way, 10 is almost absurdly cavalier in its opening command. Clutch-control is the trickiest driving skill of the lot, and almost every driver will cite it as the one s/he mastered last of all. Moreover, 10's second command is dicey in the extreme: thanks chiefly to the manoeuvre stipulated in 8, the engine is by now simply roaring away, and when the learner carries out 11, the car will shoot off at something like 30 mph.

The last three instructions are deliciously comic: the farcical potential of 12 and 13 needs no comment from me, and neither does the gloriously incompetent

---

7 There are after all three pedals, in close proximity to each other, and many new drivers hit the wrong one at some time or another. Knowing from the outset which is which is a fundamental requirement and should be properly explained at once.

14. Yet without wishing to get too solemn about it, they would all endanger life and limb if obeyed literally, especially the last one; in addition, there is no mention of checking the driver's 'blind spot' behind and to the right or indeed of checking whether the road is clear. Come to that, there is no reference to 'cautiously pulling out into traffic' or any kind of advice about how the learner should now perform that titular phrase – actually *driving the car.* It is a dismally appropriate way in which to end a set of instructions that has 'criminal nightmare written all over it!

Chapter 14

Minutes

The taking and writing of minutes is required in a limited number of situations. It is, however, a very precise skill which can demand a different format and style of writing from normal reporting and where different criteria operate.

Companies and organizations tend to have their own preferred style of minuting meetings which should be observed. Most will follow a general pattern. A meeting will be announced by an agenda giving the date, time and venue of the meeting and listing the items to be dealt with. Usually these will formally include the reading and agreeing of the previous meeting's minutes, plus dealing with matters arising from these minutes prior to any new business. Items should be numbered for convenience, the final item being any other business which allows late items to be introduced. The chairman of the meeting will normally follow the order of the agenda for his own convenience, and this will help the minuting considerably.

The depth and detail required in the minutes will depend on the style of the company. Many will wish simply to minute final decisions taken or the major points raised; some situations demand that more detailed notes are kept to record the views of individuals present. On occasion, you could be asked to record a specific point which someone wishes to stress, and this should be given verbatim.

Tone and style are also a matter of taste and choice. The apparent cold formality of minutes can be extremely useful, in that it allows all emotion and personality to be excluded from the record. This means that the minutes will present a sober, impartial report of the meeting, which leaves out arguments and personal attacks which can occur over sensitive issues. While there are times when people insist on having their views recorded, the cooling-off period between meetings often resolves differences, and it can be with a sense of relief that participants re-read minutes that give no hint of a previous battle!

Obviously, specific dates and details need to be given, but many minutes will give the bare bones of a meeting. The actual style and vocabulary used is also formalized, and always written in the third person and in the passive voice – e.g.

The decision to re-appoint the caretaker was agreed unanimously.
The Chairman suggested that a vote be taken.

A further extended example follows on page 183, together with the complementary agenda.

To be able to write accurate minutes that satisfy all parties is a valuable skill. It is also an intriguing one: you may have noticed that several of the techniques and procedures I've just outlined depart radically from most of the advice given elsewhere. (That advice stands, naturally!) You may also have noticed that my own style in this chapter has been rather more formal and impersonal than usual. That was a deliberate attempt to match form and content, for minuting is one of the very few times when the writer seeks to be anonymous. Another such occasion, the writing of a précis or summary, is explored next.

Example A

Smith and Jenkins plc
46th meeting of the Finance and General Purposes Committee to be held
on Friday 15 May at 11.30 a.m. at Head Office.

Agenda

1   Apologies for absence.
2   Approval of the Minutes of 45th Meeting held on 19 February.
3   Matters Arising from the Minutes of 45th Meeting.
4   Budget forecast. Paper to be tabled.*
5   Departmental reports and requests for funding:
    (a) Accounts Dept.
    (b) Sales Dept.
    (c) Transport Dept.
    (d) Administration Dept.
6   Chairman's Report.
7   Annual staff outing.
8   Any other business.
9   Date for next meeting.

JS/PR
2.5.90

*This would be balance sheets of the current state of business and projected figures.

Example B

> Extracts from the Minutes
>
> 1 Apologies were received from D. Brown and H. Chilcott.
> 2 The minutes of the 45th Meeting were agreed as a true record and signed by the Chairman.
> 3 [44.3.1] Salary Increases. R. Thomas (Transport) wished to know whether his Department's request for a 90% annual increase had yet been approved. The Financial Director, P. Jenkins, reported through the Chair that this oversight had been dealt with and that the increased figures were reflected in the paper to be tabled at Point 4 on the Agenda.
> 4 Budget Forecast.
> The Financial Director tabled a paper detailing the current state of business and giving outline forecasts for the coming year. He pointed out that in view of the drop in sales figures, it would not be possible to pay an increased dividend to shareholders in this quarter . . .

It is I hope unnecessary to go on. A complete example would illustrate little not already evident in this extract; nor would it add much to your entertainment, since reading minutes is hardly dangerously exciting! That of course is their strength and very function: important points and issues are logged in a neutral, low-key fashion.

Chapter 15

Précis and summary

In the 'bad old days', précis was a major and compulsory part of all O Level English Language examinations, accounting for about 20% of the overall mark. During the 1970s précis ceased to be a mandatory O Level exercise, a change upheld with the advent of GCSE. That was a cause for regret. In the main, those latterday changes in O Level were for the best, and for a while GCSE proved an exciting and imaginative replacement, allowing pupils and their teachers much greater scope. Far from slipping, standards in my judgment rose, and there is little doubt that English work at 16+ was much more enjoyable, both to teach and learn.

As anyone who has so much as glanced at my new Preface will be aware, I no longer hold that view of GCSE English, whose rapid decline since the mid- 1990s has dismayed so many. However, it is not quite all dross. There has been one development that I welcome unreservedly: the restoration of Summary as a mandatory exercise. For I would say that the ability to précis is **the** central language skill. For a start, it is a craft essential in all professions and businesses; indeed, anyone whose work includes dealing with documents at some time (and that accounts for most people) will need précis skills as a matter of course, or live to regret their absence.

Such vocational considerations, though important, are not in my view the most telling, however. The fundamental value of précis is that **it tests and exercises every aspect of linguistic competence**. To write an accomplished précis you need to have mastered eight major skills.

1 Good comprehension
To reduce a long document to its essentials requires a sound understanding of its every point and sentence. This is often more demanding [and therefore more reliable as a gauge] than any standard comprehension exercise.

2 Good prose composition
A précis should be crisp and easy to read. To achieve such at-a-glance clarity you need a muscular style, where everything is pertinent and works efficiently.

3 Discerning judgment

The prime task of précis writing is to distinguish what is really important from what is merely interesting or decorative. Regularly to achieve that requires sensitivity and discrimination.

4 An authoritative vocabulary

Although you must never invent **material** when fashioning a précis, it is entirely in order to recast ideas in your own words. In fact this is often essential, enabling you to cut down a structure of say 15 words to 5 or 6. To do that you need a vocabulary both broad and precise, supple and vigorous.

5 Literary feel

Contrary to certain prejudices, there is nothing 'airy-fairy' about good literature. Indeed, the best literature is always formidably exact; no matter how large or complex their goals, great writers are masters of nuance and precision. All good précis writers have something of such qualities; the chances are they acquired them through literary study.

6 A fierce eye for flab

Précis is a ruthless business! In most academic précis tasks, you are given an exact and mandatory word limit; in a very real sense, every word counts. And even if you are not constrained by such numerical targets, you still need to be vulture-like in your ability to tear at sentences and reduce them to their bare bones. This is

'Vulture-like in your ability to . . .'

closely analogous to the 'keyword' noting system I have described elsewhere, enabling you to 'gut' a chapter or an entire book,[1] and is a most valuable skill whatever your walk of life.

7 Sound logic
No matter how ruthlessly abridged, a précis has to make sense in its own right. This calls upon clarity of thinking and alertness to the distinct stages of an argument.

Finally, and obviously:

8 Accurate mechanical and grammatical English
This hardly requires a comment! Every task involving the use of English needs to be mechanically correct. None more so than précis, nevertheless: you can sabotage all the above strengths if you misspell, punctuate badly and perpetrate poor or clumsy grammar. Besides, if those things **do** disfigure your work, it's over-whelmingly probable that you will possess few if any of the seven skills just outlined, because each one depends on a sound knowledge of how language works and how it should be used.

Given that précis is a centrally important skill, how do you go about it successfully?

Well, précis is as much an art as a science, in that success depends more upon practice than upon the learning of fixed principles and guidelines, valuable though the latter can be. So let us start with an example.

> Gardeners are very frequently asked by persons interested in the cultivation of ornamental trees and shrubs to indicate to them some of the distinctive characters which mark off the common cypress from its near relative, the American *arbor-vitae*. These are two of the most widely grown ornamental conifers in the British Isles, and there is hardly a garden or park of any size in which one or other is not present.
>
> It is not an easy matter under ordinary circumstances to indicate to the layman the differences that exist between these two species.[2]

This passage is pleasantly written: few would accuse it of flabbiness or tedium. But while it is already tolerably concise, it can be further reduced. Let us look at it phrase by phrase.

> 1 **Gardeners are very frequently asked . . .** 'Very' does no real work and can safely be omitted. Perhaps, too, the simpler 'often' might replace 'frequently'.

1 In *Brain Train* (1996) E & FN Spon, London, pp. 104–12.
2 For the provision of this extract, I am indebted to Walter Shawcross, *English For Professional Examinations* (London, Pitman, 1947), p. 75. The analysis which follows is my own.

2   **By persons interested in the cultivation of ornamental trees and shrubs**
. . . Fair enough – except that gardeners are unlikely to be asked anything
by persons not thus interested! So if economy is the main criterion, the
whole phrase can be jettisoned.

3   **To indicate to them some of the distinctive characters which mark off
the common cypress from its near relative, the American *arbor-vitae***
. . . 'To them' has to go anyway, because we've omitted Phrase 2.
Everything else that precedes 'the common cypress' can be rendered by
the infinitive 'to distinguish between'; in addition the term 'its near
relative' can go, as it's a mere supplementary descriptor.

The amended phrase thus reads: **To distinguish between the common cypress
and the American *arbor-vitae*.**

4   **These are two of the most widely grown ornamental conifers in the
British Isles** . . . The first two words can be omitted, provided a comma
is placed after the preceding '*arbor-vitae*' instead of a full stop. In addition
'widely grown' can be replaced by the single word 'popular'.

5   **There is hardly a garden or park of any size in which one or other is
not present** . . . 'Of any size' is weak; 'or other' is similarly inessential.
And if you are feeling really ruthless – and I propose to be! – you could
argue that this whole sentence is more or less implied by the word
'popular' that I've just suggested. So we can get rid of all of it.

6   **It is not an easy matter under ordinary circumstances to indicate to
the layman the differences that exist between the two species.** Because
Phrase 5 has disappeared completely, you can render this simply by 'This
is not easy.'

The full précis thus reads:

> **Gardeners are often asked to distinguish between the common cypress and
> the American *arbor-vitae*, two of the most popular ornamental shrubs in
> the British Isles. This is not easy.**

An original total of 93 words has become 30. To be sure, some elegance, subtlety
and sheer information have been sacrificed; but the new version is a clear expression
of the salient 'bones' of the passage, and that is what any précis seeks to achieve.

That passage was quite well-written in the first place, which paradoxically made
it relatively **easy** to précis. The sentences flowed clearly and built into an
'argument' that was comfortable to follow; to dismantle them in the interests of
ruthless economy was therefore a straightforward business.

But sometimes you will have to précis material that is difficult to disentangle,
where you'll have to work really hard just to understand what the main argument

might be. Study this next passage carefully: I've used it before [p. 77–8], but on this occasion I want you just to work out what you think it means. Try to identify the key phrases that form the cornerstones of the argument:

> In the affluent society, capitalism comes into its own. The two main-springs of its dynamic – the escalation of commodity production and productive exploitation – join and permeate all dimensions of private and public existence. The available material and intellectual resources (the potential of liberation) have so much outgrown the established institutions that only the systematic increase in waste, destruction and management keeps the system going. The opposition which escapes suppression by the police, the courts, the representatives of the people, and the people themselves, finds expression in the diffused rebellion among the youth and the intelligentsia, and in the daily struggle of the persecuted minorities. The armed class struggle is waged outside: by the wretched of the earth who fight the affluent monster.

As I pointed out before, the writing here is jargonesque and top-heavily abstract, making it very difficult to identify those 'key phrases', because one is rarely sure what they actually mean! However, after (at least) two careful readings, you might come up with a list something like mine:

1   **affluent society**   An old 'buzz' term, now stale, that refers to any industrialized nation, the writer's prime focus.
2   **capitalism; commodity production** and **productive exploitation**   Capitalism is his main target; the other two phrases mean, roughly, 'the manufacture of goods' and 'the ruthless consumption of labour and resources'.
3   **all dimensions of public and private existence**   Stresses that capitalism dominates our lives in every way.
4   **available resources/have outgrown institutions**   To be candid, I still don't really know what this means: the entire sentence is an opaque mess. The suggestion seems to be that capitalism makes very poor use of the potential at its disposal, mainly because (as is implied later) its governments wish to retain power.
5   **increase in waste/destruction/management keeps system going**   See my comments for Phrase 4. The idea (I think) is that the status quo preserves itself by purely negative methods, leading to . . .
6   **opposition/suppression/diffused rebellion**   . . . direct or indirect suppression. Opposition is either tyrannically put down by state machinery or ignored because it is ineffectual.
7   **struggle: wretched of the earth versus affluent monster**   The one vibrant moment in the whole piece, graphically reducing the conflict to its ultimate alternatives.

That took me a long time, both to think out and to type, which annoyed me. Nobody minds fruitful hard work: what irritated me here was that the original seems **designed** to confuse or intimidate. However, any précis writer will eventually encounter similarly poor originals, and at least that laborious 'gutting' gives us a clearer sense of what the passage is centrally about.

The next task is to 'translate' those key phrases into fluent and comprehensible English.

Phrases 1–3 present no real problem. I suggest:

> **Capitalism, the systematic consumer of all resources, dominates affluent society at every level.**

One could omit 'all' and 'at every level'; I've included them in an attempt to retain the categorical tone of the original.

Phrases 4, 5 and 6 are murderously difficult, as already noted! The core of their argument seems to be that capitalism is by turns inefficient, deliberately destructive and tyrannical, and that its primary concern is to keep the system going for the benefit of 'the haves'. So I suggest:

> **Fundamentally wasteful and tyrannical, it enlarges the range and intensity of its influence, destroying or emasculating most potential rebels.**

This takes considerable liberties, maybe; but I do not think it distorts the original's thrust or tone, and it covers all the main ideas.

Phrase 7 is blissfully easy in comparison. It makes sense to retain the powerful 'the wretched of the earth'; 'the affluent monster' is perhaps also worth preserving. However, I suggest replacing the full stop after 'rebels' with a comma, and continuing: . . . 'leaving only the wretched of the earth to fight it.'

I've sacrificed 'affluent monster' in the interests of a simple and punchy structure, but it can be reinstated if that is your taste.

The complete précis thus reads:

> **Capitalism, the systematic consumer of all resources, dominates affluent society at every level. Fundamentally wasteful and tyrannical, it enlarges the range and intensity of its influence, destroying or emasculating most potential rebels, leaving only the wretched of the earth to fight it.**

That is 42 words; the original had 120.

Incidentally, my earlier version [on page 78] was just 33 words. On that occasion I wanted to effect a working **paraphrase** that quickly revealed the original's overall meaning. Précis, as the word itself signals, requires more **precision** than paraphrase, so here I realized that one or two extra points or ideas had to be included. Remember: précis almost always involves paraphrase, but the two are not synonymous.

Now that we've thoroughly explored two very different examples, we can begin to identify some of the principles and guidelines that inform précis writing.

1 Read the original very carefully.

If it needs two readings, give it two. You should not even start to think in terms of reducing it until you're confident that you've grasped the main points and the thrust of the argument.

All that's obvious enough, perhaps, but it needs to be rigidly adhered to. Sloppy précis work invariably hinges on imperfect understanding, and that in turn derives from excessive initial haste.

2 Once you're ready to begin, isolate the key phrases.

It's up to you how you do this: you can use highlighter pens, a separate sheet of rough paper, any method you like. However, I do not recommend the savage crossing out of everything you think you can omit, for two reasons. First, it makes your 'text' look a right mess, which will not assist clear thinking. Second, you may delete a phrase that you subsequently recognize as essential, and reinstating it in your text will both waste time and be tricky anyway.

3 Start your first draft of continuous prose.

We'll assume that your 'skeleton' is sound – that you've identified and assembled the requisite 'bones'. But even a précis needs some flesh – ideally, enough to make it attractive in its own right. What else from the original should you keep or efficiently paraphrase?

Well, knowing what to omit is more than half the answer:

3a Omit all examples, illustrations and quotations.

This is often less easy than it might sound, because such material may well be very interesting and thus memorable. However, it must be done: such things **illuminate** the argument rather than **define** it. They are **secondary**, and if you're reducing a piece to a third of its length [or even less], you can only afford to include **primary** material. That's one of the reasons why it's essential to have grasped the governing thrust of the argument before you pick up your pen.

3b Be prepared to strike out all adjectives and adverbs.

I say 'Be prepared to strike out' rather than simply 'Strike out' because some 'qualifiers' will be necessary. If you look back at the two examples analysed above, you'll see that the adjectives and adverbs that remain really pull their weight: they are definitive, not decorative. However, if you rigorously 'interrogate' all such words as to their true value, you should find that most of them do not have a good enough case.

3c Never repeat material, even if the original does

Be totally ruthless about this. The only concession you might make to an obsession with a particular point is to isolate it in a paragraph of its own, or make it into the précis's title.

4 In general, write in shortish, crisp sentences

Such a style may at times strike you as rigid and bare, and if you can construct longer sentences that are muscular and precise, go ahead. But remember that you are producing a skeleton of the original, and skeletons **are** rigid and bare! Keeping your sentences short will also promote clarity, allowing you to keep a regular check on where your argument is going and whether each word is doing some real work.

5 Try to use your own words wherever possible

In truth, this is **not** always going to be possible: most passages will include some terminology or phrasing that must remain or simply cannot be improved upon. But look to paraphrase where you can: sometimes neat wording on your part will render an idea in six words that it took the original a dozen to achieve. Besides, if you stick slavishly to what you've 'gutted' from the original, it is likely that such a residue will be stilted, tending to creak rather than flow.

Now for three important **'don'ts'**:

6 **Never** *invent material*

Whatever you put down, especially when it's in your own words, make absolutely sure that your material exists in the original, or is at the very least strongly implied in it.

7 **Never** *pass an opinion or judgment on the original*

Your job is that of a disinterested scribe **and nothing else.** Your opinion is irrelevant: furthermore, expressing it will waste words that should be devoted to central points. Even if the argument you're dealing with enrages you, keep out of it!

8 **Never** *bring the author's name into your text*

Précis takes authorship for granted. If you really believe that who wrote the piece is of fundamental importance, then find a way to mention it in your title; do not allow it to clutter up your reduced version.

There are two views about what to do if the original is in the first person. Some authorities say that a précis should always be written in the third person, and that the original must be recast accordingly. Others argue that clarity is the chief criterion, not formalism, and that if the précis will read better in the first person, then use it. I incline to the latter view, but either is tenable. Practice, experience and 'feel' will guide you best: do what seems most comfortable, provided the resultant version is clear and apt.

Finally, three guidelines concerning shape and length.

9 Should a précis be paragraphed?

It depends on the length of the finished précis.

Anything under 100 words should be presented as a single paragraph, unless there is a major switch of topic or focus therein.

For reductions of 100–200 words, a single paragraph will often still be appropriate; but be prepared to divide into two or even three, according to the material's range and your sense of the reader's comfort.

Any final version that goes noticeably over 200 words should have at least two and probably three paragraphs; four to six if it climbs to 450 and above. If the précis is any good, it will make for fiercely concentrated reading: a single chunk of prose of 200+ words is distinctly 'user-unfriendly'.

10 If you're instructed to cite the number of words you've used, do so – and don't guess or lie about it!

People who set academic précis tasks do so very carefully. When they stipulate a word target or word limit, they are not sadistically adding a further difficulty: on the contrary, they're trying to help you, for they will already have worked out that the job can best be done in the figure they cite. So keep a regular check as you go on the number of words you've used – it will sharpen your performance.

If you're too lazy to do that, don't compound the folly by making a vague guess or, even worse, inventing a number that 'looks good'. The chances are it will look **terrible**: your assessor will not need to count the words to know that you're lying. One rapidly develops a 'feel' for a version that is too short or too long, and you are most unlikely to get away with any such chicanery!

10a If given no such target or limit, what should you aim for?

The fraction most often mentioned in précis work is **one-third**, and that's what I went for in the two examples explored above. Sometimes, however, you will be asked simply to reduce a document, a report, even an entire volume to the shortest effective summary possible. This may sound forbidding in the extreme, and I won't pretend it's a doddle! Nevertheless, to be required to précis say 5000 words on a single sheet of A4 has the advantage of **simplicity**, even if it isn't easy. Such a brief means that you can – indeed **must** – be utterly ruthless, and allows you to ignore everything apart from the most basic 'bones'. Winston Churchill used to insist

'To precis 5000 words on a single sheet of A4 isn't easy'

that any document submitted for his perusal was prefaced by just such a single sheet outlining the entire case, and this was an admirable discipline, both for him as reader and for the writer.

Finally, and mainly for fun, consider the following 'brutally brief' summaries:

A **The Plot of *Hamlet*.**
   1   Young prince hates his step-father and practically everything else.
   2   Thinks and worries a lot.
   3   Does nothing.
   4   Dies, along with virtually everyone else.

B **The Causes of Germany's Defeat in World War II.**
   1   Signs non-aggression pact with Russia, 1939.
   2   Attacks Russia, 1941.
   3   Loses war, 1945.

C **The Constitution of the United States.**
   1   America is the Land of the Free and the Home of the Brave.
   2   Provided you're white.

'Forget it'.

D   **The Old Testament.**
    1   In the beginning, God created the world.
    2   And spent most of history regretting it.

E   *Civil Defence Procedures in the Event of a Nuclear Attack.*
    1   Forget it.

Chapter 16

Reportage

Reportage refers to day-by-day – even hour-by-hour – journalism. Some authorities insist that an account must be first-hand to qualify as genuine reportage; others deny that 'I was there' stipulation, arguing that the term can cover any news story based on eye-witness testimony. The purist in me makes me incline to the former view, largely because John Carey makes it the governing principle of his excellent *The Faber Book Of Reportage*. For the purposes of this brief chapter, however, I shall favour the looser or broader definition: a news story that incorporates eye-witness evidence (the writer's, others', or both), in-coming reports and background information.

Any newspaper story seeks to answer these six questions:

Who? What? When? Where? Why? How?

It could sensibly be argued that all writing seeks to satisfy the reader's curiosity in a roughly similar way; what makes reportage distinctive, even unusual, is the way this is done.

Please read the following story, taken from the Birmingham *Evening Mail* of 13 December, 1986. Does it provide answers to those six questions? If not, can you think of any reason why? And what do you notice about its structure?

PLANE IN PLUNGE ON HOME

Special correspondent

A woman passenger was killed and the female pilot seriously injured when a light plane crashed on to the roof of a private house in a London suburb today.

The plane bounced off the roof and came to rest in a field near St John's Road, Walthamstow, East London, where 40 firemen battled to free the pilot from the cockpit.

The two women were the only occupants of the plane.

Rescuers battled for over an hour to release them from the cockpit while another team searched the damaged house for occupants.

The passenger was certified dead by a doctor at the scene. The pilot was taken to Whipps Cross hospital where her condition was said to be stable.

BOTH TRAPPED

A neighbour said the single-engined plane skimmed across roofs, and crashed into the wall of a factory.

She said: 'Both the women were trapped in there. One of them was dead – that was pretty obvious. The engine had come right through the plane into the pilot's seat.

'It was horrendous. We were probably 30 feet away so we're feeling a touch lucky. They were very unlucky – there is a large field on the other side of the house.'

Another witness, Mr Adrian Pietryga, 37, said: 'I heard a bang first of all. One of them was still alive, shouting: "Get me out, get me out!"'

The plane was a Tomahawk TA38 two-seater on a flight from a pilot training school at Panshanger, near Welwyn Garden City, Herts.

Commentary

Four questions are answered: the missing ones are **who?** and **why?**

We are not told the names of the two crash victims. There are two possible reasons: either the writer didn't yet know the names, or (as often happens in such cases) they were not being made public until relatives had been informed. We also don't know why the plane crashed – a fact that may not be known for months, when the Accident Research team has completed its investigations.

The story was clearly 'hot' news: the very fact that the 'Special Correspondent' is unnamed suggests that the paper received the report not from one of its staff but an outsider who happened to be on the scene shortly after the crash. On the whole, I would say that he or she did a fine job, crisply giving all the information available and letting the incident's hideous drama speak for itself. The missing pieces stimulate our curiosity rather than irritate us: we know that in such 'Late Extra' circumstances, new information is coming in all the time, and that a later edition would probably find the story amended somewhat.

That leads us neatly to the writing's structure. The paragraphs are short – forgivably so, given the high drama of the episode. However, much more significant than their length is their **order**.

Each paragraph is progressively less important than its predecessor.

This is radically different from nearly all other kinds of writing – especially the essay and its related genres. A typical newspaper story describes the following structure.

The first paragraph, in harness with the headline, seeks to encapsulate the whole story.

Very often, as in this example, that first paragraph will also be set in heavy type, to increase its impact.

The second paragraph looks to outline most if not all or the important details.

In a really major story[1], that task may require two of three paragraphs of more or less equal 'status', but the principle remains.

Successive paragraphs will flesh out the above skeleton.

Such material need not of course be negligible: in our example, the revelation that a large field lies on the other side of the house the plane hit comes pretty late. But although that information is horribly poignant, it is still secondary to the primary facts: hence its position.

The belief that major information should be given first to ensure clarity and impact is one reason why newspaper reportage is structured in this way. The other concerns space and the 'hour-by-hour' nature of the business. Editorial staff need constantly to shift material around, to enlarge this piece and therefore cut that one, to find room for new information or entire new stories. The easiest way to effect this is to cut paragraphs – starting at the bottom and working upwards. If you study a selection of newspaper stories, I think you will find that the last paragraph is often of marginal value: usually, it can be sacrificed without doing any noticeable damage to the piece as a whole.

Longer works of reportage, or those that deal with something less immediate than our example, may not exhibit these structural characteristics in quite so obvious a way; there can even be times when there seems to be little difference, so far as procedure and shape are concerned, between a substantial piece of reportage and an essay. The criteria are different, nevertheless: in reportage, no matter how lengthy, complex and detailed, facts and information are at an absolute premium, and the structure and organization will always reflect that.

That completes this 'horses for courses' section. It has not been exhaustive. I have not, for instance, offered specific advice on letters[2] or on how to write technical explanations, although it is implicit in a good deal of the material and is addressed elsewhere in the book. Nor have I looked at descriptive or 'creative' writing – mainly because I do not believe you can instruct someone in creativity, which depends on imagination and essentially private compulsion. However, I hope that whatever your writing needs or desires may be, these chapters have made them easier to fulfil.

---

1 See for example the account of the dropping of the first atomic bomb on Hiroshima in Chapter 8, Part Three, pages 106–8.
2 Those in need of such assistance might care to consult my *Brain Train: Studying for Success* (1996), which also includes a number of Precis *Exercises*.

Chapter 17

Punctuation in speech and quotation

There is an extensive guide to most punctuation devices and skills in Part Two [pp. 26–49], but nothing on how to punctuate direct speech or its 'cousin', quotation. I have postponed the study of these important skills for one simple reason: they are extremely tricky, even for fully competent writers. Contrary to many students' beliefs and practice, punctuating dialogue or quotation is **not** just a matter of providing inverted commas at appropriate places: all the other 'normal' punctuation skills remain in play as well. This means that at any one time there is a great deal to remember, a great deal to get right; and if those 'normal' skills are not fully assured, any attempt to deal with more sophisticated tasks is very likely to dissolve into chaos.

That's the bad, or forbidding, news; the good news is that

> **Anyone who can punctuate speech and quotation correctly will invariably be entirely competent in all other aspects of punctuation.**

In other words, if you can master this section, any remaining worries you may have about punctuation should come to an end.

Note: this section deals only with the **mechanics** of punctuation when writing speech or quoting. If you are uncertain about the use of quotation in academic essays, reports and articles, please consult pages 149–55ff, where you will find advice on lay-out, when to quote and why, and how to ensure that all your quotations work to your maximum advantage.

The rudiments of punctuating speech

1 Practically everyone knows that punctuating speech requires the use of inverted commas. You can use either single or double inverted commas:

    1a 'I'm going out now,' he said.
    1b "I'm going out now," he said.

Both these versions are correct. Most publishing houses use the single version, but you are free to choose whichever one seems most natural to you. However, you should bear these two points in mind:

A   **Never mix single and double inverted commas.**

All drivers will be aware that they should never have a mixture of cross-ply and radial tyres on their car. To mix your inverted commas is a lot less dangerous but no less fundamental an error. So choose one form and stick to it at all times.

That last injunction assumes an added importance when it comes to punctuating quotation:

B   **Whichever form you choose for punctuating speech, you should use the other one for quotation.**

Following that convention will assist clarity anyway, and it is **essential** for those occasions when you need to signify a quotation within a passage of speech. This trickiest of all punctuational skills is covered later[1], but you can make a sound start by firmly establishing which form you will use for each mode.

2 Choosing your form of inverted commas and following it consistently is important, but it's also very straightforward. Other rudimentary matters are more problematic, as a return to that first example immediately illustrates:

1a   'I'm going out now,' he said.

Please note the highlighted comma. In my experience as a teacher, at least 90% of learning students fail to insert any punctuation between the passage of speech and the other components of the narrative. **Such punctuation is mandatory at all times**, whether the speech is in the form of a statement –

1a   'I'm going out now,' he said.

– an exclamation –

1b   'I'm going out now!' he yelled.

– or a question –

1c   'May I go out now?' he asked.

---

1 See below, pp. 203–6.

In addition, if the overall structure of speech + back-up narrative **ends** with the speech component, a full stop will be required if a statement is involved:

    1d He said, 'I'm going out now.'

Of those four examples, it is 1a and 1d that occasion the most frequent errors. A lot of writers comfortably observe the principle behind 1b and 1c: they can 'hear' the exclamation or the question and realize it must be drawn attention to. But those same writers are not aware of any 'break' between 'he said' and the statement itself and punctuate [or **non**-punctuate!] accordingly. I am very sympathetic about this: the need for punctuation is **not** obvious, and including it seems to serve no obvious or clarifying purpose. The fact is that the two components of the complete structure – speech and what I've just termed 'back-up narrative' – **are** separate, and a visual signal is needed to register that separateness. It may not seem to matter much in the case of the short example we've been considering; in longer passages the need to distinguish visually between direct speech and other writing becomes more pressing:

> 'I'm going out now,' he said, 'and I don't know when I'll be back.' He looked around the room. 'Where are my keys? I thought I left them on that table. Ah! Here they are – in my hand.' Grinning sheepishly, he opened the front door, muttering, 'I must be going ga-ga.'

That is quite a complex little passage. The reader has to absorb various remarks, and also various actions. Yes, they all go together; but I'm sure you can see that if the 'normal' punctuation were omitted – or even just **some** of it – your sense of what's being said and what's being done would quickly get blurred. And in any extended passage of dialogue + action [involving, say, two or three speakers and a lot of accompanying narrative] you would be quite lost within a page or so if those ordinary punctuation conventions were ignored.

3 We'll return to those issues shortly; another rudimentary point needs to be stressed first. Look again at our 'root example':

    1a I'm going out now,' he said.

I've already asked you to note the comma; please also note that it is placed **inside** the speech mark. This again is standard unvarying practice, and you should commit it to memory as quickly as possible. Many people mistakenly place such punctuation **outside** the speech marks or, even worse, **directly underneath** them. The latter practice, I always assume, is a simple case of 'bet-hedging': the writer isn't sure where the ordinary punctuation should be placed, so tries to keep all options open! I'm afraid it does not convince: don't do it.

If you think all this is mere pedantry, it isn't: when **quoting**, your 'normal' punctuation will nearly always be placed **outside** the inverted commas. As we'll see, it can sometimes be crucial to distinguish between something that has been said or asked and something which has been quoted: the conventions I've just outlined allow you to do this clearly and with a minimum of fuss.

4 Our final rudimentary point concerns **layout**. Probably the easiest way of determining how to set out exchanges of direct speech is to pick up a novel in which you know there's a lot of dialogue, find an appropriate passage and study its format. You should quickly become aware that

I   **Each new passage of speech is indented.**

And, implicit in that first principle but worth stressing on its own:

II   **Each time the speaker changes, a new line/paragraph is required.**

Two important considerations lie behind these principles, as this little passage, **incorrectly** set out, illustrates:

> 'Where are you going to, my pretty maid?' 'Mind your own business, you sexist oaf!' 'There's no need to be like that – I was only trying to be friendly.' 'Oh yeah?' 'Yes.' 'Oh well, in that case, I'm off to a meeting of my local "Emma" group.' '"Emma"?' '"Emma", yes: "Extermination of Molesting Males Association".'

That is a bare five lines, but I'd be surprised if you found it easy going. As a single block of prose it is visually taxing: there are a great number of signals to absorb, and it becomes progressively harder to work out who is saying what. As I've stressed throughout, all good writing makes life as comfortable as possible for the reader; that passage does not make comfort a priority – and you can imagine what it might be like to read **several pages** similarly set out.

Happily, it is easily put right.

> 'Where are you going to, my pretty maid?'
> 'Mind your own business, you sexist oaf!'
> 'There's no need to be like that – I was only trying to be friendly.'
> 'Oh yeah?'
> 'Yes.'
> 'Oh well, in that case, I'm off to a meeting of my local "Emma" group.'
> '"Emma"?'
> '"Emma", yes: "Extermination of Molesting Males Association".'

That is much easier to take in; in addition, in this form the exchanges somehow acquire greater flow and bite. You'll notice that the correct format is not unlike a playscript: perhaps that explains the added **drama** of the amended passage.

You'll also notice that the acronym "Emma" and the final explanation of its meaning are placed within **double** inverted commas. These instances are not quotations as such, but they are analogous to quotations in that they need to be highlighted, and highlighted in a clearly separate way from ordinary speech marks. More on this shortly.

The other great advantage of that correct format, implicit in those exchanges, can be deduced from reading this next passage. What's wrong with it, do you think?

> 'What's going on here?' demanded Susan.
> 'Nothing much,' replied Frank.
> 'Oh really?' she countered. 'There are three empty gin bottles on the floor, ash all over the carpet, and you seem to have forgotten to put a shirt on.
> 'Can't a man relax after a hard day's work?' he asked.
> 'If this is relaxing,' she snapped, 'I'd hate to see what you could manage when really making an effort. And there's another thing,' she added.
> 'What?' he enquired.
> 'I don't seem to be able to get into our bedroom,' she informed him.
> 'Well,' he explained, 'you know how that door's always sticking. Damp, I expect,' he suggested. 'You really need to give it a good shove,' he continued.
> 'Don't give me that!' she retorted. 'It's <u>you</u> I need to give a good shove,' she went on, 'out of my house and out of my life!'

This is far from bad writing, but it's **flabby** – and in a precise way:

> **Apart from the first two remarks, all the 'back-up' identifiers are unnecessary and cumulatively irritating.**

Those first two lines establish situation and personnel: it's a row between Susan and Frank. Because only two speakers are involved, and because a new paragraph occurs each time the speaker changes, the reader simply doesn't need the successive **she countered, he asked, she snapped** and so on. Furthermore, they start to get in the way, to interrupt a fast-developing storm: by the time we read the final exchange, the five verbs **he explained, he suggested, he continued, she retorted** and **she went on** are mere annoying hiccups. Susan's last remarks are a scream of rage and frustration, delivered in a single breath: to chop them up like that up seriously reduces their impact.

Be sparing with 'identifiers', therefore. Of course, if your passage of dialogue involves **more** than two speakers, you'll need to make it clear who is saying which lines. This can be done through style alone – establishing a particular 'voice' or idiom for each of several speakers – but that takes a lot of practice [and talent!], and straightforward identification is probably your best course for a while. In addition, there will be times when even if your dialogue is restricted to two speakers, you'll want to include back-up material in the form of qualifiers or narrative information, as in this amended extract from that last passage:

> 'I don't seem to be able to get into our bedroom.' She delivered each word as if biting on a stick of celery.
>
> 'Well,' he mumbled, not looking at her, 'you know how that door's always sticking.' A thought seemed to strike him. 'Damp, I expect. You really need to give it a good shove . . .'
>
> 'Don't give me that! It's you I need to give a good shove – out of my house and out of my life!' She flung the car keys at his face, catching him in the left eye, and stormed out of the room.

Even here, however, the additional material is decidedly secondary. None of it is useless; but Frank's explanation is so intrinsically feeble that we can sense without being told that he cannot meet her eye and that he's desperately improvising. Similarly, the last sentence only makes explicit the violence already implicit in Susan's words throughout. So when writing dialogue, give maximum attention to **voice**: you'll be surprised and delighted to find how much unnecessary other work it can save you.

That completes this introductory look at speech punctuation. There are further, subtle things to say about the topic, but first it is time to concentrate on punctuating quotation.

The rudiments of punctuating quotation

1 Quotation is the exact citing of someone else's words. Its most obvious instances are those where the words are famous, and they should be 'clothed' in double inverted commas:[2]

> 'To be or not to be: that is the question.'
>
> *Hamlet*

> 'It is a truth universally acknowledged, that a single man in possession of a good fortune, must be in want of a wife.'
>
> Jane Austen, *Pride and Prejudice*

> 'Really quite remarkable.'
>
> David Coleman

2 Or single, if you prefer: it depends whether you intend to use the single or double form for ordinary speech. The key thing is to keep the two usages absolutely separate.

'Let them eat cake'.

'Let them eat cake'.

Marie Antoinette

2 However, quotation is not **just** a matter of repeating a well-known phrase or saying. Look at these sentences:

1 'James said, "I'm fed up",' John recalled.
2 'She said, "Tell the kids I expect their rooms to be tidy when I get back",' their father told them.

These specimens of quotation may be mundane, but they're also pretty complex in terms of mechanics and design – far more so than their famous counterparts above. Let's examine in detail how each one works.

In 1 two speakers are involved – John and James. The latter's words were **I'm fed up**, and John is reporting them. All obvious enough – insultingly so, you might think! But see what a difference in meaning results if we omit those double inverted commas:

1a 'James said I'm fed up,' John recalled.

Instead of a quotation, we have a form of reported speech. Here John is recalling that James said he, John, is fed up. James's remark has changed from a statement about himself to a deduction about John – a notable difference.

If we wanted to preserve the original meaning but use the reported speech mode, we would need to write:

1b 'James said that he was fed up,' John recalled.

This is perfectly satisfactory, of course. But the original achieves the same effect simply by the addition of a pair of double inverted commas – clear, compact and stylish.

Sentence 2 is longer and apparently trickier; in fact, it's more straightforward, because no potential ambiguity can arise. Again, there are two speakers – the father and an unspecified female. This time, however, the audience is implicitly identified – **the kids,** which presumably makes the female speaker their mother. If we omit the double inverted commas –

2a 'She said, tell the kids I expect their rooms to be tidy when I get back,' their father told them.

– we do not change the meaning: we just end up with something inadequately punctuated. But if you think that doesn't matter much, I hope 1 has shown you that the lazy or incautious omission of quotation marks can make a crucial difference, so be meticulous at all times!

3 When quoting, you need to be especially careful about the accompanying 'ordinary' punctuation. Take another look at that familiar sentence:

'James said, "I'm fed up"," John recalled.

Please note the **order** of the **highlighted** punctuation:

A   The closing quotation marks.
B   The ordinary punctuation. [In this case a comma, but in other instances it could be a full stop, a question mark or an exclamation mark.]
C   The closing speech mark.

Ordinary punctuation is nearly always placed **outside** the quotation marks. The only exception to this is if that ordinary punctuation is itself part of the quotation:

1   'What is the meaning of "acerbic"?' Simon asked.
2   The teacher commented, 'It's amazing how many people misunderstand the line, "Wherefore art thou Romeo?".'

In 1 the question mark does not belong to **acerbic**: it signifies that Simon is asking a question about that word. But in 2 the question mark **is** part of the quotation, which is in the form of a question, whereas the teacher is making a statement. Therefore, the question mark belongs **inside** the quotation marks; and since the overall structure ends there, all that is needed thereafter is the closing speech mark.

This is a sophisticated matter, often a question of taste rather than an unvarying rule: I have found that different publishers and editors adopt differing practices, according to their 'house style'.

4 It ought to be obvious that quotation marks **advertise** a quotation neatly and on their own. But many people think it is also necessary to preface any such citation with the phrase **and I quote**. When talking, the phrase is useful [though not essential], because the listener cannot, obviously, hear the quotation marks. But when writing, it is unnecessary and irritating: don't do it.

5 Finally, read this little story – an old joke (somewhat cleaned up!) that illustrates very well the rudimentary principles we've been considering. The scene is a court of law.

> 'Where were you on the night of the 15th June?' asked the prosecution.
> 'At home,' replied the vicious-looking witness.
> 'I see. "At home", you say. Not waiting outside the Midland Bank in a dark blue van with the engine running?'
> 'No way, chief.'
> 'And what were you were doing "at home"?'
> 'Sod-all.'
> 'I'm sorry,' interrupted the judge, 'I didn't catch that last remark.'
> 'He said "Sod-all", m'lud,' the Clerk of the Court supplied.
> 'Oh, really?' said the judge. 'Funny – I thought he said something.'

I hope that amused you, and I'm sorry to descend to an analysis of it – the surest way ever devised of killing a joke. But the confusion here stems from the judge's failure to realize that the Clerk of the Court's use of "sod-all" was a quotation, not a curt statement. The reader **does** realize this, and does so before the judge makes his remark. Hence the laughter – I hope!

Further points and final reminders

Early on I stressed that the inverted commas used for identifying speech or quotation are **additional** to 'normal' punctuation, not replacements for it. You must especially be on your guard when writing passages of conversation, which are likely to require a great deal of 'normal' punctuation. For conversations feature a lot of idiomatic English and interjections or similar phrases, which must all be 'signalled' clearly.

In this example the, punctuation isn't all that bad – I've certainly seen worse. It's properly set out, with a new line each time the speaker changes; and the writer has remembered to include a 'normal' punctuation point after each spoken part, correctly placed inside the speech marks. Nevertheless, there are several omissions and at least four choices that could be improved upon. Can you identify them?

> 'Oh hello Mum,' George said nervously. 'Ken and I are just off to the,'
> 'Oh no you're not my lad,' she interrupted. 'There's the little matter of your room to tidy up and then the shoes to clean which you've been promising to do for days.'
> 'But Mum,' he began.
> 'But nothing George. You don't go out till you've done both jobs OK.'

Now study the 'fair copy' version and explanation printed below and see how it compares with what you spotted.

'Fair copy' version

Note: numbers on the right refer to the explanations below.

> 'Oh, hello, Mum,' George said nervously. 'Ken and I   (1)
> are just off to the . . .'   (2)
>   'Oh no, you're not, my lad,' she interrupted. 'There's   (3)
> the little matter of your room to tidy up; and then the   (4)
> shoes to clean which you've been promising to do for days.'
>   'But, Mum . . .' he began.   (5)
>   ' "But" nothing, George. You don't go out until   (1; 6)
> you've done both jobs, O.K.?'   (7)

1 **Oh, hello** and **Mum** are three separate components and must be punctuated as such. Of course, they are closely related; but they are grammatically distinct – the first two are interjections, the third a name. To be fair, only a pedant would insist on the comma between **oh** and **hello** (though it is correct); but a comma between **hello** and **Mum** is obligatory. The same goes for **nothing** and **George** further down.

2 George's sentence is unfinished: we never find out **where** Ken and he were off to, because he is **interrupted** by his mother. When dialogue is broken into in this way, you should signal it with ellipsis [. . .] – the comma merely confuses and thus won't do.

3 As for 1. Again, the comma after **no** is arguably optional, but the one after **not** is essential.

4 In my view the two chores – room tidying and shoe cleaning – need to be separated; hence the semi-colon, although a comma would do. It might be your

opinion that George's mother is pretty angry and delivers the whole sentence in a breathless rush. If so, fine: keep it as it was. If, however, you think her tone is one of no-nonsense firmness, then that additional signal is necessary.

5 As for 2. Notice that the use of ellipsis means that you can, if you like, scrap **he began**: that information is included in those dots.

6 Putting "But" into quotation marks is perhaps rather pedantic: I wouldn't insist on it. But it is strictly correct: she is 'throwing back' the word at him, and the extra punctuation underlines that fact.

7 Whether you insert a punctuation point between **jobs** and **O.K.** depends entirely on what you think to be the sentence's meaning. If you think **O.K.** is an adverb that goes with **done**, that George's mother is demanding that both jobs be done in a satisfactory manner, then the original version is correct as it stands. But if you take **O.K.** to mean something like 'Do you understand?' or 'Have you got me?', then additional punctuation is required. The comma I've chosen is accurate, but a full-stop would perhaps be better if you think **O.K.** is delivered with a lot of top-spin or menace!

Finally, I must again stress that if you really **listen** to what you're writing, a lot of these subtle, intricate matters will occur to you almost as a matter of course. All those seven points I've listed and discussed are matters of **voice:** once you can hear what's truly being said, everything else should fall naturally into place.

'Listen to what your are writing'.

Conclusion

As an exemplar of that last point and many others, please read this short extract from P. G. Wodehouse's *The Mating Season*, where Bertie Wooster is talking about Jeeves's uncle, a formidable butler named Silversmith.

> 'Does Silversmith minister to the revellers at the morning meal?'
> 'Yes, sir.'
> 'My God!' I said, paling beneath the tan. 'What a man,
> 5 Jeeves!'
> 'Sir?'
> 'Your Uncle Charlie.'
> 'Ah, yes, sir. A forceful personality.'
> 'Forceful is correct. What's that thing of Shakespeare's about
> 10 someone having an eye like Mother's?'
> '"An eye like Mars, to threaten and command", is possibly the quotation for which you are groping, sir.'

If you've ever found punctuating dialogue and quotation problematic, you could do worse than learn that brief passage off by heart. In its compact dozen lines it exemplifies most of the principles and techniques I've been concerned with; I would draw particular attention to lines 8 and 11, where an incautious writer might have omitted important commas or the quotation marks. As it is, the meticulously correct punctuation helps voice and meaning, thus guaranteeing the lively flow that Wodehouse intended.

There is no more concentrated writing skill than punctuating speech and quotation, especially when they occur together; as I said at the outset, if you can master all its intricacies, you should hardly ever make a mistake in punctuation of any kind.

Now on to the chaotic jungle that is English spelling!

Chapter 18

Spelling and confusibles

Introduction

In the various sections on punctuation, I have pointed out that while the skills involved may be intricate and difficult to master, they have the great advantage of being underpinned by 'rules' – rules to which there are no exceptions and which can be trusted. Teachers, or instructional books such as this, are thus able to concentrate on the **principles** of punctuation, knowing that they are watertight and that once their conceptual reasoning is grasped, comfort and accuracy should usually follow.

It goes without saying – or at least I hope it does – that spelling is important. But in my judgment there are serious limits to how far it can be taught, either in a classroom or via a book. Unlike punctuation, English spelling is not systematic in any comfortable sense. There are various 'rules', of course, and only an idiot would say they are not worth bothering with. But there are exceptions to nearly every one yet devised; furthermore, many instances of English spelling are as near to irrational as makes no difference.

Frankly, spelling has to be **learnt** – learnt privately and often one word at a time. I have yet to meet anyone whose spelling is infallible; I know my own certainly isn't. There are still words I have to look up or at any rate check, and there are others I have to think hard about before writing them down. Moreover, ever since I was in junior school, I have found that arriving at the happy state of spelling a word with automatic accuracy is often achieved only by getting it wrong several times first. Such a process of 'trial and error', or of learning from one's mistakes, may be a slow and painful one, but I'm convinced it characterizes the successful speller more than the inculcation of 'rules'.

Naturally, all that is very much a matter of opinion. If you require a detailed guide to the principles and practices of English spelling, there are plenty of useful ones about: I would especially recommend Michael Temple's *Spell It Right* [John Murray, 1985], and others are listed in the bibliography. What I offer instead of a general or comprehensive survey is a focus on specifics – words that people very often misspell and words that are frequently confused.

As a taster, here are ten words that in my experience are the most commonly misspelled in everyday usage. If your spelling is at all shaky, a good first step towards improvement would be to learn these ten, noting where the mistake usually occurs and memorizing the correct version.

Correct spelling	Usual mistake
business	s and i reversed
conscious	c omitted
definite	a instead of second i
embarrass	second r omitted
immediately	second e omitted
necessary	2 cs, 1 s [etc. etc.!]
professor/professional	2 fs
receive	i before second e
rhythm	first h omitted; n added
sentence	a instead of second e

You may also be interested in the list '20 common misspellings', which logs the most frequent errors committed in the 'Business Spelltests' conducted by the RSA during 1993.

20 Common misspellings

The words and the percentage who got them wrong

Consensus	68
Innovate	54
Practice/practise	52
Facsimile	50
Instalment	48
Supersede	47
Fulfil	47
Withhold	46
Occurred	46
Possession	44
Maintenance	44
Principal/principle	42
Grievance	42
Benefited	40
Explanatory	40
Calendar	39
Incur	39
Liaise	38
Miscellaneous	38
Transferred	36

Originally published in the *Sunday Times*, 24 April, 1994.

Improving your spelling: a strategy

As I've said, I believe that the only way, finally, to become a sound speller is to learn words one at a time – very much as one learns vocabulary when studying a foreign language. 'Rules' are useful, naturally – but as guidelines rather than anything you can fully rely on. Teachers can also help you, of course – partly [if not mainly] by marking your work strictly and drawing attention to any and all mistakes. But in the end it's down to you, to your diligent learning.

That probably sounds rather forbidding, but such an approach should produce an important and pleasing bonus. As you progress you should find that you begin to deduce certain things about how words are put together. You'll see how groups or 'families' of words behave in similar ways, and that the learning of one word will often enable you to spell another dozen or so correctly. As I've warned, there will always be exceptions, to which you must remain constantly alert; nevertheless, because of your developing grasp of how words are formed and how they work, you will find that your command of spelling rapidly increases.

Accordingly, there now follow two large lists, which I recommend you use in the following ways.

1   Have a reasonably relaxed look at them. Make a rough count of how many you don't know. Be honest about this!
2   If your 'count' is in single figures, you need neither this book nor any other spelling guide. Otherwise, take a second look – a fully-concentrated one this time – and commit to memory all those you don't know.
3   Then read the sub-section that follows the second list, where I go into further detail about the benefits such study should already have brought you.

Spelling list (1)

This first list is straightforward: it contains the 250 words which in my experience are most frequently misspelled. Especially common errors are marked *.

Words marked † can also be spelled with an 's' as in civili<u>s</u>ation and crystalli<u>s</u>e. The important thing is to be consistent throughout your work.

abandon	*across	analysis
abrupt	*address	annihilate
absorb	adequate	anonymous
absorption	*advertisement	appalling
abundant	aggravate	arrangement
accelerate	aggressive	assassin
*accommodate	agreeable	assessment
achieve	a lot of	atmosphere
acquire	although	

*beautiful
beginning
behaviour
*believe
benefit
biased
boisterous
bruise
bumptious
buoyant
*business

calculate
callous
capital
*caricature
casualty
catastrophe
ceiling
changeable
chaos
character
chauvinist
†civilization
collaborate
*committee
comparatively
concession
conjure
*conscience
*conscious
consensus
contemporary
controversy
courageous
crucial
†crystallize

deceitful
*definite
delirious
*describe
*desperate
despise

developed
diffuse
dilemma
dilettante
*disappear
*disappoint
*disastrous
dissatisfy
draught

eccentric
ecstasy
eliminate
*embarrass
emphasis
enormous
enthusiasm
erratic
et cetera
*exaggerate
excellent
exhilarate
exquisite
extremely
exuberant

facetious
fallible
February
feminist
fiery
focused
forty
fourteen
freight
frivolous
*fulfilment

gaiety
*gauge
gorgeous
government
guarantee
guardian

harass
height
honorary
honourable
*humorous
hygiene
*hypocrisy

in fact
innate
innocent
innovation
inoculate
instalment
interested
interrupt
intriguing

†jeopardize
judgment

knowledge

laboratory
latitude
liaison
librarian
likelihood
*literature
loneliness
ludicrous

manoeuvre
marriage
marvellous
meagre
meanness
medieval
mediocre
Mediterranean
millionaire
miniature
mischievous
misshapen

mysterious

*naive
*necessary
neighbour
noticeable
nuclear
nuisance

obscene
*occasion
occurred
opportunity
outrageous
overall

*parallel
parliament
particularly
perilous
permissible
persuade
*playwright
*possession
preferred
*privilege
probably
*professor
propaganda
*psychology
publicly
puerile

questionnaire
queue

†realize
recede
*receive

recipe
†recognize
*recommend
referee
relevant
repetition
resistible
restaurant
resuscitate
retrieve
*rhyme
*rhythm
rummage

sacrilegious
salary
sandwich
schedule
scourge
*secretary
*seize
seniority
sentence
*separate
sergeant
simile
skilful
slothful
sluggish
solemn
soliloquy
source
specialist
sublime
subtlety
*success
succinct
succumb
superfluous

supersede
*surprise

technique
theatre
thorough
threshold
traveller
truly

unbelievable
*undoubtedly
*unnecessary
until

vaccinate
vague
*vicious
view
visible
volunteer

weight
weird
whereas
whisky[1]
whisper
wholly
wiry
*withhold
women
woolly
writhe

yacht
youthful

zealous

1 Irish and American spelling is whiskey.

Spelling list (2): confusibles

This second list collects a large number of words that are often confused. Some are included purely out of spelling considerations, and some for subtleties of meaning; the majority are significant in both respects. The list covers a wide range, from elementary 'howlers' to highly sophisticated distinctions.

N.B. In most cases, the meanings given do not claim to be either exhaustive or definitive: they are designed merely to offer easy identification.

absorb	verb
absorption	noun
accept	to receive
except	not including; to omit
advice	noun
advise	verb
affect	to influence
effect	result; to bring about
allowed	permitted
aloud	out loud, audible
all right	O.K.; completely correct
alright	O.K. – should only be used informally
altogether	completely
all together	as one, all at the same time
allusion	reference
illusion	false image or idea
amend	to change
emend	to improve
ascent	upward climb
assent	agreement
associate	to connect
dissociate	to disconnect [N.B. not 'disassociate']
aural	heard
oral	spoken
awesome	inspiring awe
awful	inspiring awe; [colloquial] very bad
bought	past tense of buy
brought	past tense of bring

brake	copse; to stop or slow down
break	interval; to shatter, fracture
callous	indifferent to others' suffering
cruel	actively enjoying others' suffering
cereal	root crop [wheat, barley etc.]
serial	story in parts
check	to restrain; to examine
cheque	money order
climatic	pertaining to the climate
climactic	pertaining to a climax
coarse	rough
course	track; meal; series
complement	a full number; that which completes
compliment	praise
comprehensible	able to be understood
comprehensive	including much or all
contagious	communicating disease by physical contact
infectious	communicating disease by air or water
contemptuous	showing contempt
contemptible	worthy of contempt
council	assembly
counsel	lawyer; advice; to advise
credible	able to be believed
credulous	believing; gullible
curb	to restrain
kerb	edge of the road
currant	berry
current	flow; contemporary, now
dairy	as in milk products
diary	daily record, almanac
decease	death
disease	illness
definite	distinct, precise
definitive	decisive, unconditional, exemplary
dependant	noun – one who depends on someone else
dependent	adjective – depending on

disc	record, CD
disk	computer
disinterested	impartial, neutral; **not** 'bored'
uninterested	bored
dose	portion of medicine
doze	sleep
dual	of two; double
duel	a fight between two
edible	able to be eaten
eligible	suitable
legible	able to be read
illegible	unable to be read
elicit	to bring out
illicit	illegal
eminent	distinguished
imminent	impending
ensure	to make sure
insure	to take out insurance
envelop	to wrap up, surround
envelope	wrapper
excite	to stimulate
exit	to go out, leave
faint	swoon
feint	sham move; pretence
formally	in a formal manner
formerly	previously
genius	spirit; extraordinary talent or intellect
genuine	authentic
gorilla	ape
guerilla	raiding soldier
here	in this place
hear	listen
hoped	aspired
hopped	sprang on one foot
human	of our species
humane	benevolent, compassionate

immoral	knowingly flouting morality
amoral	unconcerned with or not recognizing morality
imply	to suggest
infer	to deduce, interpret
ingenious	imaginative, inventive
ingenuous	naive, artless
disingenuous	pretending to be naive or innocent
irate	angry
irritable	touchy
its	belonging to it
it's	= it is
judicial	pertaining to a judge or court of law
judicious	wise, prudent
leant	past tense of 'lean'
lent	past tense of 'lend'
licence	noun
license	verb
lightening	becoming lighter
lightning	flash of an electric storm
liqueur	sweet strong drink
liquor	any alcoholic drink
loathe	to detest
loathsome	detestable
lose	to mislay; to be defeated
loose	free; undisciplined
manual	by hand; instructional book
annual	yearly
annal	historical record
anal	of the anus
masterful	dominant, imperious; domineering, self-willed
masterly	very skilful, expert
momentary	lasting a moment[2]
momentous	highly significant

2 It is quite wrong to use the adverb momentarily to mean 'in a moment' or 'shortly'.

moral	proper
morale	confidence
official	to do with an officer's duty
officious	abusing that duty; bossy and interfering
passed	past tense of 'pass'
past	all other uses
peace	not war; quiet
piece	part
personal	private, individual
personnel	staff, employees
physician	doctor
physicist	practitioner of physics
plain	flat country; clear; not pretty
plane	level; tool; tree; aircraft
practice	noun
practise	verb
pray	to worship
prey	hunted creature
pressure	[noun **and** verb]
pressurize	to raise to high pressure[3]
pretension	noun
pretentious	adjective
principal	chief [noun and adjective]
principle	code, ethical tenet
prophecy	noun
prophesy	verb
program	used in computers
programme	all other kinds
racial	pertaining to race
racist	racially prejudiced
rain	precipitation
rein(s)	control; strap(s)
reign	rule

3 This word should not be used to mean 'to put pressure on': use **pressure** instead.

review	critique; to revise, look back on
revue	a theatrical entertainment
role	actor's part
roll	all other senses
sensual	carnal; depending on the senses, not the mind
sensuous	affecting the senses, especially aesthetically
sceptic	one who doubts
septic	poisoned, infected
sever	to cut
severe	harsh
sew	with a needle
sow	seeds
shining	luminous
shinning	scrambling [e.g. up a wall]
similar	alike
simile	figure of speech [e.g. 'as light as a feather']
sight	vision; thing seen
site	place, position
sleight	dexterity
slight	slender; meagre
specific	particular
pacific	peaceful
stationary	not moving
stationery	notepaper, envelopes etc.
story	narrative
storey	floor of a building
straight	not crooked
strait(s)	narrow channel; [plural] difficulties
stupefied	dazed
stupendous	stunningly impressive
suit	of clothes
suite	of rooms or furniture
taught	past tense of 'teach'
taut	tight
temper	mood; to modify, restrain
temperament	disposition, psychic constitution

there	in that place
their	belonging to them
they're	= they are
there's	= there is
theirs	belonging to them
thorough	complete, conscientious
through	from one end to another
threw	past tense of 'throw'
tier	row
tire	to weary
tyre	on a car, bicycle
to	towards; to do, to run etc.
too	excessive; also
two	2
urban	of a city
urbane	suave, polished in manner
vain	to no avail; physically conceited
vein	blood channel; streak, thin seam
vicious	brutal, of vice
viscous	sticky
wave	to gesticulate
waive	to forgo, not claim
weather	climatic conditions
whether	if
were	a past tense form of 'to be'
we're	= we are
who's	= who is
whose	belonging or pertaining to who
your	belonging to you
you're	= you are
yaw	to swing unsteadily [of ships and aircraft]
(of) yore	formerly

Conclusion

If you've just spent a fair time getting thoroughly acquainted with the two preceding lists, you are of course innocent of this next charge – which is that a lot of bad spelling is due to sheer **laziness**. In contrast to such sophisticated matters as sentence structure, paragraphing and the full consideration of parts of speech, or achieving crisp and appropriate syntax, accurate spelling is a simple business. One can see why it takes young writers months, even years, to acquire an authoritative style and an intrinsic understanding of how best to phrase and present their material; there is surely much less excuse for continually misspelling 'necessary', 'definite', 'conscious' and so on. Yet even the brightest and otherwise most professional students are capable of such blemishes. Why?

'Careless' is the descriptor most commonly used by teachers when commenting on poor spelling. It is an admirable diagnostic term – provided it is properly understood. For 'careless' spelling is the result of something more profound than attends such apparently synonymous terms as 'slap-dash' or 'rushed': it denotes a lack of caring. In the majority of instances, people who spell badly don't **mind** enough about getting it right: ultimately, they can't be bothered. They get away with it because, as I pointed out in Part One, a misspelling has to be grotesquely bad for the word to be rendered incomprehensible; another way of putting it is that there is perhaps not enough incentive to be a good speller. Other writing skills seem more important – and these days flawed spelling can easily be attributed to dyslexia![4]

So to rephrase a point already made, spelling correctly is your own responsibility: it is a question of how much it matters to you to be good at it. If you're still reading these uncompromising words, it's safe to assume that it does matter to you, and it's time to offer some further constructive advice rather than continue a tirade!

One reason why this section is shorter than most of the others in the Primer is that much previous material has been concerned with spelling issues – plurals, inflections, the use of the apostrophe and so on. Indeed, this whole book has been about how words work, which automatically involves how they are formed and spelled. If you've read this book with care and enjoyment, the chances are very high that a number of things have 'stuck', including a lot of spellings that you might have got wrong before. And that introduces an important point which is my first 'tip':

> If you *read* with proper concentration, you will gradually and automatically develop a 'feel' for accurate spelling.

I do not claim that such a 'subliminal' phenomenon will eventually take care of every spelling problem; but there is no doubt that attentive reading is a major help-meet to good spelling, as well as being a virtue in its own right.

Second:

> If you know that you regularly tend to make spelling errors, keep a dictionary to hand at all times.

---

4 Contrary to claims made by certain 'consultants', dyslexia is a rare and complex condition. It is a term much abused, notably by a growing army of cowboys who charge large sums of money for 'sanitizing' ordinary learning difficulties or unremarkable laziness via seductively remarkable jargon. As I remark in Part Three, euphemism is a handy device for all scoundrels.

Kingsley Amis has remarked that 'the mark of an educated man is that he's prepared to look things up'; the same goes for properly caring writers. Yes, it's a slow business at first – especially when your sense of how a word might be spelled is so vague that you're not sure precisely where in the dictionary to look! But it will soon reap benefits: the mental discipline it mobilizes should ensure that the word sticks in your memory henceforth.

Third:

Try making a *game* out of difficult spellings.

If you continue to have 'blind spots' or 'memory blanks' about certain words – and nearly everyone does – you need to find a way of making them memorable; this is best done by constructing a mnemonic, preferably one that is amusing. For example, a young pupil of mine learnt how to spell 'necessary' by constructing this mnemonic out of its letters:

never **e**at **c**hips: **e**at **s**alad **s**andwiches **a**nd **r**emain **y**oung.

I adopted the same principle for 'dilettante' – a word I previously had to look up every time I used it:

don't **i**magine **l**ife **e**xists **t**o **t**ake **a**ll **n**arcotics **t**o **e**xcess.

A bit melodramatic or pompous, maybe, but it works!

Fourth:

When spelling, *listen* as hard you can.

In an enormous number of instances, the sound of a word offers valuable clues about its spelling. To be fair, maybe that is why so many people misspell 'definite' – normal pronunciation suggests an **a** instead of the second **i**; in keeping with the exceptions that bedevil English spelling, there are other words that are treacherous in the same way. But do not let that put you off: alert 'hearing' will benefit you far more often than not. You will become aware, for instance, of the difference between long and short vowels and the effect this has on spelling, as in this example from Spelling List 2:

hoped is a **long** vowel; **single** consonant follows.
hopped is a **short** vowel; **double** consonant follows.

Fifth, and closely allied to the previous tip:

Try always to be aware of how a word is correctly pronounced.

There is a high correlation between mispronunciation and misspelling. It is true that I have hardly ever seen 'something' written as 'somethink' even though the latter is a common sound in the South of England; but I have often encountered the following misspellings, all of which derive from a mistaken idea of how the word should be spoken:

atherlete	instead of	athlete
secetary	instead of	secretary*
libary	instead of	library
particerlar	instead of	particular*
pacific	instead of	specific*
proberly	instead of	probably*
suprised	instead of	surprised*
primrally	instead of	primarily

Those marked * have already appeared in one or other of my two Spelling Lists, which emphasizes the connection between aural/oral error and written confusion.
    Sixth, and last:

Compile your own dictionary, in which you write down any word you spell wrong or are unsure of.

This idea is a more sophisticated or systematic version of something you may have encounted in junior school – doing 'Corrections'. Unfortunately, young children can associate that admirable practice with punishment for getting things wrong; don't make the same mistake. The very act of writing anything down greatly increases your chances of remembering it: what could be more sensible than to write out [correctly!] and thus focus closely on the words that don't yet come naturally to you? You can create your 'personal spelling dictionary' out of a cheap indexed notebook; peruse and add to it regularly, as you would a French or German vocabulary book, and you'll be pleased how quickly it makes a difference.

    As a final word of encouragement: remember that even highly educated and experienced professionals misspell words sometimes. One of my daughter's English reports included the rogue spelling 'developped', and two of my colleagues, at the time of writing, think there is a word spelt 'apalling'. Since one of them was commenting on a boy's spelling, this was an unfortunate mistake! Accurate spelling involves a lot of care and a lot of work – for all of us. But it's worth it, if only because nothing undermines otherwise impressive writing so obviously as a rash of mistakes that could have been avoided.

Appendix I

Answers to exercises

Exercise I

When feeding the baby with a bottle, the latter must be held at a steep angle with the bottom tilted up and the neck held firmly down, otherwise an air-bubble will form in the neck. Do not allow the baby to drink all the feed at once, but give it a rest sometimes so that it can get the wind up. Finally, when the baby has finished, place the bottle under the tap straight away or soak it in a mild solution of Milton, to prevent infection. If the baby does not thrive on fresh milk, powdered or boiled milk should be used instead.

Exercise 2

1 In the game's very last seconds, McDonald scored with a header.
2 We thought this story superb – very convincing.
3 The Channel Tunnel project seems to be getting under way again.
4 Here we are in the Holy Land of Israel – a major attraction for tourists.
5 She really excited the poolside crowd tonight.
6 No re-write possible, surely. This is a classic example of the need to shut up when there's nothing useful to say!
7 I thought the 2–0 scoreline accurately reflected the play.
8 Tell me, what is your gut feeling?

or

Tell me, how do you feel in your heart of hearts?
9 Obviously you do other things despite dedicating most of your life to ballet.
10 The atmosphere is amazing: you could cut the atmosphere with a knife.[1]

---

1 I've substituted a more than usually stale cliché here; I don't like it, but I'm hampered by the fact that I have no idea what was in Murray Walker's mind when he cited "cricket stump"!

Exercise 4

Prohibition was known as 'The Great Experiment', and it was indeed a remarkable one, occurring in the United States of America in the years 1920–33. During that time the sale and consumption of alcohol was prohibited; the people's liking for alcohol did not disappear, however, and so it was distilled illegally and sold in 'Speakeasies', clubs owned by gangsters. Some of these gangsters became enormously powerful: Al Capone of Chicago was for a time considered to be the most powerful man in the country, and although he was eventually imprisoned for tax evasion, the gangsters' control nevertheless continued. By the time Prohibition came to an end in 1933, the damage had been done: America has had to live with organized crime ever since.

Exercise 5

Counsel maintained that the allegations of some prosecution witnesses concerning the stolen articles were not very reliable; in addition, he revealed that the accused had been subject to temporary lapses of memory as a result of shell-shock sustained during the war.

Exercise 8

Cholesterol, a steroid alcohol found in certain fluids and substances stored by the body, is a potentially deadly phenomenon. It promotes arteriosclerosis; this in turn precipitates high blood pressure, which increases the chances of having a heart attack, angina, or a host of similarly dangerous conditions.

Cholesterol's main carriers are foods we eat regularly: butter, cheese, milk and salt. Cream and rich puddings are especially high in cholesterol, as are eggs and anything fried in oil or dripping. If you eat too many such foods, your arteries harden prematurely. Obviously enough, this makes it more difficult for the blood to flow; they also get coated and generally unhealthy, contaminated and weak, so that you run a high risk, at the very least, of premature illness, incapacity or even death.

Exercise 9

1 **He was fed up; the bus had left without him.**
   A colon after **up** would do just as well, as would a comma plus the conjunction **for** or **because**.
2 **His promotion was not due to any particular skill or merit: he had bought his way up.**
   A perfect example of when to use the colon, which 'signals' an intimate, direct link between the two clauses.

3   Stuck out here in the heart of the Yorkshire moors, in the vicinity of a
     bog, there is no problem parking the car; a little difficulty extricating it
     may be experienced, though.

     Some might prefer a full stop after **car**: it depends how <u>long</u> a pause you think
     the 'speaker' might take. Either device is accurate.

4   **The fridge worked; the food stayed fresh; the milk remained cold; the little
     light came on when you opened the door.**

     The original commas are not seriously faulty, perhaps, but semi-colons are
     better: four separate clauses occur, and one should try to avoid the comma
     where one can, to prevent a profusion which irritates and distracts.

5   **He was caught in a vicious circle: nobody would hire him as a portrait-
     painter until he was well-known, but he couldn't become well-known until
     people hired him.**

     The colon sets up the full explanation of the opening statement. The comma
     is wrong anyway, being too weak to separate two full clauses.

6   **The recent BAFTA awards prove one thing if nothing else: when it comes
     to excruciating self-indulgence the TV industry has no equals.**

     See explanation to 2. A full stop after else would be technically correct but
     stylistically much inferior.

Exercise 10

1   In fact this can be punctuated in *three* ways. **1a** suggests a court of law and that
     the policeman, on oath, is certain that the driver turned across oncoming
     traffic; **1b**, totally different, presents us with the driver's equally assured
     contention that the policeman committed this traffic offence;[2] and **1c**, very
     different again, indicates two separate events – the policeman indulging in
     profanity and the driver turning across oncoming traffic. To repeat: all are
     perfectly correct, but they illustrate the need to decide what you want to say
     before you attempt to express it.

     1a   The policeman swore (that) the driver turned across oncoming traffic.
     1b   'The policeman,' swore the driver, 'turned across oncoming traffic.'
     1c   The policeman swore; the driver turned across oncoming traffic.

2   More straightforward than 1. **2a**, which simply adds a final full stop to the
     original, indicates that the speaker has experience in both hunting and
     shooting and as a result knows how dangerous guns can be. The pair of dashes[3]

2 The inverted commas are optional; it could be a piece of dialogue, but it could equally be part of a
   written report, where that device is not needed.
3 A pair of brackets or even a pair of commas would do very well instead, but I think the dashes are
   best – more dramatic, which is appropriate in this instance!

added in **2b** means that the speaker is an experienced hunter who on one occasion (at least) managed to shoot *himself*, which presumably makes the claim that he knows all about the dangers of guns hard to refute!

2a   **I have hunted and shot myself and know the dangers of guns.**
2b   **I have hunted – and shot myself – and know the dangers of guns.**

3   **3a**, again adding nothing but the final full stop, means that it was Simon's opinion that his mother should go to the hospital. **3b** reverses that sense: here it is Simon's mother who thinks *he* should go to the hospital. In each case, whether that trip is for treatment or to visit someone is not clear, but while perhaps a touch tantalizing, that issue doesn't affect lay-out and sense.

3a   **Simon thought (that) his mother ought to go to the hospital.**
3b   **Simon, thought his mother, ought to go to the hospital.**

4   follows a pattern very similar to 3. **4a** adds only a final full stop; as in 1a and 3a above, the bracketed 'that' confirms the sense but is not grammatically necessary. It thereby records David's opinion that Susan was no longer able to cope with her professional tasks or whatever; **4b** turns the sense right round, indicating that it is Susan's view that *David* can no longer 'cut it'.

4a   **David decided (that) Susan was no longer up to the job.**
4b   **David, decided Susan, was no longer up to the job.**

Exercise 15 '40 errors' exercise fair copy: mistakes numbered and annotated

My friend and I (1) were lying (2) around on the floor when the bell rang (3). It was the postman, who was in a very stroppy mood: (4) he said that the parcel he was delivering to me was extremely awkward to handle, and that £2-40 was due (5) because the sender hadn't handed over enough money. I was uninterested (6) in his problems, but his manner was so unpleasantly masterful (7) that I thought I'd better behave judiciously. Undoubtedly (8) he'd have been even more unpleasant if I'd stuck to my principles (9) and told him where to get off. After all, he is a public servant and has no business being so officious: (10) it wasn't my fault that the parcel was so tricky for him and it's (11) no use blaming the innocent recipient if the sender has been too mean to pay the correct postage. I therefore offered him my condolances (12) on having such a pressured (13) job, paid the excess (14) postage and shut the door on the villain. (15)

When I opened the parcel, I was incredulous (16): it was a priceless diamond (17). The reason it was so bulky was that (18) it was wrapped in yards and yards of paper – tissue paper, newspaper, brown paper, even corrugated cardboard.

No wonder the postman had found such a lot of stationery **(19)** awkward to carry! My friend was fascinated by the jewel and said I could probably **(20)** retire **(21)** if I sold it to the right buyer. I told her not to be so venal **(22)**: **(23)** it was a treasured present and I would never part with it for anyone **(24)** Then she asked me who it was from. **(25)** I scrabbled around in all that paper, looking for a card or a letter, but could find nothing **(26)**. I was so upset at not knowing who my benefactor was that I needed an immediate stimulant **(27)**, and so I dived for the brandy. I poured out a good measure for each **(28)** of us, but she complained that mine **(29)** was bigger than hers and implied **(30)** that I was greedy. I said she was unique **(31)** in being the nastiest, most grasping little rat-bag I had ever come across and that if she had the intelligence required to find the door, she might like to use it at her earliest convenience. People like that embarrass **(32)** me: they're **(33)** full of criticism for others but never practise **(34)** what they preach.

Oh, I eventually found out who sent the diamond. There *was* a letter after all, tucked into the outer wrapping **(35)**: it was from a Belgian **(36)** I met on holiday, who's **(37)** the most gorgeous man I've ever clapped eyes on. Anyone who doesn't fancy him must be off her **(38)** head: he's the sort of phenomenon **(39)** that makes me go weak at the knees **(40)**.

Explanations

Some of these are so obvious that they almost require an apology for their inclusion! However, a comprehensive list is the safest course.

1   You can't use **me** as the subject of a clause/sentence.
2   'laying' is transitive. If they *were* 'laying around on the floor' they were either transmogrifying into chickens or being just plain dirty!
3   **'rung'** is the past partciple (as in 'I had rung the changes.') The simple past form is always 'rang'.
4   CNE (= Comma Not Enough). There are two discrete clauses here, and while a full stop would be accurate, the colon is better because the second sentence complements and 'explains' the preceding one.
5   '£2-40' – self-evidently a sum of money – makes *either* **to be paid** *or* **due** *tautologous* (see **15**). One or the other is sufficient, and it's neater to plump for the single-word 'due'.
6   **disinterested** = 'impartial, neutral". Here she is clearly bored or indifferent, so **_uninterested_** is required.
7   **masterly** = 'expert, superbly well done'. A different 'master' association is at issue here – that of 'boss / in authority' and therefore **_masterful_** (= 'bossy, imperious') is needed.
8   There is no such word as **undoubtably**. Maybe there *should* be, but there ain't!
9   **principal** = 'chief' (either as noun or adjective). If intending 'moral or ethical tenet', **_principle_** is required.
10   CNE. See **(4)** – the principle here is identical.

11 **its** = 'belonging to it'. Here the sense is 'it _is_', so **it's** is needed.

12 Simple spelling error – probably brought about by lazy received pronunciation.

13 **pressurised** = 'raised to high pressure and should only be used of (e.g.) a soft-drink can or an aircraft cabin. If you _literally_ were to 'pressurize' someone, you would cause them instantly to explode! The simpler **pressure** functions as a verb as well as a noun, and is both simpler and right.

14 Simple spelling error, doubtless caused by pronunciation-confusion.

15 **wicked villain** is an example of _tautology_ – a phrase where at least one word is redundant/literally useless. A **villain** is by definition **wicked**, and the adjective is therefore not only a waste of space but harmfully weakening

16 **incredible** = 'incapable of being believed', and therefore can refer only to the object of disbelief. The _subject_ doing the unbelieving is 'incred_ulous_'.

17 Another (very hefty) tautology. Since it's already been established that the diamond is **priceless**, the clause 'that must have cost a pretty penny' is not only redundant but to some degree undermines the absolute quality of 'priceless'.

18 **The reason** _includes_ the whole idea of **because**: one or the other, never both. The fair copy version is the neatest and simplest.

19 A 'confusible'. **stationary** = 'standing still'; if intending 'writing paper, envelopes & c', **stationery** is required.

20 I have no idea why so many people write **proberly**, but they do! Maybe it's the lazy-received-pronunciation syndrome again; in any event, the word is of course **prob_ab_ly**.

21 Perhaps pedantic, but . . . The concept **retire** surely connotes **for life** to such an extent that the latter is tautologous.

22 **venial** = 'forgivable, minor, excusable' (usually used of a peccadillo/small sin). **Venal** = 'unhealthily interested in money' (the sense intended here) or 'financially corrupt, open to bribes'.

23 CNE. See **4** – the principle here is identical.

24 Naff double negative in the original.

25 Full stop, _not_ question mark. This is **_reported speech_**, and the question mark is not only wrong but misleading: it almost suggests that the writer is questioning his/her own prose! That's not _really_ a problem here, naturally – but in other circumstances where reported & direct speech are confused, it could well be.

26 **absolutely nothing** may be fine in casual speech, but it is in fact another tautology: like **unique** (see **31**) **nothing** is an _absolute_, and cannot be qualified/added to.

27 **stimulus** = 'anything which rouses energy, activity or interest'. It's not _obviously_ 'wrong' here – but the subsequent mention of **brandy** makes it clear that the meaning intended is that of 'a stimulating _agent_, as in quickening drug, article of food or (especially) alcoholic drink' – and that requires **stimul_ant_.**

28 If the measure was for **both** of them, the only true inference (see **30**) is that she poured **a good measure** into a _single_ glass which they then shared in some fashion (taking turns, slurping from opposite sides, whatever!).

29   You cannot have a **bigger half**! The use of the pronoun **mine** is the simplest and neatest way out.

30   **infer** can only be used of reader/listener, and means 'deduce'. It is writers/speakers who **imply**, meaning 'hint, suggest'.

31   See **26.**

32   Simple – but *very* common – spelling mistake.

33   Ditto: **their** = belonging to them. Required here is **they're** (= 'they are'). Complicating the issue further, of course, is the adverb of place, **there**. A splendid triple example of why spell-checkers should be used with the utmost caution! [See the **Interlude** section between Parts Three and Four.]

34   A prime instance of how *silly* some English spelling is. At present, *English* English (as opposed to the more sensible American and Canadian English) uses **practice** only as a *noun*; if the verb is required, then it must be **practise.**

35   Another simple spelling error: **rapping** = 'striking, hitting' or (at the time of writing) 'churning out a river of drivel masquerading as "street poetry" to a remorseless backing of thudding drums and bass guitar.' The sense required for 'pertaining to a parcel' (etc.) is **wrapping.**

36   **Belgium** is the country; its nationals are **Belgian(s)**. I never cease to be amazed by how many (educated) people get this wrong; maybe it's because they can't be *bothered* to get right anything to do with the place!

37   **whose** = belonging to who(m): it is a *relative adjective*. If intending the elided form of 'who is', then **who's** is required.

38   A problem of *number*. **Anyone** is singular, so the sequent **their** (plural) won't do. Sometimes, putting this right is very tricky/clumsy, requiring the new androgynous structure **his/her**. In this case, however, since the speaker is female and is clearly talking in exclusively 'hetero' terms, the simple **her** is fine.

39   **phenomena** is plural; the singular *phenomenon* is obviously required here. An object lesson in the danger of using 'exotic' words to impress: that aim is instantly annihilated if you get your 'exotic grammar' wrong! Analogous instances include **criterion / criteria** and of course **media**, which at least 90% of the population seems to imagine is singular.

40   The American suffix **-wise** *can* be neat and useful. More often than not, however, it's employed in a way both needlessly ugly and clumsy, as here: the well-known idiom **weak at the knees** is just as clear, neater and a lot more euphonious.

Exercise 16

1   Throughout the chapter . . .

2   The incident with which the chapter ends . . .

or

The chapter's final incident . . .

3   These factors combined to produce . . .

4   It was no more than a passing thought . . .
5   After a while, however, he realized . . .

or

But after a while he realized . . .
6   He can do no more than follow blindly . . .

Exercise 25

Verb	Definition
Account for	Explain the cause of
Analyse	Separate down into component parts and show how they interrelate with each other
Comment on	Make critical or explanatory notes/observations
Compare	Point out the differences and similarities
Contrast	Point out differences only and present results in orderly fashion
Describe	Write down the information in the right order
Discuss	Present arguments for and against the topic in question; you can also give your opinion
Evaluate	Estimate the value of, looking at positive and negative attributes
Explain	Give reasons; say 'why' rather than just define
Identify	Select features according to the question
List	Item-by-item consideration of the topic, usually presented one under the other
Outline	Give the main features or general features of a subject, omitting minor details and stressing structure
Review	Make a survey of the subject, examining it critically
Summarise	State the main features of an argument, omitting all that is only partially relevant

Appendix II

A grammatical and technical glossary

This is an edited and freshly annotated version of the 'Glossary of Terms' used in the *National Literacy Strategy Framework for Teaching* published in 1998, and it serves as a kind of final check-list of all the matters I've been concerned with in this book. But I have another reason for including it, one which returns me to some of my observations in the Preface.

The *National Literacy Strategy Framework for Teaching* was and remains an excellent document, but there is something very disturbing about it nonetheless. Even a cursory glance at the pages which follow will show that the amount of teacher-knowledge the authors assumed to be essential for the Strategy to thrive is formidable, indeed daunting. I have a high regard for those thousands of professionals who teach English at all levels and in all circumstances, so I hope it is neither cynical nor condescending to think it most unlikely that more than a handful of them knew beforehand *all* the terms which follow or that quite a number did not know a sizable percentage of them. Grammar has not been taught formally in schools – or to training teachers of English – for well over a generation, and I suspect that in order to teach the Literacy Hour and its various subsequent spin-offs, many teachers had to learn their stuff pretty quickly, and in the main on their own.

The fact that the Literacy Strategy has been one of the few real successes in two feverish decades of 'innovation' and 'improvement' suggests that those auto-didact crash courses in grammatical and technical terminology were effected impressively well. However, I believe this glossary may help teachers as well as students; compiling it has certainly sharpened and at times increased my own knowledge. Finally: I have omitted some sixty items from the original while also adding a few entries of my own.

In the right hand column, a **bold-highlighted** word means that the term is further annotated elsewhere in the list.

abbreviation	A word which is shortened. This may be a word which has passed into common usage – *phone* for *telephone*, *fridge* for *refridgerator*, *bus* for *omnibus*. Other abbreviations may be **acronyms** – *NATO/North Atlantic Treaty Organisation; modem/*

means of delivering electronic mail. And others have passed into speech or writing in universally-understood abbreviated form, such as three standard Latinisms – *e.g./for example* (exempli gratia), *i.e./that is* (id est) and *etc./and so on* (et cetera) – or *BSE/Bovine Spongiform Encephalopathy.* [See also **contraction.**]

accent
Features of pronunciation which vary according to the speaker's regional and social origin. All oral language is spoken with an accent (including **standard English**) and speakers may use different accents in different situations. **Accent** applies *only* to pronunciation and should not be confused with **dialect.**

acronym
A word made up from the initial letters of the phrase in question: *SWOT/Strengths, Weaknesses, Opportunities, Threats; DRINKY/Double Regular Income No Kids Yet*

acrostic
A poetic form which is organized by the initial letters of a key word, either at the beginning of lines, or with lines arranged around them:

Whistling wildly	*Blowing*
In a	*rain*
Northern	*round*
Direction	*and round*

adjective
A word or phrase added or linked to a noun to describe or modify it.

adverb
A word or phrase which modifies a verb, an adjective or another adverb.

affix
A **morpheme** which is not in itself a word but is attached to a word. See also **prefix; suffix.**

agreement
Linked words or phrases must agree formally with each other in terms of **number, gender** and **person.** For example: *The girls collected their belongings* (plural forms agreeing) or *Yesterday I began a new job* (agreement of words concerning time).

alliteration
A phrase where neighbouring or closely connected words begin with the same letter or sound: *several shining ceilings; one weird witch; big burgers banish the blues.*[1]

ambiguity
A phrase' or statement which has more than one interpretation.

---

1 **Alliteration** should not be indulged too freely and certainly not for the sake of it. Any fool can alliterate – there are, after all, 400,000 words in English but just 26 letters of the alphabet! **Alliteration** is only effective if it *adds* something to the idea being expressed, as in this line from Philip Larkin's 'Bridge For The Living'

Wind-muscled wheatfields wash round villages . . .

where the repeated **w**s increase one's sense of nature's power and of the vulnerability of the *villages* as well as the latter's beautiful setting.

	Often unintentional and / or the result of careless writing, as in the (authentic) headline quoted in the very first section of this book – *Police Help Dog Bite Victim* – where the omitted hyphen between *dog* and *bite* has a ludicrous result.
anagram	A word or words made up from the letters of another word or words: *marriage / a grim era; carthorse / orchestra; mother-in-law / woman Hitler.*
analogy	The perception of similarity between two things.
antonym	A word with a meaning opposite to another: *hot – cold; light – heavy; imply – infer.* A word may have more than one antonym: *cold – hot/warm; moral – immoral/amoral; like – dislike/unlike.*
apostrophe	A punctuation mark indicating the omission of a letter or letters. Contrary to widespread belief (and teaching guidance) the so-called 'possessive apostrophe' is <u>also</u> an instance of omission – in this case the dropping of the **e** from the Anglo-Saxon-derived genitive: *the womane̲s handbag* becomes *the woman's handbag.*
appendix	A section added to a document offering secondary or illustrative information.
article	(1) A (mini) essay, usually commissioned for a newspaper or journal. (2) The most basic form of **adjective**, incarnated in two forms – the *definite article* ('the') and the *indefinite* ('a', 'an').
assonance	The repetition of vowel sounds; sometimes this involves a **rhyme** or **internal rhyme** – *dream team; fine wine* – but assonance can occur in non-rhyming forms too: *crying time; cool dude.*
asterisk (*)	A punctuation mark used most often to organize text, highlighting a point explained or followed-up elsewhere. It may also be used to **euphemize** taboo or risqué words by replacing letters.
ballad	A poem or song that tells a story. One of the oldest (but still employed) of English poetic poems, it is characterized by short regular verses with a rhyme scheme, often with a refrain.
bibliography	A list of texts provided for readers. Providing such an inventory of *texts consulted* is fast becoming an absolute requirement for student essays, but **bibliography** also applies to a list of texts on a particular subject (as in my own 'Further Reading' section) or texts written by a particular author.
blank verse	Poetry written with rhythm and metre but without rhyme. Traditionally held to be the 'highest' form of English verse – not surprisingly, since its two most prolific practitioners are Shakespeare and Milton.
calligram	A poem in which the calligraphy – i.e. the formation of the letters or the PC font selected – represents an aspect of the poem's subject, as in:

thin　　　　　　growth

[See also **mimesis**.]

cinquain A poem with a standard **syllable** pattern, not unlike a haiku. Invented by the US poet Adelaide Crapsey (!), it has five lines and 22 syllables in the sequence 2, 4, 6, 8, 2. [See also **quatrain**.]

clause A distinct part of a sentence including a finite verb.

clerihew A four-line comic verse with two rhyming **couplets**. Named after its inventor E. Clerihew Bentley (ob. 1956) its first line should be the name of the person about whom the rhyme is written

> *Cap'n Bob Maxwell*
> *No tycoon could excel;*
> *But it all went to pot*
> *When he fell off his yacht.*

So Hilaire Belloc's otherwise wonderful

> *How odd*
> *Of God*
> *To choose*
> *The Jews*

does not strictly qualify as a clerihew.

cliché An over-used phrase or opinion. [From the French *clicher* meaning 'to wear away/wear down'.]

colloquial Typifying speech/language used in familiar, informal contexts.

colon (:) A punctuation mark used to introduce a list, a quotation or a second clause which expands, illustrates or demonstrates the first.

comma (,) A punctuation mark orchestrating the relationship between parts of a sentence. Often abused, it is too weak a 'stop' to separate sentences and for all but the most assured punctuator is probably best confined to separating words or phrases.

commentary A set of notes – or an extended essay – which explain or give further information on a text. The purpose of a commentary is to deepen **comprehension**.

compound word A word made up of two other words – *football, binliner, seatbelt*. Also found in hyphenated forms – *drugs-related crime, a bitter-sweet experience*. [See also **hyphen**.]

comprehension The level of understanding of a text.

> **literal** the reader has access to the surface details of the text and can recall material which has been directly related.

<dl>

inferential the reader can deduce meanings which are not directly explained, making explicit information which is only latent or implied.

evaluative the reader can offer an opinion on whether the text fulfils its purpose.

</dl>

Also, more mundanely, **comprehension** denotes those 'reading for meaning' passages set in most exams up to Key Stage 4 and at times beyond.

conditional A clause or sentence which expresses the idea that the occurrence of one thing depends upon another. This can be effected through the form of the verb itself – _Should it be wet, we shall hold the picnic in the Scout Hut_ – or via **conjunctions**: _If you go, I shall be sorry._

conjunction A word used to link **sentences** or **clauses** or to connect words within the same **phrase**; from the two Latin words _con_ ('with') and _junction_ ('a joining'). Their use is normally as straightforward as enabling, but sometimes the choice of conjunction can crucially affect – indeed determine – meaning:
  He was in a good mood until Jane asked him to sponsor her.
  He was in a good mood so Jane asked him to sponsor her.
  He was in a good mood because Jane asked him to sponsor her.

contraction Words which are shortened – _fax_ for _facsimile_, _cello_ for _violincello_ – or through **elision** reduced from two words to one: _can't_ / _cannot_; _could've_[2] / _could have_; _won't_ / _will not_. [See also **apostrophe**.]

couplet Two consecutive lines of poetry paired in length and rhyme. Poems of near-**epic** length have been written in couplets – the _locus classicus_ is the work of Alexander Pope – and the same goes for some sizable speeches in Shakespeare's plays: almost all of the verse spoken by Hermia, Lysander, Helena and Demetrius in A _Midsummer Night's Dream_ is in couplets, as is a good deal of _Richard II_. But from the earliest English poetry to the present day the most frequent occurrence of the couplet is as the completion of a **stanza** or the full poem itself.

dash (–) Used _singly_ to indicate an (often significant) afterthought or _in pairs_ as an alternative to brackets. See also **parenthesis.**

decode To convert a spoken/written message into language readily understood. The process is as old as language itself, but at the time of writing mobile phone text-messaging is probably the most prevalent instance.

derivation The tracing of the origin of a word or saying.

---

2 **Not** (please, for pity's sake!) _could of_ – possibly the naffest illiteracy of them all!

dialect	Regional variations of **grammar** and **vocabulary**. These change over time, naturally; some disappear, often with disturbing speed. Dialect should on no account be confused with **accent**, an apparently similar but in fact wholly distinct matter.
dialogue	A conversation – spoken or written – between two or more parties. [See **duologue**.]
digraph	Two letters representing one **phoneme**: *ba<u>th</u>*; *br<u>ai</u>n*; *<u>p</u>sy<u>ch</u>olog<u>y</u>*
diminutive	A term implying smallness. Most often employed as a term of endearment or fond familiarity – *my lovely baby-girl, Babs* (instead of *Barbara*) – but sometimes used as a tougher indicator of status: *star<u>let</u>, lectur<u>ette</u>, under<u>ling</u>.*
double negative	(1) Illiterate use: two negative forms which effectively cancel each other out: *they don't go sit in no waiting rooms; I never took nothing.*
	(2) More subtly, a way of 'holding back' from a fully positive statement. *Not unimpressive* is less of a compliment than *impressive*, while *never untruthful* is considerably weaker than *always truthful.*
draft	Preliminary version of a written document.
duologue	A conversation/exchange between *only* two parties. [See **dialogue**.]
edit	To modify – and presumably improve – written work, either one's own or another's. Follows **drafting** but precedes **proof-reading**.
elegy	A poem or song that is a lament, usually for someone or something that has died/is no more.
elision	An act of compression whereby a letter or **syllable** is omitted or suppressed. All **contractions** involve **elision**, but the latter also frequently occurs in verse for reasons of **scansion**, as in these celebrated lines from *Macbeth*:

> If it were done when '<u>t</u>is done, then '<u>t</u>were well
> It were done quickly. If th'<u>a</u>sassination
> Could trammel up the consequence . . .

ellipsis (. . .)	Signifies a place where something has been omitted, or there is a pause for (immediate) interruption.
embedding	Placing a clause within a sentence rather than appending it with a conjunction. For example:
	Trevor lives in Luton. He is a dentist. becomes
	Trevor, a dentist, lives in Luton.
empathy	Identifying with another – a character in a story, a historical figure, so forth. Literally 'feeling in', it denotes the ability to see situations wholly from another's point of view.

epic	A poem or story relating the adventures of a heroic or legendary figure, often relating to national identity – e.g. Odysseus or Arthur – or even mankind itself (*Paradise Lost*). Usually as grand in size as in scale.
epigraph	A short quotation or motto placed at the commencement of a book, chapter, or essay. The most telling epigraphs signify something of central significance in the forthcoming material; one of the more dramatic and illuminating is *Vengeance is mine, and I will repay* which heads Tolstoy's *Anna Karenin*.
epitaph	An engraved inscription on a tombstone.
eponymous	Derived from Greek, this means 'giving (his/her) name to something'. Its chief relevance here is to works of literature whose title is also the name of the central character – Agamemnon, Emma, Macbeth, Tom Jones, Jane Eyre. If when writing you mean to refer to the character, then use the normal typography just employed. However, if your intention is to refer to the *work*, then it must be either italicized, underlined, or placed between inverted commas. In such cases, and using the first of those three options, the above examples now should appear as *Agamemnon, Emma, Macbeth, Tom Jones, Jane Eyre*.
etymology	The study of the origin, history and development of words.
eulogy	Writing or speech designed as a paean of praise to a named person or thing. In the USA, it refers specifically to funeral oration.
euphemism	The substitution of a mild or vague or roundabout expression for a harsh or blunt or direct one.
exclamation	A sentence – or sometimes a single word – expressing emotion. Concluded by an exclamation mark.
exclamation mark (!)	Punctuation mark used to signify great emotion – joy, anger, surprise, humour, pain, so forth. Also often accompanies **interjections**.
eye-rhyme	As far as I know, this term was coined by a friend and colleague Robert MacDowell. It refers to a pair of words which *look* as if they rhyme but whose *sounds* are not the same. An example occurs in Gillian Clarke's poem 'My Box':

> . . . *I leave it there for you to read,*
> *or them, when we are dead* . . .

Sometimes an 'eye rhyme' will come about through a change in pronunciation. This famous couplet from 'The Rape of the Lock'

> *Here thou, great Anna! whom three realms obey,*
> *Dost sometimes counsel take – and sometime Tea.*

– was a full rhyme when Alexander Pope wrote it in 1714; nowadays, of course, we pronounce 'tea' to rhyme with 'see', not 'say'.

Some 'eye rhymes' are therefore inevitable, and even when they are not, there is nothing necessarily *inferior* about them. It might, however, be said that it is unfortunate if they appear too frequently or indeed regularly; most poets would want to use the device sparingly.

fable A short story written to convey a moral lesson. *Aesop's Fables* probably remain the most renowned, but a great deal of literature has a **fabular** dimension.

fact Accepted, observable or demonstrable truth. Facts must be supported by evidence; without it they can only be granted the status of opinion.[3]

fairy tale A story written for or told to children which includes elements of magic and the supernatural.[4]

fiction Text which is invented by writer or speaker. [See **fact**; also footnotes 4 and 5 below]

figurative language The use of metaphor or simile to create a particular impression, mood or effect. At least 90% of all language – be it spoken or written – is figurative. The opposite of figurative is *literal* – and the fact that the latter accounts for less than one-tenth of our linguistic activity is one of several reasons why the incautious use of *literally* must be resisted![5]

footnote (endnote) Additional information or comment which is printed at the bottom of the page rather than in the main body of the text. If

---

3 Those two sentences, a slight adaptation of the *NLSF*'s entry on **facts**, form a perfectly decent, dictionary-style definition. But to my mind the matter is much more slippery and difficult than they imply, and one needs to dig deeper, which I can best do by quoting the psychologist William James. These words were written ninety years ago, but they are just as relevant to our own time, and particularly to what any writer's life is about:

> '*Facts*' themselves are not true. They simply are. Truth is the function of the beliefs that start and terminate among them.

That is very difficult: what it means, I think, is that the real significance of facts – of all data, if you like – is how they are interpreted, how they are used by an individual discerning human brain. That is how people arrive at the 'truths' which inform and direct their lives; it is also how they arrive at knowledge as opposed to mere information.

4 Some would contend that **fairytale** is an absolute synonym for **fiction** and therefore defines *all literature*, not just a specific child-orientated genre. Even the greatest literature (so goes this argument) is 'but shadows': it is not and never can be part of the 'real world'. I have neither the time nor the space to deal with that view as I would like to, so will settle for declaring that it is as near to rubbish as makes no discernible difference.

5 See 'Waffle and Padding', Part Three p. 72–3.

	footnotes become sufficiently numerous to risk typographical awkwardness and/or reader-distraction, it may be better to present them all as **endnotes**.
free verse	Poetry which eschews patterns of rhyme and rhythm.
gender	In a specifically grammatical sense, the division of nouns into masculine or feminine forms. Universal in several languages, it is only occasional in English but still important when it arises. Gender in English manifests itself most frequently in personal **pronouns** and possessive **adjectives**; it also characterizes *personal animate nouns, some inanimate nouns* and some *nonpersonal animate nouns*
genre	French for 'kind/type', this term refers to different *types* of writing. In literature the three 'major' genres are poetry, drama and the novel, but there are many other 'sub-genres' – the short story, the novella, the **sonnet**, the **ode**, the **monologue**, tragedy, comedy, so forth. Diversity of genre is just as much a feature of non-literary writing: this book has addressed letters, essays, articles, reports, minutes, reportage and précis, and there are many others.
glossary	Often in **appendix** form, a list of technical terms (which can include abbreviations and acronyms) that the writer thinks may be unfamiliar to the intended audience and/or of confirmatory and referential help to those readers.
grammar	The conventions which govern the relationship between words in any and all languages. It is worth re-emphasizing here a point made in my main text – that *grammar serves language: it is never the other way round.*
haiku	Japenese poetic form comprising three lines and 17 syllables in the pattern 5, 7, 5.
half-rhyme	Words which almost rhyme but not quite: *polish/relish; ever/river, weird/wild.* [See also **eye-rhyme**.]
homograph	Words with the same spelling as another but different meaning: *the calf was slaughtered / my calf was aching; Are you going to welsh on that bet?/He is Welsh.* Amongst the more spectacular examples is *cleave*, which can mean either 'to cling to, adhere' or 'to split violently asunder': *His tongue cleaved to the roof of his mouth / You cleave my heart in twain.*
homonym	A word with the same spelling or pronunciation as another but different in meaning or origin. A **homonym** will be either a **homograph** or a **homophone** – sometimes *both.*
homophone	Words which sound the same but have different meanings or spellings – *read/reed, we're/weir, threw/through.* **Homophones** underscore most **puns**; they are also responsible for a sizable proportion of spelling mistakes committed by even the most literate!

hyphen (-)   The least powerful of all punctuation-points, but no less valuable for that. Its applications are various:

a. To make a single word or expression: *well-known*; *index-linked*,

b. To prevent ambiguity – *re-cover/recover*; *re-sign/resign*; *correspondent co-respondent* – and no less useful in preventing a different aspect of reader-confusion: *co-operate* is visually much more congenial than *cooperate*, as is *re-entry* instead of *reentry*.

c. To join a prefix to a proper name: *anti-Darwinian*; *post-Renaissance*.

d. To clarify meaning: *all-consuming lust* as opposed to *all consuming lust*, where the first denotes intense passion while the second seems to signify some kind of sexual equivalent of McDonald's. Similarly, *twenty-odd guests* denotes something quite different from *twenty odd guests*.

e. To divide lines at the end of a line of printed text. Even the brightest writers/editors/type-setters can make ridiculous reader-unfriendly mistakes here!

idiom   A non-literal phrase whose meaning is understood by the people who use it but cannot be inferred from knowledge of the individual words: *over the top*; *under the weather*; *beside oneself*; *out to lunch*.

imagery   The use of language to create a vivid sensory image, often visual. See also **figurative language, metaphor** and **simile**.

imperative   A sentence which constitutes a command or a (strong) request for action. *Get out of here* is a direct order; *Please get me my tablets* is still a command even if the tone is much gentler. In the first person the effect is 'softer' still, but *Let's go to the pictures* still qualifies as an imperative.

inflection   An **affix** which alters a word for changing tense, number, part of speech, so forth: *walk, walks, walked, walking, walker walkers*.

interjection   An **exclamation** uttered by a listener which interrupts the speaker (sometimes oneself). Usually marked in the text by an **exclamation mark**.

internal rhyme   The siting of rhyming words within a line of poetry: *Though the threat of snow was growing slowly* . . .

intonation   The tone of voice selected by a speaker or reader to impart further information to the listener, adding a further dimension to the words themselves.

jargon   Language used by a particular profession or interest-group. May – sometimes deliberately – include vocabulary unknown to the non-initiate.

jingle   A short verse or slogan used to attract attention and to be memorable. May be based on **alliteration** or **rhyme** and often makes use of music too. Most commonly associated with advertising.

legend	(1) A traditional story about heroic characters; it may be based on truth, but will have been embellished and enriched over the years.
	(2) The wording on maps, charts and other forms of guide, explaining the symbols used.
limerick	A five-line comic verse following the syllable-pattern 8, 8, 6, 6, 8 and rhyming *aabba*.
metalanguage	The language we use when talking/writing about language itself. This particular **glossary** is almost entirely **metalingual**.
metaphor	Any usage in which meaning is not literal, where the writer/speaker alludes to something as if it were something else: *He is an ass; the ship ploughed through the waves; the rain was rodding down*. It has been illuminatingly defined as 'imaginative substitution' (Fowler). See also **figurative language**.
mimesis	Originally 'a figure of speech whereby the words or actions of another are imitated' (*OED*), **mimesis** as a literary term refers to moments or passages in the text where form imitates, and thus strengthens, meaning. Two examples might be Tennyson's *The Lady of Shalott*, whose insistent (even hectoring) rhyme scheme mirrors the tension and monotony of the **eponymous** heroine, and the massive paragraphs which on occasion characterize Conrad's *Heart of Darkness*, which are **mimetic** of the huge Congo river that is the novel's central locale. This difficult term is more easily grasped if one takes full note of its first four letters: though more sophisticated, literary **mimesis** echoes that original definition in being an act of *mime/mimicry*.
mnemonic	A memory aid. Particularly valuable when learning to spell – a *piece of pie; there is a rat in separate*; and *never eat chips, eat salad sandwiches and remain young*, an imaginative formula to ensure the correct spelling of *necessary*.[6]
monologue	A text spoken by one speaker. Can refer to a formal dramatic piece or to a speaker who monopolises the conversation and/or never shuts up!
morpheme	The smallest unit of verbal meaning. A word may consist of one morpheme (*joy*), two morphemes (*joy`ous*) or three or more morphemes (*joy`ous`ly, penn`i`less`ness*).
myth	An ancient traditional story of gods or heroes; more complexly, any idea which has operational significance. A **myth** does not have to be 'true' to acquire currency or even governing importance: in the words of American critic Richard Poirier, 'If enough people believe in an idea, it exists.'

6 If your problem is limited to remembering the number of times **c** and **s** appear, *one coffee, two sugars* might help.

narrative poem	A poem which tells a story – *The Charge of the Light Brigade; The Rime of the Ancient Mariner*.
noun	A word which names a thing or a feeling.
number	**Singular** or **plural** form. Straightforward enough, perhaps, but matters of number can occasionally ambush the unwary. Strictly speaking, *the army are retreating* is incorrect, since *army* is a singular noun, for all that it implies many – members. Similarly, one should write/say *Not one of is ready* rather than *Not one of us are ready*. See also **agreement**.
object (direct)	The recipient of an action in a sentence: *Fred caught the ball; The bulldozer destroyed the house*.
object (indirect)	A 'secondary' object identifying someone or something affected by the controlling verb. In *He played me a tune*, it is the *tune* that is played, not the listener, but the latter is obviously involved. The indirect object can usually be prefaced (and thereby recognized) by 'to' or 'for' even when those words are not formally required. *He played (for) me a tune; She passed (to) him the salt*.
ode	A lyric poem addressed to the subject and thus written in the second **person** ('you). There is no fixed pattern of rhyme or rhythm.
onomatopoeia	A word whose sound is the same as its meaning: *cuckoo, hiss*. Full onomatopoeias are rare, but English abounds in words that have considerable onomatopoeic properties, particularly those denoting anything violent – *crash, bang, wallop, crunch, crush, squash*. . . .
palindrome	A word or phrase which is the same when read forwards or backwards: *mum; dad; rotor; pip; noon; Madam, I'm Adam*.
paragraph	A section of a piece of writing, marking a change of focus/ time/place/topic, or a change of speaker in a passage of **dialogue**.
parenthesis	A word or phrase inserted to explain or elaborate. May be placed in brackets or between commas or dashes.
parody	A literary caricature which emphasizes particular aspects of style or form to create a humorous effect.
participle	(1) Present participle. Invariably ends in *-ing*, but beware: such words do not always help form verbs. They can be independent adjectives (*a passing thought*) or nouns (*bedding, kindling*). (2) Past participle. Usually ends in *-ed, -d, -t, -en, -n* and follows the words *has, have, had* or *was*. Like its (1) counterpart, the past participle can also be used as an independent adjective (*fallen arches, driven snow, past participle* itself!
passive voice	A sentence in which the subject is the person or thing acted upon by the verb rather than the one who performs the action.

person	A text may be written in
	    the **first person** (*I, we*)
	    the **second person** (*you*, singular or plural)
	    the **third person** (*he, she, it, they*)

personification	A form of metaphor in which language relating to human action, capability, motivation or emotion is ascribed to non-human things or abstract concepts: *Mondays always seem to be in a bad mood; love is blind; the branches bent down and touched the window-pane.*
phatic	Refers to speech where the *act of communication/contact* is the key thing, much more significant than what is actually said. Everyday examples would include the words we use when introduced to someone, *How do you do?*[7], going into a room and saying *Hello, it's me*, or (in the UK especially) remarks about the weather. In literary contexts **phatic communion** can be very funny or, equally, highly poignant: in the work of Harold Pinter it is often both.
phoneme	The smallest unit of sound in a word. It can be represented by one, two, three or four letters: *go*; *sh<u>ow</u>*; *th<u>ough</u>*.
phrase	Two or more words that act as one unit.
plural	The form of a verb, noun or pronoun which indicates that there are more than one.
portmanteau	A word made up from blending two others: *smoke + fog = smog; breakfast + lunch = brunch; sham + amateurism = shamateurism.*
predicate	The part of a sentence which is not the **subject**.
prefix	A **morpheme** which can be added to the beginning of a word to change its meaning: *in`finite; dis`appear; in`famous; ig`noble; mis`lead.*
preposition	A word describing the relationship between two nouns, pronouns, or a noun and a pronoun.
pronouns	A word used instead of a preceding noun or noun phrase to prevent or reduce repetition, thus improving stylistic flow and readability.
proof-read	To check a piece of work thoroughly before publication or submission.
proverb	A saying which states a belief about the world: *once bitten, twice shy; look before you leap; pride comes before a fall.*[8]

7 The longer I live, the barmier this structure seems. It is incomplete, mystifying gobbledegook, surely prompting the query 'How do I do *what*?' – and, maybe, the additional rejoinder, 'And mind your own business anyway.'

8 As you will have gathered from the section on **Proverbs** above (pp. 72–3) I am not keen on them! However, I am a great devotee of the 'alternative proverbs' often coined on Radio 4's *I'm Sorry I Haven't A Clue*; two favourites are 'It is easier for a camel to pass through the eye of a needle if you've put it through the liquidizer first' and (of course) 'If you can't beat 'em, what's the point of teaching?'

pun	A play on words; the use of words with similar sounds but different meaning to humorous effect. Often – mystifyingly – considered 'the lowest form of wit'. See also **homophone**.
punctuation	A way of marking written text to help (indeed *ensure*) readers' understanding.
quatrain	A **stanza** comprising 4 lines. Distinct from, and quite unlike, the **cinquain**.
question mark (?)	Punctuation mark used at the end of a sentence to denote a question.
rap	A form of oral poetry which has a very strong rhythm and *rap*id pace (the pun is functional). Now also a musical genre, very popular at the time of writing.
redundancy	A situation where a word does no work and is either merely decorative or (more likely) should be deleted. See also **tautology**.
rhetorical expression	An utterance in which the intended meaning is expression different from that which might be inferred by a listener unaware of certain linguistic conventions. For example, *Do you know his name?* is not an enquiry concerning the listener's stock of knowledge but a request by the speaker to be told that name. Many rhetorical expressions are questions disguising imperatives: *Would you like to be quiet?* means *Shut up*, just as *Where do you think you're going?* is in effect a command forbidding departure.
rhyme	Words which contain the same **rime** in their final syllable are said to rhyme: *frown/clown; fangs/meringues; cheques/sex*.
riddle	A question or statement, sometimes rhymed, that forms a puzzle to be solved by the reader/listener.
rime	(1) That part of a syllable which contains the vowel and final consonant or consonant cluster: *at* in *cat*; *ourn* in *mourn*; *ringue* in *meringue*. Some words consist only of rime: *eel, or, us*.
	(2) A now-archaic term for a tale told in verse: *The Rime of the Ancient Mariner*.
root word	A word to which prefixes and suffixes may be added to make other words. In *dependent, dependant, independently, dependable* and *depending* the **root word** is *depend*.
scan	(1) To look over a text very quickly, trying to glean information by focusing on key words.
	(2) A line of poetry which conforms to the rhythm (or metre) of the rest of the poem is said to scan. **Scansion** depends, strictly, on an exact **syllable**-count; hence the need at times for **elision**.
semi-colon (;)	A punctuation mark used to separate phrases or clauses in a sentence. Much stronger than the comma but weaker than the full-stop, it is an invaluable 'stop'.

sentence	A unit of written language which makes complete sense on its own.
simile	An image comparing two things through the agency of *as* or *like*: *as* dull *as* ditchwater; he drinks *like* a fish.
singular	A form of a noun, verb or pronoun indicating that there is only one agent involved.
skim	To read quickly so as to get an initial overview of the subject matter. Both analogous to **scan (1)** and subtly different from it in both aim and procedure.
slang	Words and phrases used in an informal context, often linked with regions or used by groups of people as a kind of code.
sonnet	A poem of fourteen lines. There are two titular kinds:

> The Petrarchan sonnet is divided into 8 lines and 6 (called *octave* and *sestet*). There may though does not have to be a space between the two sections, but the division invariably telegraphs a switch in focus or tone.
>
> The Shakespearian sonnet comprises three **quatrains** and a concluding **couplet**.

A sonnet may follow any rhyme scheme. Its mixture of compression and elasticity has made it the most durable of poetic forms, still in frequent use nearly a millennium after its creation.

speech	(1) Direct: words actually spoken, as indicated by speech marks: '*Go away!*' *I yelled.* (2) Indirect or Reported: The writer/speaker reports what has been said but does not quote it. No speech marks are necessary: *I yelled at him to go away.*
standard English	The language of public communication, distinguished English from other forms of English by its vocabulary and by the rules and conventions of grammar, punctuation and spelling. Contrasts with **dialect**, with archaic forms and global variations (e.g. Australian or American English).[9]
stanza	An Italian term denoting the sub-section of a poem sometimes referred to as a 'verse'. The latter is perfectly acceptable, but since *verse* also means the kind of language in which the poem is written, **stanza** is a valuable substitute that prevents any confusion.

---

9 Standard English has recently come under fire in a number of quarters as elitist, confining and uncreative; one does not have to denigrate any of the other manifestations of our language to find such a view pretty silly. As in so many things, the most productive attitude is 'both/and' rather than 'either/or'. Besides, like it or not, Standard English is more or less the required register for a host of situations, so any writer needs to be properly aware of it.

subject	The agent in a sentence – i.e. whoever or whatever is 'in charge' of the verb.
suffix	A **morpheme** added to the end of a word.
syllable	Each beat in a word. Words with only one beat are **mono-syllabic**; words with more than one beat are **polysyllabic**.
synonym	Words which have the same, or very similar meaning.[10]
synopsis	A brief summary or outline of a paragraph, chapter, book or lecture.
syntax	The grammatical relationships between words, phrases and clauses; also (more narrowly) to do with matters of word-order.
tautology	A word or group of words which uselessly repeats an idea already established, either through ignorance or carelessness: *new innovation*; *this is an annual event held every year*; *throughout the whole play*.
tense	The time-zone which a verb occupies, telling us *when* something is/was/will be happening.
theme	The subject of a piece of writing. It is a good idea to get used to citing **theme** rather than **subject**, since the latter has a quite separate grammatical meaning. The former will reduce any chances of confusion in either reader or writer.
thesaurus	A reference text which groups words by meaning. An indispensible aid to all writers, but one to be used with care and intelligence; see footnote 10.
trigraph	Three letters representing one **phoneme**: *high*; *judge*
usage	Refers to the way in which a word or a grammatical structure is commonly used; such practice may not be strictly 'correct' but is so widespread as to be accepted.[11]
verb	A word or a group of words that names an action or state of being.

10 This is the NLTF's primary definition, and it is perfectly accurate. But writers of English need to be careful about synonyms, not least because – such is the richness of our language – there are so many. In fact, the number of synonyms that have *exactly* the same meaning is small: most contain subtle differences, either in shades of meaning or when they can be most gainfully employed. To be properly aware of that means, amongst all else, that you will use a **thesaurus** productively and that you will never run the risk of assuming, for example, that all these 'synonyms' for *break* – *shatter, demolish, interrupt, crack, fracture* – are interchangeable, and that these sentences are anything other than comic idiocies:

> *To make an omelette, first demolish four eggs.*
> *He interrupted his leg playing rugby.*
> *I shattered my journey at Sheffield.*

11 A contemporary instance is the almost universal acceptance of *like* as an alternative to *as if*. *He looks like he's seen a ghost* would have been marked as wrong by any and every English examiner twenty years ago, but not any more (even if some of us still consider *He looks as he's seen a ghost* more elegant and euphonious).

vocabulary   A collection or list of words; the sum of words composing a language; the range of language of a particular person, class or profession. It is the third which is of chief interest here, mainly because virtually everyone has (1) an active vocabulary and (2) a passive one. The former is the number of words that you can use with certainty, comfort or confidence. The latter is the larger aggregate, for it adds words you may recognize when you hear or read them or whose meaning you can contextually infer, but which you would probably not (as yet) use yourself.

voice   (1) A grammatical term relating to verbs, which are placed in either the **active** or the **passive voice**. The latter is very useful in certain situations or contexts, but in nearly all good writing the active voice predominates

(2) Less formal or precise, but still very important: the sense a piece of writing gives of the author's personality, tone, standpoint or point of view. All good writing will communicate that authorial voice in a fashion both clear and pleasing – which is one reason why successful writing works equally well when read aloud (and *vice versa*). And since indeed one of the central preoccupations of this book has been the importance of voice in that sense, it is appropriate that those observations form the very last entry in this Glossary.

Further reading

I've subtitled this book 'A guide to good English'; there are many other books which will help you achieve that goal. Indeed, the field is enormous, and considerations of space make a comprehensive bibliography impractical. What follows is a list of the books I have found valuable and instructive while preparing my own text. Titles that are particularly recommended are marked*.

Standard dictionaries

* *The Oxford English Dictionary*. Still beyond compare, but the financial outlay is prodigious! The *Concise* and, especially, the *Shorter* editions are excellent, and reasonably priced.
  The Oxford American Dictionary.
  Webster's New Collegiate Dictionary (Merriam-Webster).
  Oxford Dictionary of English Etymology, ed. C. T. Onions.
* *Collins Cobuild English Language Dictionary*. Cobuild denotes the Collins Birmingham University International Language Database, and this dictionary is imaginatively and helpfully put together.
* *Roget's Thesaurus of Words & Phrases* (many publishers).

Major guides

* *Fowler's Modern English Usage*, revised by Sir Ernest Gowers.
* Sir Ernest Gowers, *The Complete Plain Words*.
* *The Right Word At The Right Time*, ed. John Ellison Kahn (Reader's Digest, 1985). An invaluable recent addition.
  The Oxford Guide to the English Language (1985).

Specialist dictionaries

* John Ayto, *The Longman Register of New Words* (1989).
  Ambrose Bierce, *The Enlarged Devil's Dictionary* (Penguin, 1983).
* Bill Bryson, *The Penguin Dictionary of Troublesome Words* (1984).
  Mary Edwards, *Dictionary of Key Words* (Macmillan, 1985).
  Jonathon Green, *The Cynic's Lexicon* (Sphere, 1986).
  Daphne M. Gulland & David G. Hinds-Howell, *The Penguin Dictionary of English Idioms* (1986).

* R. W. Holder, *The Faber Dictionary of Euphemisms* (1989).
  Kenneth Hudson, *The Dictionary of Diseased English* (Macmillan, 1977).
* B. A. Phythian, *A Concise Dictionary of English Slang* (Hodder & Stoughton; 3rd edition, 1985).

Grammar, mechanics and usage

  S. H. Burton, *Mastering English Language* (Macmillan, 1982).
* G. V. Carey, *Mind The Stop* (Penguin, 1971).
  David Crystal, *Who Cares About English Usage?* (Penguin, 1984).
* David Crystal, *Rediscover Grammar* (Longman, 1988).
  D. J. Collinson, *Writing English* (Pan, 1982).
  Gordon Humphreys, *Teach Yourself English Grammar* (Hodder & Stoughton, 1945).
* Eric Partridge, *Usage & Abusage* (Penguin, 1981).
* Philip Davies Roberts, *Plain English: A User's Guide* (Penguin, 1987).
* Michael Temple, *Spell It Right* (John Murray, 1985).
  O. M. Thomson, *Essential Grammar* (Oxford, 1978).

Style: general

  Philip Howard, *A Word In Your Ear* (Penguin, 1985).
* Philip Howard, *The State Of The Language* (Penguin, 1986).
* O. M. Thomson, *A Matter Of Style* (Stanley Thorn; 3rd edition, 1992).
  John Whale, *Put It In Writing* (Dent, 1984).

Style: technical, commercial and scientific

  Edward P. Bailey Jr., *The Plain English Approach To Business Writing* (Oxford, 1990).
  John Kirkman, *Good Style for Scientific and Engineering Writing* (Pitman, 1980).
  Walter Shawcross, *English for Professional Examinations* (Pitman; 3rd edition, 1947).
* Christopher Turk & John Kirkman, *Effective Writing* (E & FN Spon, 1982).

Miscellaneous

This final selection has no connecting thread other than my own pleasure. However, each is excellent in its own way and should prove a rich source of both enjoyment and instruction.

  Robert Burchfield, *Unlocking The English Language* (Faber, 1989).
* *The Faber Book Of Reportage*, ed. John Carey (1987).
* H. L. Mencken, *The American Language* (1936; 1977 Knopf paperback version, including the two supplements of 1945 & 1948).
* David Lodge, *Write On* (Penguin 1986).
* David Lodge, *The Art of Fiction* (Penguin 1992).
  Logan Pearsall Smith, *All Trivia* (USA 1945; Penguin, 1986).
  Christopher Ricks & Leonard Michaels, *The State Of The Language: 1990 Edition* (Faber).
  Christopher Turk, *Effective Speaking* (E & FN Spon, 1985).

Indexes

II: Subject index

Bold type signifies an entire section
devoted to that topic.
Readers are also referred to the Glossary
that comprises Appendix II.